The Smaller English House

The Smaller English House

Its History and Development

by
LYNDON F. CAVE

ROBERT HALE · LONDON

ISBN 0 7091 8866 8

Robert Hale Limited
Clerkenwell House
Clerkenwell Green
London EC1R 0HT

Photoset and printed in Great Britain by
REDWOOD BURN LIMITED Trowbridge, Wiltshire
Bound by Hunter & Foulis

Contents

Illustrations

Picture Credits
Paul Woodfield: 1, 2, 3, 4, 7, 14, 15, 16, 19, 20, 21, 26, 28, 29, 30, 31, 32, 33, 37, 38, 39, 42, 46, 47, 48, 49, 50, 58, 59, 65, 68, 69; Max Ellerslie: 5, 9, 12, 13, 18, 34, 66; G. F. Cordy: 6; Ben Darby: 8, 11, 17, 22, 23, 64; Neville Hawkes: 10, 24, 56, 57, 61, 62, 63, 70, 72, 73, 74; J. Allan Cash; 25, 43, 44, 51; W. R. Mitchell: 27; G. Douglas Bolton: 35; E. Hector Kyme: 36; Ronald Goodearl: 40; J. H. B. Peel: 41; Humphrey and Vera Joel (late); 45; Guildhall Library, City of London: 52, 53; The Greater London Council Photographic Library: 54, 55; Geoffrey N. Wright: 60; BCIRA: 67; National Monuments Records: 71

Line Drawings in the Text

Acknowledgements

In preparing this survey of the development of the smaller English house the author acknowledges the help given by the work of many writers particularly Ronald Brunskill, M. W. Barley, Alec Clifton-Taylor, John Penoyre, Nikolaus Pevsner, John Summerson and John Woodforde, as well as others mentioned in the text and elsewhere. The views expressed are solely his own and not those of the people mentioned in the book. The assistance of Max and Beryl Ellerslie, Neville Hawkes, and Paul Woodfield in providing photographs was essential to the completion of the book as was Mr Woodfield's help in preparing the diagrams. The author would also like to thank Mr R. J. Brown for giving permission for the five maps (Figures 1, 4, 10, 16, 20) to be reproduced here which originally appeared in his own book, *The English Country Cottage*.

1
Introduction

The aim of this book is to be a guide to the development of the smaller English house and cottage, the type in which most people live, in contrast to the large mansions which, for a variety of reasons, their owners are now increasingly abandoning to the visitors or demolition men. There are few references to these houses in this book because even when newly built they were as unlike the rest of the country's houses as the stately homes are today; the difference being that we now accept them as part of our heritage but once they were brand-new, modern-looking buildings being admired, perhaps, or disliked, by the people living at that time.

It is almost impossible to write a history of the smaller English house or cottage as each person, using the available local materials, built a house to suit the needs of his family, so homes varied from district to district and often from one village to another. It should be remembered that wherever the house is mentioned, the cottage is in most cases also included, these small locally built dwellings which have in recent years become popularly known as "vernacular architecture". This has no connection with architecture in the modern sense as very few of these buildings were consciously designed. Following the publication of the first two pioneer books, *The Evolution of the English House* by Sidney Addy as long ago as 1898 followed by C.F. Innocent's book, *The Development of English Building Construction* in 1916 almost no interest was taken in the subject until the late 1930s, since when there have been many detailed studies of the smaller houses in particular areas of the country. This book attempts to bring together much of this work as a guide for the non-professional reader wishing to know more of the way in which these smaller dwellings developed up to the present time, bearing in mind that the Oxford Dictionary's definition of the word "vernacular" is "that which uses the native or indigenous language of a country or district". The dictionary definition can be also "the arts native to a particular country or locality", and it appears that the word was first used in connection with the cottage building of the day as long ago as 1857, so the modern usage of the word has a rather longer history than is usually suspected.

Although the subject of this book is the houses of England it should not be assumed that the development of Welsh and Scottish, or for that matter Irish, houses differed much from the English pattern. Ideas cross geographical and national borders albeit slowly, and houses in other parts of the British Isles evolved in a similar way but perhaps slower and later than in southern England.

Although man has for ages needed to make a shelter, such dwellings appear as they are because of the materials found in the locality and man's understanding of how to use them by cutting and moulding them into convenient shapes. The type of house was always limited by man's knowledge at the time, bearing in mind that many small cottages were built by uneducated yeomen and that then, as now, "jerry-building" was not unknown. It was in the large important houses that innovations and experiments were tried, not in the small houses and cottages which were always conservative in their layout and construction, adopting the ideas incorporated in these larger manor-houses perhaps after an interval of several decades. Standard, mass-produced dwellings were virtually unknown until the Georgian period, and nowadays the family has to fit into a standard, mass-produced house space, whereas formerly except perhaps for the very poorest labourers, families always built houses to suit their needs and those of their cattle or the trade of the occupier.

When considering the development of such dwellings all modern romantic notions of thatched cottages with roses round the door must be shelved for the realization of the important fact that all such houses were once new, surrounded by scaffolding with workmen laying bricks or stone, or cutting timber, in very much the same way as they still do. Buildings generally now referred to as houses and cottages usually date from the last two centuries or so as the original flimsily constructed medieval cottages have long since disappeared. The older the small house, the more important it was when first built, so what we call a "medieval cottage" was really an important yeoman's house; nineteenth-century cottages of the same size were built only for poorer labourers. According to the Oxford Dictionary the word "cottage" only came into general use, meaning "a small erection for shelter, a cot, hut, shed, etc." as late as 1796, and in the U.S.A. a few years earlier, in 1765, so its present usage was unknown during the Middle Ages.

The development of different methods of construction and internal layouts does not fall into clear divisions like chapters in a book, as the various stages merge and overlap for a considerable time in parts of the country furthest from the south-east. Techniques which today appear to belong to widely separated periods, were often being used at the same time, and in buildings almost side by side in the same district, perhaps because some builders were more old-fashioned than others, and some owners wanted to appear more new-fashioned than their neighbours; ideas rooting in one part of the country might take a hundred years to flower in another. During the Middle Ages the technique of making timber-framed buildings was used for several centuries but by the Georgian period each generation saw changes, and the speed of change has now become so rapid that revolutions in construction may take only a decade to spread throughout the country.

In days when man had to use whatever materials were to hand his houses matched his surroundings, thus on one side of a hill could be found stone houses and on the other side, perhaps in a river valley, timber-framed or cob houses covered by thatch. In the space of a few miles these differences are dramatic and obvious and in many remoter rural areas are still apparent to the observant visitor. An example of this can be seen when travelling out of Wales and Radnorshire into Herefordshire or Worcestershire; on some roads the point where the stone buildings of the uplands give way to the timber houses of the Midland Plain is clearly seen, a swift change without overlapping of the two building types.

Geologists divide the British Isles into two parts, the highlands and the lowlands, the highlands comprising the western side of the country from the Scottish border to Devon and Cornwall, the Tees to Exe line, the lowlands east of the highlands and facing the English Channel and the North Sea. The lowlands occupy the London and Hampshire Basins, an area of gravels, sand and clay lying in the once well-wooded area between the chalk hills of the Chilterns and the Hog's Back of the North Downs, and westwards to Salisbury Plain, the characteristic local building materials being timber, flint and brick clay. Adjacent and extending from Hampshire through Surrey, northern Sussex and Kent is the Weald, once covered with forest, the natural materials being timber, clay for bricks, some stones and flint.

To the north and east the Fens and East Anglia were chiefly known long ago for timber, flint and brick clays, though development was restricted until the Fens area was adequately drained in the seventeenth and eighteenth centuries. The Yorkshire Plain, facing the North Sea, had brick clays and timber but a limited amount of good building stone. The Midlands cover a central undulating plain stretching from the mouth of the Severn to Lincolnshire and the south Staffordshire coalfield, an area with vast deposits of brick clay, good building stones and coal seams, which eventually became the birthplace of the Industrial Revolution.

The highlands comprise two areas, often divided by river valleys which formerly provided adequate supplies of timber for buildings. The highest areas, the top of the Pennines and the Welsh Massif (the hills of Wales, Monmouth, Herefordshire and Southern Shropshire) were too barren for any farming except perhaps sheep-rearing, and so were never properly developed. These areas and the similar areas of Exmoor and Dartmoor have plenty of building stone but very little timber or other suitable materials, and the granite, slate or millstone grit being hard to cut were never used on a large scale until better stone-cutting equipment was developed in the last century. The other part of the geologists' highlands, the English scarplands, is a broad belt of stone-bearing country supplying all the best building stones which provide a single material for both walls and roof coverings.

This division of England into highlands and lowlands is a much simplified view and as always in practice the evidence on the ground is not so clearly and precisely defined. It is obvious that in the highland areas there must be low-lying valleys or coastal lands which contain building materials vastly different from those on the hills, and these are often easier to use than the stone on the higher ground, while the lowlands of the eastern part of the country have hills which are sources of more useful stones than some found in the higher lands to the north and west.

But it is no use having a building material unless the resources and techniques to work it are available, so the earliest builders used what was lying on, or just below, the surface of the ground or what was easy to cut, like timber, therefore the early buildings were of cob and timber rather than the harder stones like granite.

As areas of habitation began at the coastline, extending gradually over the lowlands towards higher ground, it follows that different styles of building made a similar progression. Until the Industrial Revolution distorted the pattern, the lowland Britain of softer stones, flint, clay and the woodlands, south and east of the line from Yorkshire to Exeter, was also the most densely populated area and therefore politically the most important during the Middle Ages. The medieval wheat-growing region was here, overlapping and competing with wealthy sheep-rearing, originally confined to the lower hills surrounding the Midland Plain, so that this part of England supported the largest and richest towns, the markets for farmers and merchants. Therefore most of the ancient large houses or mansions were in the southern and eastern counties and where there were large mansions and estates there were most of the smaller houses, many of which survive today. The highland soil was poorer and farming harder even when conditions were suitable, and as these areas developed much later, most of the smaller houses date from a century or so later than in the richer lowland England.

In the lowland areas the Enclosures brought many new farmhouses and workers' cottages, a trend which continued during the eighteenth century, and many survive unaltered in some remoter villages, recognizable by their simple Georgian style. During this period of agricultural improvement many timber-framed houses and cob cottages disappeared, and despite their elegant air many of the new dwellings were badly built, especially those provided by landowners for their workers.

The second invasion of the rural areas occurred in the Victorian period when the railways made the countryside more accessible to the business-men; and for their new houses they rejected the local materials, using the mass-produced bricks then becoming available all over the country. These houses are usually found grouped near a railway station, which may now have disappeared, or in all sorts of unexpected places as they had no connection with the agriculture of the district.

In the highlands however the position was different as seventeenth- and eighteenth-century farming conditions were bad and most farmers could not afford to build new houses or replace the existing ones, many of which survived until well into the present century. Many of the other longhouses and cob cottages still stand alongside rows of nineteenth- century brick houses built as the result of industrial activity rather than for farm workers; nowadays rural areas like the moors of North York- shire and Cornwall may appear pleasant and undisturbed but this was not always so. The pattern of industrial development has changed so that factories are now largely within existing urban areas, but in the last century Cornwall provided much of the world's copper and many of the houses built for the large workforce of miners have survived though the mines closed down years ago. The same thing happened with the iron workings of North Yorkshire, the lead workings of the Pennines and the slate quarries of Cumberland and North Wales, where the workers' villages still remain after the decline or closure of local industry. Many of these groups of small houses built in the highlands are usually easy to identify as they are often in districts where agriculture, except perhaps sheep-farming, would be very difficult, and are rarely built of local materials, but almost always of mass-produced red brick.

Although most of the older, smaller houses date from the eighteenth and nineteenth centuries it should be remembered that the older the house the greater its importance at the time of building. The earliest labourers' cottages of cob have long since disappeared but more solidly built houses survived, namely the ones erected by the wealthier people of the community who could afford better materials and craftsmen to do the building. These older buildings certainly do not represent the ordi- nary houses of their period, no matter how the building may have been used afterwards.

As well as the availability of suitable materials the other factor deter- mining the type of house built was the economic situation; the possibility of choice of a particular type or design had little influence. Innovations in design always originated with royalty, noblemen or the church and by the time these ideas were adopted by merchants or farmers they had become rather commonplace and old-fashioned. What was more essential was the right economic climate to enable the builder to develop the skill to build more elaborate houses, which usually meant using less materials in a more efficient way, and having the right tools to use the materials properly.

Almost the first tools available to medieval craftsmen were those for cutting timber, and museum specimens show that these had hardly changed in shape from those used by the Romans, the chief difference being improvements in the metals used. During the Middle Ages there was certainly a very highly organized building industry but as tradesmen's tools were expensive and their training long, only very wealthy patrons could pay these craftsmen for the long periods necessary to erect the large and important buildings they required.

Given tools for felling trees and shaping wood into convenient sizes, the earliest houses of the timber-framed type had massive timbers and simple pegged joints, the cutting kept to a minimum so that small trees were often used untrimmed especially in places where the timber was not exposed, a practice followed under thatched roofs until the late nineteenth century. But such buildings are not all of the same date throughout the country, as those in the northern counties were built long after those in the south. Then as time went on tools were improved, each craftsman often making his own, so they could make more efficient joints as well as carved or moulded timberwork. The result was the elaborate timber-framed houses of the fifteenth to seventeenth centuries, although carvings in wood had appeared much earlier in many ecclesiastical buildings.

A similar evolutionary process applied to masonry, the first buildings being largely of rubble picked off the ground and used as it was since lengthy and arduous stone-cutting was avoided unless absolutely necessary. The first stone-cutting tools helped to build the castles and churches of the Saxon and Norman periods but even the very wealthy merchants or landowners had to be content with houses of a very simple type. The older the elaborately carved stonework the more important the building, as such decoration proclaimed the great wealth of the owner and apart from moulded arches around doors and windows, all other early carved stonework is found in churches. This remained so throughout the medieval period and domestic buildings were of plain and simple stonework until the arrival of efficient stone-cutting saws in the eighteenth century. These made possible the fine ashlar-faced houses of the Jacobean and Georgian periods with their classical pilasters and cornices, and afterwards cheap worked stone became available for quite modest houses, characteristic of many of the stone areas of the country.

Again it was the national prosperity from the sixteenth century onwards which encouraged the steady improvement of kilns ensuring the reliable and fuel-saving production of bricks. Efficient kilns resulted in brickmaking on a scale large enough and cheap enough for the needs of the whole country with the ensuing rejection of local styles of building dictated by local materials.

Before the early nineteenth century, small houses and cottages whether urban or rural were not specifically designed by architects, as might be the case today, but were the result of the builder's interpretation of the requirements of the owner of the property. Most people formerly lived in the same type of house, the one and only difference being the size and number of rooms, so that up to the end of the eighteenth century anyone requiring a house could ask the local builder to produce one with so many rooms and, by specifying the use of the Building Acts laid down by Parliament, would know what type of house would be built. In the medieval period it would have been timber-framed, in the Georgian period it would be a simple brick or stone house with no decoration externally, having sash-windows and a plain tile or slate roof. After this things were different partly due to the advent of better printing methods so that books became available to more people, not only building owners but also the master builders.

It was these "pattern" books which, from the Georgian period onwards, enabled the local builder to adapt the prevailing fashionable style of London houses to the needs of people in his own area, possibly far from the capital, which he and his clients probably never saw. The first of these books dealt solely with the designs of the façades, leaving the builder to adapt them to his own requirements, fitting in the rooms behind the front wall as best he could, often with the odd results still seen today.

Later volumes, particularly in the nineteenth century, contained designs for cheaply built cottages for farm labourers following the example of John Wood, the builder of much of Bath, whose book, *Series of Plans for Cottages and Habitations of the Labourers*, was first published in 1781.

Before the eighteenth century the appearance of smaller houses and cottages was governed by their location, the local building materials and the economic development of that part of the country; in the nineteenth century these influences weakened as local materials were rejected as being comparatively more expensive. In most districts the turning-point, and the houses built before and after that point, should become obvious to anyone who studies his locality and detects the differences in the materials employed, and this book may help in understanding the changes and the reasons for their occurrence.

2

The Early Builders

For many centuries after the departure of the Romans the ordinary yeomen lived in dwellings of unbaked earth or cob, to use the well-known Devon name, which should not be despised as it is the oldest building material known to man. If such dwellings are to survive for any time the earth has to contain sufficient lime to enable it to harden, as well as being mixed with straw or heather, to give it extra strength. The oldest buildings of this type are found in districts where the soils contain natural lime, particularly Cumberland and Westmorland as well as Dorset, Devon and Cornwall although rarely in south-eastern England. This is strange as large deposits of chalk very suitable for this kind of building are found here, but perhaps in this earliest inhabited part of the country the tradition of using cob disappeared before it did in the rest of the British Isles. For centuries cob was not exclusively a poor man's material; for example the old manor-house at Hayes Barton near East Budleigh, birthplace of Walter Raleigh in 1552, is built of it. The house, still existing and probably not new when Raleigh's parents lived in it, was later altered and rendered with cement mortar; not the traditional method of finishing such buildings.

The old Devon saying that cob needs "a good hat and a good pair of shoes" means that this type of wall needs a roof and a plinth to keep out the rain and rising damp. Once the thatched roof ceases to keep out the weather the walls disintegrate, leaving only piles of earth and a few traces of the supporting timber posts, and therefore cob huts have disappeared but the more important houses of timber, stone or brick survive, some isolated in rural areas often with no indication of the small villages which used to surround them. Modern archaeological excavations reveal the remains of these houses, but not the humbler homes which have gone leaving almost no trace.

But traditional methods of building rarely disappear completely and in 1956, over fifteen hundred years after the Romans left the country, excavations at Verulamium, near the modern city of St Albans, revealed the remains of a house built by them whose lower walls were of flint, with lime mortar, the tops being flat and crossed by slots to hold timber shuttering. This was used to retain the yellow clay of which the upper parts of the walls were built before being plastered, and so little do things change, that a similar form of construction was still being used in parts of eastern Europe up to the beginning of the present century.

There is documentary evidence that as late as 1212, walls of mud were being extensively used in London and their use continued until at least 1419 when a building law decreed that chimney-stacks should only be of stone, brick or tiles and all stacks of mud, often reinforced with timber beams, should be demolished. It is unlikely that everyone complied with this regulation, as right up to the Great Fire of 1666 efforts were being made to enforce such rules. As fashions changed, rather than demolish the older cob dwellings, builders often encased them in stone or brick to form more up-to-date-looking houses, and not only domestic buildings, as in 1925 when the bulging walls of the fifteenth-century church at Cold Ashby were being repaired, an infilling of local mud was discovered between the two exposed stone skins.

According to eighteenth-century writers it was quite common for the poor to live in mud cottages, and some of the best descriptions of cob as a contemporary building material are to be found in the agricultural survey of England made for the government early in the nineteenth century. The material is known to have been used in Devon since the thirteenth century and Charles Vancouver in his *General View of the Agriculture of Devon* (1813) refers to whole villages of whitewashed cottages, Devon having perhaps more buildings of this type than any other county except perhaps Cumberland. William Stevenson in the companion volume for Dorset, written in the previous year, states that about a week was allowed for drying out between the successive layers of cob, taking between five and six weeks to finish the walls. This contrasts with other accounts that as long as a year was required, but it is obvious that the time varied as the work had to be fitted in between the normal farming activities, and Frederick Eden in his book *The State of the Poor*, written in 1746, related how whole villages would turn out to erect the walls of a cottage for a newly-wed couple, a communal effort taking a single day and ending with a feast.

Hutchinson, in his *History of Cumberland* of 1794, writes about such dwellings found over a large area of this county and a survey made about twenty years ago recorded over a hundred cob dwellings in the Solway district, one in ten dating from before the 1840s and several as early as 1672. Up to 1856 all Naseby was described as being of mud construction and during the preceding two centuries Lye in Worcestershire was locally called "mud town", all the miner's houses being built of clay lump. Also up to the start of this century cob buildings could be found all over the industrial Midlands, particularly in the Black Country, a rare survival being found at Foleshill, not far from the centre of modern Coventry, as late as the 1960s; its construction was recognized only when it was being demolished.

Cob was also widely used without shuttering, the clay mixed with pebbles and straw before being used, and traditionally this was done in the winter, the material being left in the open to weather before the walls were built in the spring or summer months. The walls were raised slowly, each section being allowed to dry out and harden properly before proceeding to the next layer, about 2 feet being the maximum practical to deal with at one time as the walls were lined up by eye as work went on.

The more usual, and quicker, method was to use a clay mix laid between shuttering of planks, logs, twigs or hurdles. The wet clay and pebbles had layers of straw reinforcement, and this type of building can sometimes be recognized by the thin layers of clay, usually about 7 to 12 inches thick, with chopped straw in between. The walls were normally 2 to 3 feet thick, although examples are known as thick as 4 feet, and when the walls were finished the loose ends of straw were cut off flush with the cob. All the later, and thus surviving, buildings have plinths of about 1 to 2 feet high, different stones being used according to the district; in Devon stone or pebble, in Leicestershire boulders from the Boulder Clay, in Rutland rubble sandstone, in Cumbria blocks of slate and in East Anglia flint followed later by brick.

The strongest material is earth containing chalk, or pure chalk, which forms a very hard wall. The best area to discover such buildings is Buckinghamshire where in some places a chalky earth, known as 'wichert' can be found just below the surface. This, when mixed with straw, forms a strong cob and examples can still be found from Aylesbury westwards, particularly near Haddenham and Dinton. The best locality for pure chalk cob, however, is near Andover and on the edge of the Salisbury Plain where, as late as the 1920s, efforts were made to revive the technique to provide cheap homes for ex-servicemen. The scheme was started by the Government near Amesbury in Wiltshire, and some thirty-three dwellings were built, each on its five-acre small holding. These homes of either chalk cob or chalk blocks are still standing, the walls of the two-storey houses being 1 foot five inches thick, while in other cases chalk and ordinary soil were mixed and used dry, being rammed between shuttering.

The material used for cob walls varied from place to place depending on the local clays and experience of the builders, but it was essential that the earth used should contain the right proportion of clay. The agricultural surveys of the last century state that in Hampshire and Dorset the mix was three parts chalk, one of clay and straw, and where chalk was not easy to obtain it was only used as a finishing coat. In Dorset loam, gravel and sand were used with heather as a binder instead of straw, and in Cornwall two loads of clay were used to one of broken slate, while barley straw was commonly used in this district.

Since cob walls were rough they were built to project 1 inch or so beyond each side of the stone or brick plinth, and were then pared down smooth with a special tool like a baker's shovel but made of iron rather than wood. This was done when the walls had completely dried out, allowing the natural colour of the cob to show up, which varied according to the type of clay used; for example in red sandstone areas it was red, while in chalk areas it would be white. This kind of dwelling was usually given a protective covering to prevent rain penetrating the walls, lime-wash and plaster were generally used but traditionally sand thrown onto wet tar was used in East Anglia. A mixture of clay and cow dung was also used as a protection and cases have been recorded, particularly in Naseby in 1792, of cob houses being coated with dung which after it had dried was removed and used for fuel, the covering being renewed for this purpose every year.

A further use of unbaked earth, *pisé-de-terre*, may sometimes be found but more rarely in this country than in Europe and Africa where it is still in common use. *Pisé-de-terre*, or rammed earth, was first used by the Romans although the few surviving examples in this country only date, as far as can be told, from the earlier years of the last century when it was first introduced from the continent. Unlike cob, the earth is cleaned of all vegetable matter and stones, being used dry, rammed between wooden or other shuttering.

All dwellings of earth have thick massive walls laid either directly on the ground or on a stone plinth, later examples having brick instead of stone in this position; the thickness of the external walls preventing them spreading outwards when the roof beams and coverings are placed on them. The walls also have to be tied together by cross walls, usually of other materials, as due to the thickness required cob walls would take up too much space. Cob is sometimes used as a filling in these internal stud partitions before being plastered, but as all the rooms are small and as the strength of the material is reduced by every opening, there is a limit to the size, and number, of door and window openings; generally speaking the smaller the windows, the older the building, while in later examples the larger window openings were spanned by lintels of timber buried in the clay walls. Originally the roof-covering was always thatch, or reed, but from the Tudor times these inflammable materials became increasingly unpopular so that they have nearly always given way to clay tiles in town centres. Walls as thin as 18 inches are known, but although normally 2 to 3 feet thick, walls as thick as 4 feet have been discovered in some buildings. Cob is usually used for single-storey dwellings but walls as high as 30 feet have been recorded, and all buildings of solid clay usually have the corners rounded off to prevent cracking, while ovens may still be found in semi-circular projections below the chimney-stacks.

Even today many cob cottages survive although some are hard to distinguish having been faced at a later date with plaster, limewash, cement
or brickwork, while in Northamptonshire ironstone was also used.
Some examples also exist, perhaps dating from the seventeenth century,
of cob walls at first-floor level and ground-floor walls of stone or brick, as
well as houses with the front walls of stone with cob at the rear. In Pitt's
View of Agriculture in Leicestershire, written in 1809, the use of road scrap-
ings for building cottages is mentioned, but old records show that this is
not new, as in 1587 people were tried in Northamptonshire for taking up
clay from the Queen's highway for building their houses.

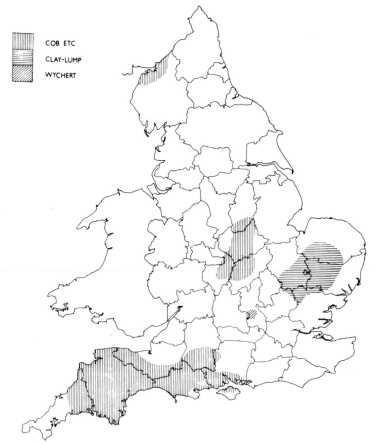

COB ETC

CLAY-LUMP

WYCHERT

Fig. 1 Main districts where earth houses and cottages still survive

The other common use of clay for building – in its unbaked form – is
for bricks or clay bats, also known as clay lump in the eastern counties.
Even this is of ancient origin as in recent years a Roman building was

excavated in Leicester where the walls were of mud bricks, $17 \times 11 \times 3$ inches bedded in a loamy sand before being rendered with a rough coat of lime and straw, later decorated in colour. Examples of this technique are now generally restricted to East Anglia though widely used in the early part of the last century until the mass-production of cheap bricks, easily transported by the railway, superseded this material. Chalk and clay marl, mixed with straw, was moulded into bricks about $18 \times 12 \times 6$ inches which were dried in the open air rather than being baked in a kiln. Walls were then built using soft clay as mortar, the outside covered with a thin coating of clay or limewash and the inside often plastered, although these walls often had to be quite thick to allow for the weight of the roof-covering as mud, in itself, is not a very strong material when used to carry weights.

In the specification for work at Fersfield, Norfolk, carried out for the Duke of Norfolk early in the nineteenth century, the method was described as follows:

> The clay to be raised on the farm within a quarter mile of the site, to be properly picked so as to leave no large stones and to be trodden in with long hay or straw and made into lumps 1½ feet long, 1 foot wide and 6 ins. deep, the lumps to be carefully dried and built up in a workmanlike manner jointed with a mixture of clay and mud and the lumps to be keyed on both sides while soft for plastering.

Later examples of this kind of building have flint, or brick, plinths to keep out the rising damp and often a tar and sand finish before being colour-washed traditionally white, red, pink, yellow and buff. Instead of colour-washing, the outside was often finished with a thin skin of bricks as may be seen in East Anglia and Cambridgeshire.

A study of the large-scale editions of early Ordnance maps may also suggest places to search, for example Mud Town near Walton-on-Thames which had some early nineteenth-century clay cottages, and cob buildings of the same date still survive elsewhere providing comfortable homes now that they have been modernized, contrasting with the vivid descriptions of such cottages by writers like Edwin Chadwick, the great sanitary reformer. In 1842 he visited some dwellings in the Vale of Aylesbury and wrote: "the vegetable substances mixed with the mud to make it bind rapidly decompose leaving the walls porous. The earth of the floor is full of vegetable matter, and from there being nothing to cut off its contact from the surrounding mould, it is peculiarly liable to damp . . ." Although it should be said that by then the long tradition of cob building was at a very low ebb, being replaced in most cases by brick, and today almost all that the observant will see, particularly where rural

Northamptonshire runs into Leicestershire, are farmyards surrounded by cob walls, once with a thatched coping but now almost always covered with the ubiquitous corrugated-iron sheets. But for the diligent searcher with local knowledge, examples of cob houses can still be found over a wide area of northern Northamptonshire, though less frequently elsewhere in the Midlands.

All these early buildings had earth floors, later replaced by brick or tile, which in their turn have been replaced by concrete required under the modern building regulations to prevent rising damp. The use of earth lasted for a very long time in rural areas although this was replaced many times during the life of the dwelling as, being porous, it tended to absorb nitrous waste materials. In order to search for the nitre required in the making of gunpowder, and only known in its natural form at this period, the 'saltpetre man' had power to dig up floors in his search for this material. These officials often exceeded their powers and acted in a very high-handed manner so that during the sixteenth and seventeenth centuries, in particular, many cases of abuse are recorded and these increased until saltpetre digging was discontinued during the Commonwealth. To keep down the dust, earth floors were often strewn with rushes or green plants, and in the sixteenth century the practice of mixing the earth with bullocks' blood, which made it hard and black, became popular, this material also being used as plaster. Another method of hardening floors was to mix the earth with crushed bones, but later the finish was improved by mixing lime with the earth to help its setting properties. This method was described by William Marshall in his *Rural Economy of Yorkshire* (1787), showing that such floors were still quite common in all types of rural dwellings.

As far as can be established the earliest covering for these huts was a crude form of thatch using turf, heather or reed on a simple form of wooden roof. Thatch has a limited life so none of these original coverings remain, most having been replaced by cheaper mass-produced clay tiles. Few existing thatched roofs are older than fifty to seventy years, as thatch will not normally last longer, and though the number of thatchers now exceeds the supply of straw or reed, ironically, modern building regulations make it almost impossible to put a thatched roof on a new dwelling.

Thatch has a long history, being mentioned by Bede who died in 735, and today it is a rich man's material, more expensive than almost any other roof-covering; this was not always the case as during the last century it had become the poor man's material used on almost all small cottages. Due to its continual decay, and the need to renew it every fifty years or so, the use of thatch declined when tiles became cheaper to produce and their use more widespread. This was only part of a continuous process accelerated by its prohibition in towns from very early times due to the risk of fire.

Everyone has heard of the Great Fire of London but this was only one of many fires which took place in almost every town of any size. Fires occurred in London in the years 1077, 1087, 1135, 1136 and 1161, while Canterbury also suffered in 1161 as did Exeter, followed by Winchester in 1180 and Glastonbury four years later. Chichester suffered in 1187, Worcester in 1202, Chester in 1140, 1180 and 1278 and almost the whole of the centre of Warwick was destroyed in this way in 1694. These events, with many others, resulted in continual efforts by the Crown and city burgesses to discourage the use of thatched roofs in the centre of congested towns. Many building laws were introduced, mostly dating from a period immediately after a "great fire" and a London building law of 1189 required that where existing buildings had thatched roofs, these should be coated with lime plaster to try and prevent the spread of fire by sparks, a practice still continued in some parts of rural Wales.

In this same Act, Henry Fitz-Alwin, the first Lord Mayor of London, decreed that the walls between all new houses should be built of stone and the roofs covered with slate or burnt lime, the use of thatch on such buildings being forbidden. It was of little avail because, being cheap and with the materials easily obtainable locally, most houses continued to be thatched until about 1570–1640 when national prosperity stimulated a great period of rebuilding so that all except the poorest were rehoused. These new houses were largely roofed with stone or clay tiles, thatch only surviving in rural areas where reed and straw were plentiful, although it is known that flax, broom and heather were also used. By the end of the Tudor period most towns had banned the use of thatch as, for example, in Hull in the reign of Elizabeth I, although the tradition lingered on and at the beginning of Victoria's reign there were about two hundred and seventy wholly or partly thatched churches in East Anglia. The number today has diminished and there are only about sixty in Norfolk and twenty in Suffolk with a few others scattered elsewhere in the area. Though thatch was banned in Cambridge in 1619, some towns had more difficulty in prohibiting it and as late as 1825 the Act for Improving the Town of Leamington Priors in the County of Warwick (now known as Leamington Spa) forbade its use on the new buildings of the Regency spa town, indicating that it was still in use in the district.

The banning of thatch meant that most of the buildings roofed with it were in country areas where natural stone for "slates" was not easily available, particularly in East Anglia and parts of the West Country, and as thatch was the lightest of the traditional roof-coverings it was extensively used on cob houses where the walls could not support other heavier coverings. It is therefore usual to find thatched roofs and cob buildings in the same districts, but it should be realized that all the trim thatched roofs seen today are "modern". These are certainly not older than some time this century as long straw only lasts about fifteen years, wheat reed for about twenty and Norfolk reed for about seventy-five, depending on the care taken to maintain the roofs.

Although thatching methods have changed very little the materials used have altered considerably with changes in farming. In medieval times short straw was used, each layer of it being spread with wet clay as the roof was covered, while heather was widely used in the same way. Variations to the common pattern were found in places where other materials grew, such as flax in Derbyshire, sedge in Fens around Ely and reed in Norfolk and Suffolk. Later, when the drainage of the dykes reduced the reed-beds in the Fens, reed was replaced first by the distinctive hand-made clay pantiles of East Anglia and later by the less attractive plain machine-made tiles. Heather was traditionally used in the northern counties of Yorkshire, Durham and Northumberland and around Exmoor and Dartmoor in the south-west, and was cut in the autumn while still in flower. It is not much used today, although less liable to rot than straw, as it tends to blacken and look less attractive after being exposed to the weather for a number of years.

The most reliable contemporary estimates suggest that there are about 50,000 thatched buildings still in use and these all have one characteristic in common, which is the roof with a steep pitch between forty-five and fifty degrees to allow the rain to run off quickly rather than soak into the thatch. So unless the roof trusses are to be unusually large, they cannot have a very wide span which results in the buildings being long and narrow with small rooms inside. There is also always a large eaves overhang to allow the water to drip clear of the walls as damp is the enemy of both thatch and cob walls. More buildings of this kind survive in Norfolk and Suffolk than perhaps anywhere else, mostly roofed with the natural reed found in the river estuaries and marshlands of the Fen district. This is cut, when between 3 and 8 feet long, during the winter when the leaves have been stripped off by frost, and afterwards it is stored to dry before use. Due to the improved drainage of the dykes, natural reeds are scarcer and commercial reed-beds are now cultivated on the Norfolk marshes and cut as a crop to provide regular supplies of this long-lasting thatching material, but to meet the demand it now has to be imported from such places as Holland.

Leaving East Anglia, thatched buildings become fewer but do not disappear completely as one journeys across the Midland Plain towards the Welsh borderland. It is here, in Worcestershire and Herefordshire, that this form of roof-covering appears again, wheat straw being commonly used. This in turn is uncommon the further north one travels towards

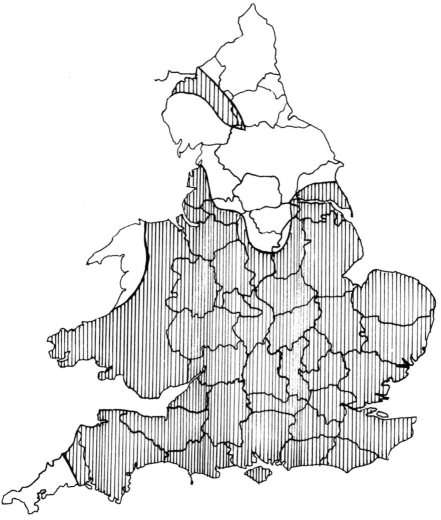

Fig. 2 Districts where thatched buildings survive in varying numbers. (Based on Brunskill)

Lancashire and Cumbria where rye straw was sometimes used, but the covering was more probably heather, although this is rarely seen today. In Dorset and Devon thatching in wheat reed was once common; this material is not to be confused with the natural reed of East Anglia although it is hard to tell the difference once a roof is covered. The wheat reed derives its name from being laid in the same way as natural reed with the ends exposed and showing all over the roof, whereas with straw the stem shows along the line of the slope. Today, due to its durability, more reed is being used on roofs than formerly and in many districts beyond its original home in East Anglia is replacing the traditional straw thatch.

But whatever type of straw is used the wheat, barley or rye has to be cut in a way which prevents the stems being crushed or broken. The modern combine harvester breaks the straw which renders it useless for thatching and today, as a result of modern farming methods, straw for thatching has to be grown as a special crop and harvested with the old-fashioned binder and baler before being threshed with a reeding or combing device to prevent breaking, and leaving the stems about 3 feet long. This makes the material expensive as modern wheats have short stalks, so special varieties have to be grown and harvested by what are now almost museum pieces. Only a few farmers grow straw especially for thatching and they always have full order books, supplying the same thatchers year after year. It has been estimated that on average a single thatcher uses annually the straw from up to forty acres of wheat, and it is becoming increasingly difficult to obtain. Although straw from wheat, rye, oats and barley were once all used, modern harvesting methods mean that wheat now takes preference, rye sometimes being found on buildings in northern England.

3

The Medieval House

Originally all buildings were of cob or unbaked earth, sometimes re-inforced with timber uprights buried in the walls. Later farmers used more permanent building materials and from then distinctions depend on where the farm was situated as well as on what materials were easily found; stone in the highlands of northern England and various escarp-ments of the southern parts of the country, with timber in the forests of the lowland plains. No real communications existed between these districts as the roads, laid out by the Romans, gradually fell into disre-pair after their departure leaving large areas of the country isolated, served only by rough tracks. This meant that all building materials would have to be found very near the site, and therefore distinctive buildings would be grouped together in quite a small area. To under-stand the development of building it is important to realize the diffi-culties of transporting materials any distance by ox-carts, and as travelling in winter was practically impossible everything would have had to be moved during the rest of the year. Records tell us that, for example, the commissioners of Henry VIII reported that the lead from the roof of Jervaulx Abbey in Yorkshire "cannot be conveyed away until next summer for the ways in the countie are so foule and deepe that no carriage can pass in winter". If this was the case for the King's property, the small yeoman had no possible means of moving his ma-terials, but in better conditions some building materials required by the Crown were carried great distances. We know that in 1177–8 timbers were taken from York to help repair the Tower of London, while in the years 1100–35 beams used for the building of the abbey at Abingdon came from Wales, taking six weeks on the journey.

The first statute dealing with roads was the Statute of Winchester in 1285 stating that highways leading from one market town to another shall be enlarged "so that there be neither dyke nor bush whereby a man may lurk to do hurt within two hundred feet of either side of the way". So at least up to this period communications for the ordinary man were almost impossible unless they were able to take several days, or some-times weeks, on the journey.

Improvements were slow to come, and an Act of 1621 forbade the use of four-wheeled wagons and the carriage of goods of more than one ton in weight, because vehicles with excessive burdens so spoilt the highways and the very foundations of the bridges, that they were a public nuisance.

A further Act in 1629 stated that no more than five horses or oxen were to be used for one vehicle, but by 1662 the use of seven horses or eight oxen was permitted, although such restrictions continued well into the eighteenth century when turnpike roads, and canals, made the carting of materials easier. So it is evident that up to this period, when the canal system began to expand, the transport of materials for building to places not on rivers or canals was very difficult and expensive, and local styles of building continued for many centuries until the pattern was disturbed by modern methods of transport evolving over the last two hundred years or so.

All these difficulties meant that ideas also travelled slowly, with the result that forms of building being used in parts of southern England within the influence of London and the major ports, extended gradually along the trading routes from town to town so that building styles used in the southern counties were not in common use in, for example, Cumberland until a hundred years later. For this reason the evolution of the traditional house does not fall into clear-cut sections, like chapters of a book, since various forms of construction and plan types often overlap for long periods, but as far as can be established the next distinct form of timber building was the use of crucks, or curved tree branches, used in bays to support the roof-covering, a development to be discussed in the next chapter. Here it should be noted that there are two methods of building, still used today although the materials may be different; these are mass construction and framed construction, the type of material employed depending on the choice of the system.

In mass construction, the type of material used depends on the choice of the system as the roof and floor loads are carried down to the foundations by means of the walls which also give protection from the weather. Materials used for this kind of building include stone, flint, brick, unbaked earth or cob, and, in modern times, concrete. The material used for the frames of traditional buildings was always timber, in either the form of crucks or by jointed beams. In this case the panels, which do not carry any loads, were filled in with wattle and daub or, in later times, brick, leaving the frame exposed, or sometimes covered with a cladding of tiles, weather-boarding or lath and plaster. Therefore early in the Middle Ages there were examples in this country of two types of building techniques which have continued to the present day.

It would also be wrong to think of the early medieval period as lacking skilled builders or craftsmen. This is a false idea as old records provide an immense amount of information about the large numbers of building craftsmen working throughout the country, and there were many carpenters and stonemasons who travelled, often in large numbers, along the poor roads connecting castles, monasteries and major towns. These

Manor House, Hayes Barton, East Budleigh, Devonshire. The birthplace of Walter Raleigh in 1552. This large cob house was constructed some time before that date and is still in existence, although a little altered

A small farmhouse in cob and thatch, typical of the Devonshire countryside

The Jew's House, the Strait, Lincoln, built between 1170 and 1180 and one of the earliest surviving stone houses in the country although altered on the ground floor

The Manor House, Boothby Pagnell, Lincolnshire, a fine example of an early medieval stone house built about 1200

A cruck house, Weobley, Herefordshire, an example of the early cruck houses of the western Midlands, dating from almost any time between the fifteenth and seventeenth centuries

Weavers' cottages, Lavenham, Suffolk. A general view of timber-framed cottages
built between the fifteenth and sixteenth centuries

Two-bay, timber-framed house off the Market Place, Lavenham, built in the
fifteenth or sixteenth centuries

The Priest's House, West Hoathly, Sussex. A fifteenth-century, timber-framed house with the roof covered in stone slabs from the Horsham locality. The first-floor windows are in the original state

(*Above*) Preston-on-Stour, Warwickshire. Timber-framed house dating from the sixteenth century with close studding on the ground floor, square studding above and gables with their ornamental infilling probably dating from early in the following century

The Old White Horse Inn, High Street, Henley-in-Arden, Warwickshire. Sixteenth-century close studding over an altered ground-floor wall of brick

The Preacher's House, Ewhurst, Sussex. A sixteenth-century, close-studded
house with later tile-hanging concealing the first-floor timbering

(*Above left*) Orleton, Herefordshire. Timber-framed house with large panel framing and a slightly projecting seventeenth-century central bay, a development characteristic of that period. (*Above right*) Abbots Morton, Worcestershire. Sixteenth-to seventeenth-century house, with close studding and square framing used in the same building. A later brick chimney has been added to the timber-framed gable wall

Haddenham, Buckinghamshire. Seventeenth-century square framing with brick infilling of various dates. Probably this building always had brick infilling rather than the earlier wattle and daub

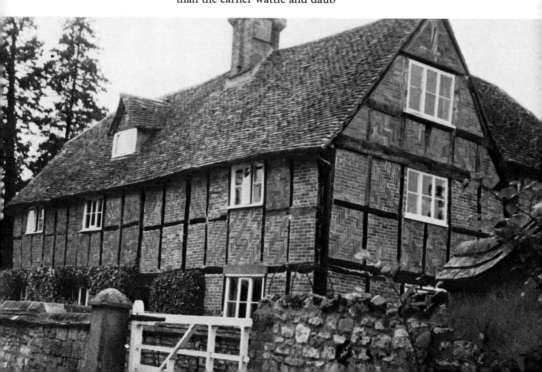

The Abbot's Fireside, Elham, Kent, built in 1614 using close-studded walls with a continuous jetty, the framing only being exposed on the upper floor. The jetty, and the wide overhanging roof eaves, are supported on elaborately carved brackets. The south end gable wall, just seen in the photograph, is a fine example of seventeenth-century brickwork

Lady Hill, Lavenham, Suffolk. Detail of a house with a continuous jetty at first-floor level, the overhang being supported on the projecting floor joists

craftsmen never worked on the small houses built by the yeomen, but local people working alongside them naturally learned new techniques while engaged on large and quite complicated building contracts, and since such buildings often took several years to complete these craftsmen might live in a particular locality for a long time.

What is certain is that with few exceptions small houses built in England up to the thirteenth century were of turf, earth or timber. In the early period this applied even to the royal palaces, from evidence provided by excavations on the site of the royal palace at Cheddar. Only in the more important Anglo-Saxon churches and some defensive works was stone used in any quantity, at least before the coming of the Normans, and all those buildings which have survived have now been so well recorded that it is unlikely that other Anglo-Saxon churches or larger houses could be found standing above ground.

The earliest homes were the farmsteads scattered over the lower plains of the country where cattle sheltered under the same roofs as their owners, until the later periods when cattle, and some farm crops, were kept in separate buildings, leading to the now normal situation of a farm-house away from the general farm buildings. Excavations show that there were two kinds of small Anglo-Saxon house where some stone was used, sunken huts and those at normal ground level which had low stone walls acting as a base for cob and crude timber walls. These dwellings, both sunk and at ground level, were circular with one, or perhaps two, poles in the centre to support the simple roof. Some later buildings used an elementary form of construction, inclined poles tied at the bottom to a log, or sill beam, resting on the ground or with the poles pushed into the ground itself. There were no vertical walls and a later example of this type of building was "Teapot Hall" in Lincolnshire, but it was obviously an inconvenient form of building without vertical walls. This was eventually overcome by placing a horizontal timber, just above head height, across the sloping poles to support the top of a vertical wall. These walls of cob were sometimes thinner as wattle was placed in the centre of the earth to give it strength, or timber planks used instead. There is evidence also that some of the larger important buildings had first floors; at the meeting of the Royal Council at Calne in 978, the floor collapsed and, according to Anglo-Saxon documents, many of King Edward's noblemen were injured by the collapse of the timbers, leaving Archbishop Dunstan sitting safely on a beam in mid-air.

There are indications that some houses were boat-shaped, one example being found in excavations at Thetford where the house, 50 feet long and maximum width 15 feet, was divided into five rooms. It has been suggested in the past that this shape evolved from the experience of the Norse boat-builders. Whether this is so cannot really be proved, but the shape would provide protection against damage by high winds on exposed sites in eastern England. Some buildings did have massive posts, spaced about 8 feet apart, linked by horizontal or vertical timbers slotted into the posts, later examples of the planks having grooves down the sides to allow them to be connected by a tongue of wood or the tapered edge of a thinner alternate plank. In this country the only surviving example of such Anglo-Saxon timber construction is found in the nave of Greensted Church in Essex, now very much restored. Here the uprights are split oak logs with the curved bark-covered portions exposed externally, the corners being formed by a log with a part cut out to give an internal right angle. The timbers are let into a wooden sill which, when renewed in 1869, was discovered to be grooved with tongues of oak let in between the timbers. Such buildings must have been quite common, some having survived elsewhere in Europe until much later, but no example of a small house built in this way has yet been excavated in England.

Early stone houses are, however, not as rare as once thought, recent research having shown that there are some twenty examples of domestic buildings dating from Norman times which include at least some fragments of stonework from that period. Most of these date from the second half of the twelfth century, after the unrest caused during the reign of Henry II, and are mainly found in the oldest settled parts of southern England. There are also the remains of several hundred larger stone houses built in the early medieval period scattered all over the country not fitting into any pattern relating to present-day settlements which is that of a number of cities, with small towns and villages distributed around and very dependent upon these larger centres for all kinds of services. But at the period under discussion there were thousands of villages and hamlets spread evenly over the whole country although many of these have now disappeared, remembered as deserted medieval village sites or names on large-scale maps. It seems to have been unusual for even the more important market towns to have a population of over six hundred. These settlements grew up around a market-place or fairground, a river-crossing or port, at a defensive position or an intersection of major trails and were usually of a single street with building grouped round a market and church or, in the more important places, a castle.

An example of such a town is Warwick where in 1086 the Norman king owned one hundred and thirteen of the houses in the ancient borough, and his barons almost as many, crowded within the town walls which extended from the castle dominating the important ford and later the bridge built over the River Avon. In similar towns the lanes were usually less than 10 and often as little as 6 feet wide, resulting in considerable congestion as goods were carted to market. The house plots might be six times as deep as wide, the short side facing the street to save space, although narrow lanes were not inevitable as some towns were laid out with very much wider streets such as Stratford-upon-Avon where the Bishop of Worcester laid out his "new" borough with a main street 50 feet wide containing the market. Eventually the lines of market booths up the centre of this street gave way to permanent buildings dividing the original wide street into two narrow lanes, and similar developments due to overcrowding can be traced in many other ancient market towns.

Some form of control was essential and as early as 1189, the first year of the reign of Richard I, a building Act was introduced in London by Henry Fitz-Alwin, the Lord Mayor. While this controlled the building of walls between houses, known today as "party-walls" it only did this when owners actually wanted to build in stone, and the Act could not in itself prevent timber buildings being erected in ever-increasing numbers within the confines of the town walls. Each adjacent owner was required to give up 18 inches of his land on which they were jointly to build, at their own expense, a stone wall 3 feet thick and at least 16 feet high to help prevent the spread of fire. There were also rules dealing with such matters as the collection of immensely valuable rainwater from the roofs of the houses, the digging of pits for waste or basements for storage. An adjoining owner who could not afford the cost of building a wall was to give the neighbour who decided to obey the regulation 3 feet of his land to enable the work to be done.

But this Act had little effect on the style of buildings erected in London and other large cities, and a similar Act was introduced in the reign of King John after a fire in July 1212 destroyed London Bridge and a large number of houses. Records show that such shops and houses had very small frontages, often as narrow as 12 feet, and shops opening directly onto the street were as little as 10 feet in depth. Some examples have been excavated showing ranges of four houses built on a site 84 feet by 20, each with a shop underneath the living quarters, and in most provincial towns the buildings were only two storeys high. But by 1300 London was being rebuilt with three-storey houses and regulations existed to ensure that the projecting "jetties" of the timber-framed houses were at least 9 feet above ground (to allow a person on horseback to ride underneath) and no shop stalls were to project more than 2½ feet into the street and were to be movable. But such was the demand for land that only the richer people could build houses long side on to the street, as in the case of the Jew's House in Lincoln, and these landowners had to pay higher taxes as a result. In 1155, for example, the king decreed that for each house in Scarborough whose gable was turned to the street the tax was four pence, but when houses were built with the long side turned to the street the tax was six pence.

The only surviving Norman houses in anything like their original form are the so-called "Jews' Houses" or "King John's Houses", the tradition being that these stone houses were occupied by Jews, the only people allowed to be money-lenders or debt-collectors in the reign of King John. Although not all are in towns and few are unaltered, the locations of these stone domestic buildings, of which there are about twenty still existing, are well known and their construction has in recent years been the subject of much detailed research.

The stone used was found in the locality, generally picked up near the surface, and used in the form of rubble. The working of stone to square it up was then difficult and expensive and such stones were only used to form the corners of buildings as well as round the windows and door openings. The houses were rectangular, two storeys high, the usual size being about 20 feet by 40, split up into two or three bays. The living quarters or hall were always at a defensible height on the first floor, raised on a solid basement or undercroft reached by an external staircase of timber, and later stone, built parallel to the walls, but eventually this was constructed inside the house or in a projecting turret. Originally the lower storey was reached by a ladder through an opening in the first floor and there were no external door openings at ground level, this area being used for the safe storage of goods. Later, in more settled times, there was a doorway into the building at ground level facing the street and at first the upper floor was constructed of planks laid across the base of the tie-beams of the roof truss. But around the twelfth century these floors were independent of the roof and supported on beams propped underneath by central posts or stone columns to enable the span to be increased as the houses became larger. In time the wooden floors were superseded by bays vaulted in stone supporting a stone first floor, and, in the case of the larger buildings, one or two rows of columns down the length of the ground floor. Such houses were more fire-proof and so the owners were able to put a fireplace on the first floor which was lighted by shuttered windows, often of the oriel type, in the north end or one of the sides, but rarely in the southern end due to the belief that plague would enter a dwelling on the south side.

The Jew's House on the Strait in Lincoln is one of the best known of these houses and although the ground floor of this late twelfth-century house has been converted into a shop its original form is still recognizable. The house is unusual in having a northern entrance door at street level, its opening surrounded by an elaborate carved Norman archway. This doorway opens onto a passage leading to a rear yard where there was originally an outside timber staircase to the upper rooms which had two two-light windows. Although such houses are scarce the importance of Lincoln during the early medieval period is reflected in the fact that there are three twelfth-century stone houses still surviving in the city. As well as the Jew's House there is not far away a house of similar style known as "Aaron the Jew's house", named after the rich Jew who died in 1186, although there is no evidence that it ever belonged to him.

Other examples of such houses are Moyses Hall at Bury St Edmunds, built about 1180, whose lower floor is divided into aisles with stone columns forming six bays which support an upper floor made of the same material. The oldest domestic building in the town, and originally connected with the abbey, it has two storeys with a nineteenth-century east wall of flint and stone, but was drastically restored in 1858.

Records also show that in the thirteenth century, thirty similar stone houses existed in Canterbury. Little is left of them, but so unusual were stone houses even then that special reference is made to them in contemporary documents, the common timber-built houses receiving slight notice. One of the best examples of this type of house, outside the cities, is the Old Manor House at Burton Agnes, a few miles from Bridlington. This building, about 40 feet by 20 in size, is close to the Elizabethan Burton Agnes Hall, built in 1598, and was left standing when the family moved into their large new house. Today the Old Manor House is under the guardianship of the Department of the Environment who have recently restored it and although a later front was added to this Norman house most of the original two-storeyed building is visible. The upper floor is supported over a basement by a series of stone vaults held up by two rows of stone columns and is reached by a spiral staircase in the corner of the undercroft or basement.

But in spite of the increasing use of stone for buildings the danger of fire was still of great concern as most roofs were still thatched. After the fire of 1212 King John prohibited ale houses in the City of London, and unless built of stone, all existing buildings used by bakers or cooks had to be whitewashed or plastered both inside and out. As early as 1189 other fruitless efforts were made to have the thatch replaced by slate, shingles or baked tiles and an Act of 1221 also had to prohibit the use of thatch and require all new buildings to be covered with wooden shingles, lead, stone slabs or clay tiles. All existing houses which were covered with reed or rush had to be plastered over within eight days or failing this the sheriff's men would demolish the buildings on the spot. It is interesting that in rural Wales the practice of whitewashing thatched roofs to help prevent the spread of fire continued until the early years of the present century. But in spite of all efforts London remained a city of timber buildings up to the time of the Great Fire, which was the case throughout the whole country as, for example, it was not until 1509 that Norwich made the use of tiles on roofs compulsory and the last of the thatched buildings were replaced in that city.

As thatch became rather less popular wooden shingles came into use, particularly on church roofs. Shingles were cut by hand from local trees and overlapped to prevent water getting into the buildings in much the same way as tiles are used today, a method probably copied from the tiles used by the Romans although the art of tile-making had been lost after their departure. Shingles, though widely used, were never as common as thatch owing to the difficulty of getting suitable wood. They were made of oak and records show that by 1248, if not earlier, Henry III generally used them for roofing the royal palaces, but by 1260 stone tiles were taking preference. It is recorded that in 1236 shingles were 2s. per thousand, but, as timber increased in price, by 1386 the cost had risen to 13s. 4d. for the same quantity. This increase made stone tiles more popular, but at this time clay tiles were not in general use even on the royal palaces or monasteries, the largest buildings of the period.

The Saxons, having seen tiles on the roofs of the surviving Roman buildings, must quickly have realized their value as a roof-covering and there are examples of Saxon re-use of tiles and bricks taken from Roman sites. Although as early as 1290 tiles were being made in London most supplies at that time came from Flanders and these were almost the same size as those being used today.

In 1477 an Act introduced by Edward IV standardized the size as $10\frac{1}{2} \times 6\frac{1}{2} \times \frac{5}{8}$ inches thick, these being fixed by a peg whereas the same-sized modern tile is fixed by nibs, but this Act only really confirmed what is shown by other evidence to be the size already in regular use, so that one can say that the size of clay tiles has hardly changed in the last five hundred years and recent changes have only come about due to metrication. After the Act of 1477 there were still local variations, mostly in southern England; in Kent tiles were 9×6 inches, in Sussex $9 \times 6\frac{3}{4}$ inches while northwards in Leicestershire the size was as large as 11×7 inches and this type of variation continues to the present time, still being found in tiles made by hand rather than by machine.

In the medieval period vast quantities of tiles were being produced in such places as Hull where in 1303 the annual production was 54,000 tiles in addition to large numbers of bricks being produced in the same area. But where a suitable clay was available it was not uncommon for the tiles, and later bricks, to be made on the actual building site or as near as possible to it. Small gangs of craftsmen travelled the country making tiles in one area until the clay – or the demand – was exhausted and they moved on to another area. Tile-making was introduced, or perhaps more correctly re-introduced, into this country long before brickmaking, bricks being harder to bake in kilns than the thinner plain floor and roofing tiles.

During the thirteenth century tile-making was well established in the east and south-east of England and the technique spread slowly west-wards, so that tiles are known to have been made in Nottingham, Coventry and parts of Buckinghamshire during that century, while the first tiled roofs appeared in Worcester in 1467, which was rather later than in most cities of this size.

Anyone who has seen an old roof covered with hand-made tiles will appreciate the difference in texture and appearance between these and modern, machine-made tiles. Not only are there variations in size and texture, but the tiles were not hung, as today, on regular-sized battens which are of a standard size required under the modern building regulations. In the past riven and roughly shaped oak or elm laths were used and these were never straight or level, no one caring about a wavy line to the roof, which today causes many people to worry. The old tiles were then fixed by pegs through the tiles, until late in the nineteenth century a projecting nib was provided on the tiles to hang them over the battens, the pegs being eliminated. Early examples of fixing by nibs have rarely survived to the present day, except perhaps as museum exhibits. But in spite of the increasing use of tiles during the five centuries which followed the arrival of the Normans, thatch was still more common than tiles, particularly in rural areas.

4

The Cruck Tradition

The oldest types of timber buildings are those with curved tree principals, or "crucks" as they are commonly called. The earliest houses were originally all roofs as the framework was simply sloping pairs of tree-trunks stuck into the ground and tied together at the top to form tent-like structures. Later the trunks were crossed at the top to form a fork, being tied or pegged together with the pairs of trunks linked up at the top by a ridge pole which helped to stabilize the "crucks" as well as to support the smaller sloping branches which carried the thatch-covered roof.

The crucks were originally naturally curved tree-trunks as it was found these allowed more headroom in the dwelling and although it might appear to the casual observer that these timbers are curved, this is not really so. Over the centuries a distinct shape developed and all the crucks we see today, many surviving from the fifteenth century, are "elbowed" rather than curved as this gives the maximum height to the upright external walls. Such was the value of suitable trees that in order to economize on timber, matching pairs of crucks were obtained by slicing a trunk down the centre. There is documentary evidence indicating that trees were specially grown for use as crucks, the trunks being trained into a curved outline, and since such hardwood trees take a considerable time to mature this suggests that this traditional form of building had a very long history, eventually dying out perhaps through its uneconomic use of timber which was to become very scarce over the centuries.

Where this form of building started is uncertain, but its development extended from Saxon times, and possibly before, to the eighteenth century, although by this time the crucks had diminished in size or were formed of two sections of timber pegged together at the elbow. This type of construction thus overlapped the later timber-framed and jointed buildings so that for a long period both types were being built concurrently, the cruck gradually being abandoned as it became rather old-fashioned in appearance.

The first serious study of cruck buildings was in 1898 when Sidney Addy wrote his book *The Evolution of the English House*, a social and historical study of the house rather than the development of its construction. After the appearance of this book arguments began about where the cruck was first developed and one theory offered by Mr Addy was that cruck construction, although known to the Romans in a modified form, developed from similar shapes found in upturned boats, possibly those of the Viking settlers in England.

The fact that the full cruck may have been widely used only in northern England is supported by the evidence of old dialect expressions meaning "crucks", found in the same counties. The oldest non-classical form is "cruck" and in ancient times variations were found among the Teutonic languages describing the ribs of a boat, or a bent wooden post with a forked end. The English word has the same meaning and has passed from "crucken" to become cruck, while in Derbyshire such curved supports were known as couplings; in Durham the word used is forks and in Cumberland siles or sile-blades. The word siles is interesting as it also meant columns in some parts of Europe, and Mr Addy pointed out that the Anglo-Saxon word *gaflas* meant forks which were in some areas called gavels or gavelforks. This term was also applied to the forks, or crucks, at the two ends of a building which in time came to be called the gable ends. The word gavel was in common use in Scotland as late as 1788 and in some remoter areas until late in the nineteenth century referring to the end of a building. Numerous examples remain of buildings where crucks were only used at the gable ends, where they could be seen, with the intermediate supports formed of members pegged together and not cut out of solid tree-trunks, thus saving valuable timber.

The earliest discovered documentary evidence of a cruck in this country refers to a building in Essex mentioned in Estate Rolls of 1225. The first crucks were usually in large buildings of all types, as references in Crown records indicate; for example in 1245 a new garderobe containing six crucks was built for the queen on the west side of the courtyard at a royal residence at Brill in Buckinghamshire, while at Harlech Castle in 1306 seven great crucks were used for a new bakehouse. Records also show that in the medieval period the king, from time to time, instructed the custodian of the king's forests to allow various people to cut oaks to make crucks, this privilege being of great importance to local landowners.

The distinguishing feature of a cruck building is that these inclined timbers rise from ground level to the roof and this is supported on the crucks standing independently of the outside walls, which in other forms of construction take the roof loads. Whereas the later jointed buildings could be built up in panels on site it was not possible to do this with a cruck frame which had to be put together lying flat on the ground with the arch, and tie-beams, being pegged together before being raised upright. To do this the members had to be jointed so that the large timber pieces did not fall apart in the process of being heaved upright, therefore arch blades, and tie-beams, were usually fixed together with a notched-lap or halved dovetail.

It was usual to erect the end gable cruck first, and to assist in lifting up these heavy timbers levers were inserted in holes, normally about 18 inches above the base. If the bottom of the crucks has not rotted away these holes can sometimes still be seen in place. It is also sometimes possible to find numbers carved on the members showing the sequence in which they were erected, the numbers being put on in the builder's yard to help erection on site. (*See* Figure 3.)

Originally all crucks were in one piece of oak but where timber was scarce, two or more pieces were joined at the elbow to form a curved timber upright. This was done with pegs, and all pegs used were usually a square, or octagonal, shape about an inch in diameter, and while the pegs used in the mortise and tenon joints of a framed building could be knocked out if necessary, those in crucks were formed so that this was not possible. (*See* Figure 3.)

While full crucks were rarely used in south-east England, other forms of curved timbers which do not rise the full height of the building can be found in dwellings which have survived in those counties; modern experts call these base crucks, raised crucks and upper crucks. While the full cruck was open to the roof, forming in most cases the structural supports of a single-storey building, the base cruck normally formed the ground floor of a two-storey type. These crucks rise from the ground or a low plinth wall, but finish below the normal apex of the roof, being joined by a large tie- or collar-beam which in later examples supports a floor at the upper level with a simple truss over this holding up the roof and its covering. The raised crucks meet at the apex but start some way up the outside walls, into which they are built, rather than from the ground while the upper crucks are set on top of a tie-beam built between walls, and rise up to the apex of the roof, perhaps forming the upper storey. Since large oaks were becoming scarce in the south earlier than in the north these other cruck types, less than the normal 15 feet high full crucks, may have originated in part from a shortage of timber.

However it does seem doubtful whether the style was introduced by the Vikings, as the distribution of the surviving full cruck buildings does not coincide with that of places with Scandinavian names but rather the reverse. These buildings tend to be in places with ancient British names which may be due to their accidental survival in some districts rather than others, but it supports the idea that crucks were developed by the British rather than being introduced across the North Sea. Evidence shows that these buildings appeared over a wide area so it is more than likely that over the centuries crucks just developed from the natural way of erecting small huts by fastening tree-trunks to support a sloping thatched roof.

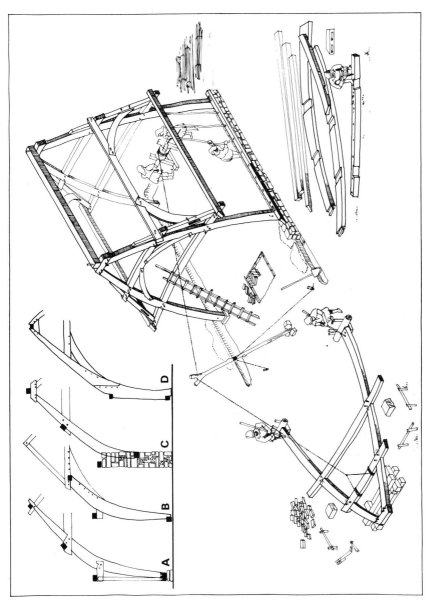

Fig. 3 Assembly and erection of a small, three-bay cruck house based on a house at Walsgrave in Coventry: A. full cruck with spur tie and halved apex joint; B. base cruck; C. raised cruck with saddle-type apex; D. jointed cruck with yoke-type apex. All types of crucks are found with any of the apex types illustrated

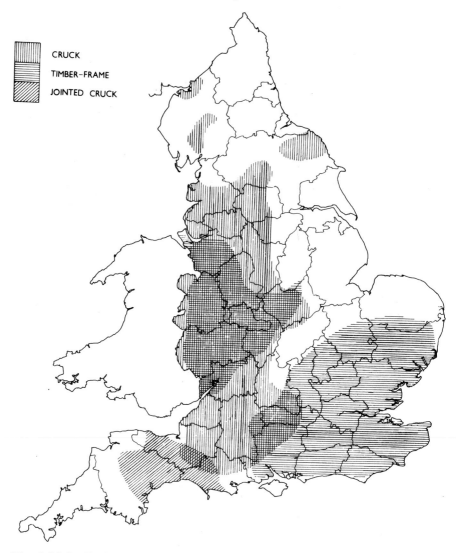

CRUCK

TIMBER-FRAME

JOINTED CRUCK

Fig. 4 Main districts where cruck and timber-framed houses and cottages are still to be found.

Whatever their origin full cruck buildings are found roughly north and west of a line from the Wash to the Solent and are almost non-existent in East Anglia and the eastern counties of Bedfordshire, Cambridgeshire, Hertfordshire and parts of Lincolnshire, and a few to the north of the Humber. Such buildings are also rare in the three south-eastern counties as well as westwards from Devon into Cornwall where it is known that from the early medieval period trees suitable for constructing timber buildings were hard to find. The county with the most examples is undoubtedly Herefordshire, particularly the district north and west of Weobley reaching into the borderland of Wales.

The space or gap between two pairs of crucks was known as a "bay" and since the ridge-pole tended to sag if the width of the bay exceeded about 16 feet, this distance tended over the years to become the normal width used between crucks. A lot of folklore has developed around the bay and Mr Addy suggested that the distance was dictated by practical considerations as from 12 to 15 feet was needed to allow a team of four oxen pulling a cart or plough to pass into the building. (*See* Figure 5.)

Normally a small cottage was only one or two bays in length and since buildings were often taxed according to the number of bays, extensions tended to be erected at the rear of the building, the roof slope being continued down over them to form what is called an "outshut". From early medieval times surveyors regarded the bay as a standard measurement and records of a survey made about 1737 of the Earl of Arundel's Yorkshire estates refer to "a dwelling house of four bayes, a stable being an outshut and other out houses are seven little bayes, beside a barne of four bayes". Just as buildings were measured by the bay they were also sold or let by the bay, and in deeds of sixteenth- and seventeenth-century houses the buildings are often described by the number of bays they contain.

In pre-metric days people would be used to hearing of rods, poles and perches used for land-surveying since Saxon times. An important development in land tenure was in 1277 when Edward I made the first attempt to standardize weights and measures. During the Norman period the rod length varied between 12 and 24 feet but in 1277 the length of the Statute English rod was set at 16½ feet, the bay width then in common use. This measure was first adopted as 16 Rhineland feet, approximately 16.4 English feet, which was adjusted to become 16½ feet, and this standard rod survived as a measurement of land well into the present century. The Statute acre was set as 160 square rods. There are many examples of buildings being measured with this unit, for example the Great Barn at Walton which was 10½ rods long by 3 wide. Mr Addy describes how the rod was originally fixed in Germany, an old book on surveying stating that:

to find the rod [or perch] in the right and lawful way you shall do as follows, stand by the door of the church on Sunday and bid sixteen men to stop, tall ones and short ones, as they happen to pass out when the service is finished; then make them put their left feet one behind the other and the length thus obtained shall be a right and lawful rod to measure and survey the land with, and a sixteenth part of it shall be a right and lawful foot.

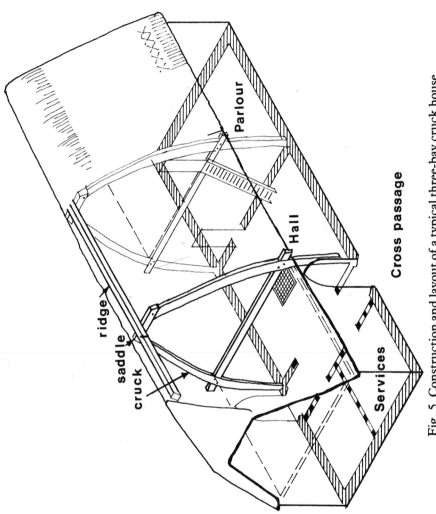

Fig. 5 Construction and layout of a typical three-bay cruck house

In this way the original bay width was determined and established in use for several centuries until the rod disappeared completely when metric units were employed in this country.

In later dwellings the bases of the crucks were placed on continuous balks of timber which, because of their tendency to decay from damp, were in time raised on stone plinth walls thus providing more headroom inside the building itself. This method of construction also allowed the use of smaller crucks at a time when large oak trees were becoming scarcer and crucks less available to the poorer yeoman. In many buildings still existing the bases of the crucks, and the supporting beams, have rotted away and have now been replaced by low walls of stone or brick often built at a much later date than the original timberwork which is supported in this way.

As techniques improved one or two beams were also placed across the crucks, usually at the same height as the curve or elbow, and pegged to the uprights to help prevent these spreading outwards, with the ends of the cross-beams projecting no further than the base of the cruck itself. These beams, the upper one known as the collar- and the lower as the tie-beam, also supported at their ends continuous pieces of wood holding in place the top of the vertical uprights in the outside walls, which finished at eaves level. The lower of these cross-beams, the tie, was also used to support boards forming a permanent upper floor for sleeping or storage purposes, a simple form of construction lasting until the use of crucks declined some time in the seventeenth or eighteenth centuries, although there is evidence that such buildings were still being erected in the Lake District as late as 1800.

Those buildings which still have base crucks are often found in the Midlands and southern counties where full crucks are unknown or have not survived, which is not the same thing. Only several hundred crucks still exist, a few north of the Humber, and while the earliest examples appear to date from about 1300 this form of construction was, as far as can be established, no longer widely used after the fifteenth century, unlike the full crucks which continued for a much longer period. Evidence confirms that base crucks were used for a fairly short period which makes it possible to date such buildings with some accuracy; not so with full crucks without documentary or other evidence relating to a particular building or site. Some scholars suggest that cruck buildings may be dated by the type of joints used, the crucks being mortised to take the tenon on the end of the collar- and tie-beams up to the middle of the sixteenth century. From then onwards this joint was replaced by a lapped joint, or halved dovetail, and though the type of joint used may have some significance, such theories depend on all craftsmen being advanced enough to use the same joints at the same time throughout the whole country, whether in isolated rural areas or important towns – an assumption which would be hard to accept.

In all early forms of timber construction the amount of timber used was by present-day standards wasteful, but when crucks were in general use England had a supply of timber sufficient to meet all the needs of the time. During the thirteenth century there were still at least sixty forests in this country and estimates show that by 1500 there were still about four million acres of forest mostly consisting of hardwood trees, many of which had never been thinned out or felled. Gregory King writing in 1688 states that there were then about three million acres still in existence. The surviving older crucks are almost all oak as were the later fully developed timber-framed buildings, with a few rare examples of chestnut being used in some of the larger medieval buildings.

Documentary evidence establishing the date of crucks suggests that the earliest examples were of well-shaped heavy timbers, but the inferior ones may simply have disappeared being of less durable wood. What is certain is that as crucks became a less important feature in the houses of the wealthy yeoman the timbers became smaller until they ceased to be used in the late seventeenth or early eighteenth centuries. But up to about the fifteenth century the better crucks, which still survive, were in the southern parts of the country where farmers were richer than those who worked the poorer land of the northern highlands. As the use of stone increased the use of crucks declined, until all the later ones are found in buildings which originally had cob walls rather than stone, particularly in northern England. But it should be remembered that some of the original cob walls have been replaced at a later date by stone or brick walls, so that without other evidence the precise dating of such buildings remains difficult. In most cases it is probable that the smaller cruck buildings now found in our villages are not older than the seventeenth century; earlier ones are comparatively rare.

The first cruck houses were open to the roof, which allowed the smoke from the central fire to escape through a simple hole in the roof covering. This presented problems when the need for increased accommodation required the building of an upper floor, so what is now called the open hall type of house developed. In the three-bay house, as well as the rather more commonly built four-bay type, the floor was placed over the end bays only leaving the central bay, or bays, forming a hall still open to the roof, and as the fire was still in this room it became the most important part of the house. This type of building was commonly used over a large area of the northern and Midland counties spreading as far south as the Surrey/Hampshire borders. But not all such houses had crucks as this plan form was also used in the timber-framed houses built of jointed panels, although not many survive in their original form. Except for a few rare examples, all the open halls have had later floors added at the same level as those in the end bays, while at the same time plaster ceilings were often inserted throughout the upper part of the building, either just below or just above the level of the collar-beam. This was usually done sometime in the seventeenth or eighteenth centuries when it was obvious that there was no reason for the open hall to be retained, as the building of stone or brick chimney-stacks and fireplaces removed the need for the open fire, originally a feature of the open hall.

So altered are some of these earlier open-plan houses that almost the only evidence that an open fire ever existed are traces of smoke or soot-encrusted beams found among the roof timbers hidden for many centuries by the plaster ceilings inserted below them. These traces are often only uncovered when in their own turn the old ceilings are being renewed in the process of restoration or modernization. As with all building developments this was a gradual change and at the same time, to prevent smoke from the open fire spreading into the side bays of the cottage, partitions were often built around the hall to close it in at ground level. Apart from the discomfort of a smoke-filled hall and open roof space there was also the ever present threat of damage from sparks and so smoke hoods, of timber and plaster, were placed over the central fireplace to help direct the smoke through the hole in the roof, and later stone or brick chimney-stacks became more common. They were built against one of the external or cross walls while in the case of timber-framed cottages the stacks were placed projecting outside the beams of the external walls to prevent these being damaged by fire. Since flimsy screens provided the only protection for any windows in these early cottages, and the other door opened directly into the hall, timber or wattle and daub screens were built projecting out from the fireplace, to shield those by the fire from draughts, and over the centuries this evolved into the still popular ingle-nook fireplace, whose development will be discussed later.

Timber buildings are normally formed of a series of bays, one between each pair of crucks, or roof trusses, with one room on each bay placed on each side of the central hall or reached by going through the adjacent rooms. This simple but rather inconvenient plan gave a series of rooms placed in a straight line, as it was impossible to produce other layouts, such as L or E shapes, until the builders of the period learnt the art of making quite complicated roof trusses capable of dealing with varying spans. The use of crucks to support the roof restricted the width of the building which could be covered in this way, and any additions to the single-room-deep cottage came to be made by adding bays of a similar width to either end. Extra rooms which could not be formed in this way were placed in small projections, or outshuts, at the rear of the original house and these were covered in by extending the original roof slope down over them towards the ground. But this was not very convenient as it reduced the headroom in such rooms below that of the original dwelling which was never much more than 6 feet, in contrast to the 7 feet 7½ inches, or 2.3 metres, required under modern building regulations.

The size of these long narrow houses was dictated by the width of the building plots found in the village along the lanes near the church and village green, where many of these old cottages still survive. There were at this period few farmhouses standing in their own holdings, a feature of the landscape only after the Enclosures of the seventeenth and eighteenth centuries. Before that each farmer lived in the village and went out to his land which was part of the strips laid out in the common fields. The plots along the lanes were usually less than 30 feet, or two bays, wide, resulting in a long continuous terrace of cottages along the whole frontage, and the cross passage which later developed when the interior was divided up, became essential to reach the rear. If the wealthier yeomen required larger dwellings, plots were joined together to allow these to be built, or the houses turned round on their plots so that the gable faced the street, a feature common in medieval towns.

Previously, chimneys were built on to the side of a house, or in the case of timber-framed buildings projecting outside the framework, but there is no evidence of the use of chimneys in England before the twelfth century, and in London's first building regulations made in 1189, or those of 1212, no reference was made to fireplaces although the regulations were designed to prevent the spread of fire. Twelfth-century fireplaces can still be found in such buildings as Rochester Castle, the King's House Southampton, and Boothby Pagnell Hall in Lincolnshire, but it was much later before they appeared in the small cottages used by yeoman farmers.

The first known flues date from about 1280 and were carried up stone shafts at Aydon Castle, Northumberland; soon afterwards similar flues were built at Stokesay Castle, these dating between 1285 and 1305. Such flues were covered with various types of louvred hoods although by the twelfth century there were examples of round pots, and some early examples of hoods and chimney "pots" may be seen in the Sedgewick Museum at Cambridge; on the whole, examples are hard to find but a few may be discovered among museum collections in medieval cities. The best modern book on the subject, *Chimney Pots and Stacks* was written by Valentine Fletcher in 1968, which incredibly was the first book to deal exclusively with this subject since the early nineteenth century.

After the sixteenth century the central hall became less important as its original purpose diminished, and rooms tended to be divided up by partitions eventually leading to the development of the cross passage with an internal fireplace alongside this. Fireplaces were often placed back to back in a central position between the two main rooms, the kitchen and the parlour. Instead of a ladder to reach the upper rooms a small spiral staircase would be positioned at the side of this fireplace, and it remained in this place until well into the nineteenth century, by now the cattle no longer being housed under the same roof as the farmer and his family, but as today in other buildings separated from the farmhouse. Typical cottage plans of this kind may be seen in Figures 3 and 5, as commonly used in small cottages throughout the country whether using crucks, timber frames or in later periods, stone or brick load-bearing walls. It was not until some time in the seventeenth century that builders evolved the complicated trusses which enabled them successfully to roof houses two rooms deep.

Before looking at the more developed timber-framed houses it is advisable to consider the evolution of wattle and daub, the universally known material used to fill in the panels of "black and white" buildings. Wattle work is made by weaving twigs in and out of uprights, generally hazel rods about an inch in diameter complete with their bark, and it was used by prehistoric builders, followed by the Romans and the Saxons. It was first used, with clay daubed on both sides, to form the walls of small huts without the timber-framing characteristic of later periods, and some of the earliest English examples were found in the last century by General Pitt-Rivers while excavating prehistoric settlements on Cranborne Chase. But from the early medieval period until the nineteenth-century advent of cheap mass-produced bricks, the construction of wattle and daub infill panels changed very little, although in time the original material decayed and needed renewing, which in some cases was done with brick nogging.

The method used to make wattle and daub varied depending on the sizes of the panels and the materials available in the locality, but in all cases the sides of the beams forming the panels have grooves or a series of holes cut into them to hold the wattle work. If the brick filling of the panels of a timber-framed building has to be removed it is then possible to examine the sides of the beams for traces of grooves or holes and if these are visible it is evident that the brickwork replaced earlier wattle and daub panels. If such features cannot be found it is likely that the panels were always filled with brick, and so the building will be comparatively late, probably dated after the seventeenth century. (*See* Figure 6.)

In the earlier buildings the timber uprights were set close together and the twigs were inserted direct into the holes of grooves cut into the timberwork, normally hazel or ash twigs, as these were flexible enough to be bent to get them into the panels. But when timber was plentiful, split oak

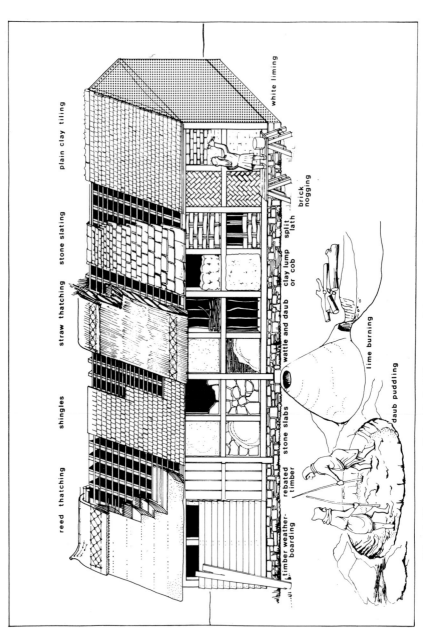

Fig. 6 Types of traditional cladding materials used on timber-framed buildings and roofs although never used together as illustrated

or elm laths were sometimes used in the grooves in place of woven twigs. These laths were of heart wood, although later sap wood was also used, which was riven and often fastened to the posts with nails. This occurred as early as the reign of Edward III as contemporary regulations fixed the size of the laths to be used as 1 inch wide by ½ inch thick. As the timber panels of the later buildings became larger and square-shaped the filling was often of twigs attached by green withy bands or leather thongs to upright rods or staves of split oak or elm. These panels, very like the hurdles still used by farmers to pen sheep, were woven to the right size and inserted complete as the building was erected, but in no case was the material used structurally since it was, and still is, possible to remove all the infilling from a timber house without causing the collapse of the jointed framework.

No matter how the wattle was made or fixed, the covering was always the same; clay was just daubed into the infilling and the plasterer who practised this ancient craft was originally known as the "daubator". To hold it together the clay was mixed with a binding material, usually straw but other substances such as cow dung, mutton fat, any kind of animal hair or flax stems and the waste left over after the flax was worked, were all commonly used for this purpose. The clay was then thrown or daubed on to the twigs in layers and left to dry before the final coat was smoothed down to form the outside of the panels. The material tended to shrink or crack as it dried and although it was sometimes left like that, in later periods it was finished with lime plaster mixed with cow hair which covered the panels and sealed the cracks. The panels are now usually found finished flush with the face of the timber frames but the earliest examples have recessed panels, although this trapped the rain in the edges of the framework which as a result tended to rot away.

Recently, at the Avoncroft Museum of Buildings, near Bromsgrove, the wattle and daub panels of a re-erected fifteenth-century house were first repaired with a mix of sand, lime, cement and animal fat using sawn oak laths as infilling. But this mix soon cracked and had to be replaced after only ten years when hazel twigs were used covered with a daub of one part of cow dung, one part of sand, one of lime, and a little cement covered with a lime wash of eight parts of lime, one part of cow dung and one part of mutton fat, which protected the exterior from cracking.

5

The Timber Tradition

Incredible as it seems in an era of widespread timber shortages, there have never been enough trees in this country to meet all needs and the position has been deteriorating since the Tudor period when oak was beginning to become so scarce that elm was used for rafters and floor joists, when these were concealed from view, and this was considered a very inferior way of building.

After the sixteenth century the price of oak rose very steeply restricting its use to the larger and more important timber-framed buildings, while in some regions such as Yorkshire and the Fens, oak was rare and it is never found in the older small buildings which still survive there. But until that time oak was the favoured building material used everywhere in vast quantities, and records of the fourteenth century provide details of the payments made for such items as three thousand oak trees required for the building work then taking place at Windsor Castle. During the same period large amounts of timber were also being imported from the Baltic for work on other royal residences and among the extensive medieval court records are many cases of craftsmen being fined for using other woods, considered as inferior, in place of oak. For example in 1317 a carpenter of Bytham in South Lincolnshire was sued for having built a house of willow instead of oak, and a timber-framed house built in 1543 by Thomas Sherman and William Becham was found to be of inferior timber, causing it to fall down, and the London Carpenters' Company made them rebuild it in oak.

Oak was the timber normally used even if it had to be brought from long distances and Dr Oliver Rackham has calculated that an average timber-framed farmhouse, built about 1500, contained some three hundred and fifty trees, mostly oak. Half of these were less than 9 inches in diameter, with thirty-two as small as 6 inches in diameter and only three exceeded 18 inches, the normal size of a mature oak, while on the other hand the mid-fourteenth-century Old Court of Corpus Christi College, Cambridge, contained about fourteen hundred oaks, mostly less than 9 inches in diameter. So it can be seen that young, and unseasoned, timber was normally used as it was only after a building had been designed that the timber could be found to make it. So common was the use of unseasoned timber that a number of medieval contracts for the larger and more important buildings stipulated that only seasoned wood should be used, resulting in suitable oak being transported many miles to the site.

In 1577, during a time of great change when medieval England was disappearing, William Harrison, an Essex clergyman, wrote in his *Description of England* about the timber-framed houses still to be found, saying that "in times past men were content to dwell in houses built of sallow, willow, plum tree, hornbeam and elm so that the use of oak was almost wholly for churches, noblemen's lodgings, and navigation". It should be remembered that at the time Harrison was writing most English towns, apart from London, were almost entirely filled with timber-framed houses and although it might now be hard to believe, up to the eighteenth century even places like Manchester were made up of timber-framed houses as is Chester today.

From the reign of Elizabeth I the scarcity of oak throughout eastern England meant that old timbers were re-used to save timber, giving rise to the tradition, largely without foundation, that old ships' timbers were used in the construction of houses. This may have been true in some coastal areas, but it is unlikely to have been widespread as the number of ships being broken up would hardly supply enough timbers for all the houses reputed to have been built in this way. Still, at that period stone and brick were becoming more fashionable, partly through necessity, and the wealthier merchants, following the example set by the Crown, started to demolish their old timber-framed manor-houses and replace them with buildings of these newer materials. Many of the oak beams salvaged from older houses no doubt found their way into the humbler timber-framed buildings still being constructed by the poorer people.

The development of the timber-framed houses still existing depended upon the invention, or long-term development, of satisfactory joints and their improvements over the following centuries. Up to about 1,600 wooden pegs, usually of oak, were used to hold these joints together; wrought-iron was too expensive for general use, and if used untreated as bolts in joints made of unseasoned oak, the iron was affected by corrosion due to the acid found in the wood. After about 1600 the art of timber building started to decline when builders, for lack of wood, had to use other materials, although timber framing was often used together with brick or stone. In these cases the rear, and sides, were of timber leaving the more important elevations to be in brick or stone, to indicate the wealth of the owner.

Judging from the surviving examples it seems that about this period the old 16-foot bay was generally being abandoned by builders in favour of a 3-yard module of 12 feet; the present yard of 3 feet was a later introduction based on the standard measurement of woollen cloth. But it should be remembered that the distribution of the surviving timber-framed buildings has no connection with the universal employment of wood in the medieval period, even in districts such as the Cotswolds, today thought of as being only "stone" areas. The number of really old timber buildings surviving is very small compared with those actually built by our medieval forbears and as far as is known from old records the only county at that time lacking in timber was Cornwall.

There are no known surviving timber-framed houses dating from before the fourteenth century and very few before the fifteenth. Those that do survive are the larger buildings in districts where there are numerous later timber-framed structures and it is rare to find really old buildings of this type in areas where the timber tradition was comparatively short-lived. The majority of our existing timber buildings, including the larger well-known houses as well as the humbler ones, belong to the sixteenth and seventeenth centuries, and even in the north country such buildings dated earlier than about 1600 are rare. In the west Midlands the date is even later and many cottages, as well as barns, are mid-Georgian in date despite the general shortage of timber large enough for beams and roof trusses.

Before looking at the various types of joints which developed, the frame itself should be considered to see what may be learnt by observing the building on its site. The older the building the more likely the timbers are to be bent, or warped, and in some cases the whole building may be tilted at quite a frightening angle although many acquired this position soon after being erected. This is because green, or unseasoned, oak had to be used when the building was put up as only in this state is the wood soft enough to allow it to be cut, the joints formed and the building framed up and erected. As the oak gets older the sap dries out and the wood hardens until eventually it is almost too hard to cut and in the process it shrinks or expands, pushing joints out of their original positions and causing the panels to lose their shape. Very few old dwellings are straight and as this results from the ageing of the oak the older dwellings are more likely to show defects than more recent ones where the timbers used were smaller due to the shortage of wood.

Efforts were often made to avoid excessive movement by partly seasoning the timber, leaving it to soak for a year or more in rivers or mill-ponds, which allowed the water to replace the sap and reduce warping. It was also done by using very large timbers, but both methods relied on adequate supplies of oak and this became increasingly difficult. It is known that when a shop was built in London in 1369 the carpenters were instructed to use 7 × 12 inch sill beams, 14 × 12 inch principal uprights and floor joists, with the walls consisting of 9 × 7 inch intermediate studs 6 inches apart. Evidence shows that these sizes were common throughout the country but after the Great Fire of London the average size of floor joists was down to 7 × 3 inches and rafters to 5 × 4 inches, 12 inches apart in most cases, while timber uprights in walls were not allowed due to the fire hazard.

In general terms the larger in size and the closer together the vertical timbers, the older the building, but this generalization must be qualified by other local variations, e.g. the distance of the dwelling from the south of the country where such buildings first developed, and the abundance of oak forests in that district when the house was constructed. As the panels became squarer different types of infill timbering developed, much being of a structural nature to give more rigidity to the vertical and horizontal members which over the centuries tended to become smaller in section.

The vertical posts, the sill, the cross rails and the wall-plate, just under the roof, form the main panels of the framework and these are often divided further by intermediate members, either vertical or horizontal, or with curved braces of various designs. The larger panels usually have sides of between 6 or 7 feet divided up as shown in Figure 7, and a house of large panels is only two panels high with the horizontal division normally at floor level in the case of a two-storeyed building, while cottages are often only one panel high.

In other buildings the main horizontal and vertical members form smaller squares divided up with different patterns of infilling as shown in Figure 7. This diagram shows all the variations known to have been used in the older, and original, timber-framed buildings, but other designs were often used when copying timber-framed buildings in later periods, particularly during the late Victorian era when timber-framed houses and cottages of no previously known style were popular among the newly rich industrialists. But perhaps the most easily recognized type of framing, and certainly one of the oldest, is the close studding common from the fifteenth century onwards. The name stud is derived from the old English work *stuthu*, meaning a pillar or post, and in this case the panels between the uprights are rarely more than twice the width of the studs and frequently only the same width.

Evidence shows that in London this type of framing was common in the fifteenth century, for in 1497 an Italian visited and described the city in his *Itinerarium Britanniae*, and a translation made in 1953 by C. V. Moffatti states that "there were also many mansions which do not seem very large from the outside but inside they contain a great number of rooms and garrets and are quite considerable. Six-inch beams are inserted in the walls the same distance apart as their own breadth."

This may have been true of London but the distance between studs often varied in other areas where this kind of framing usually appeared in the more important buildings. The distance apart of the timber uprights also varied even in buildings of the same date found in the same district;

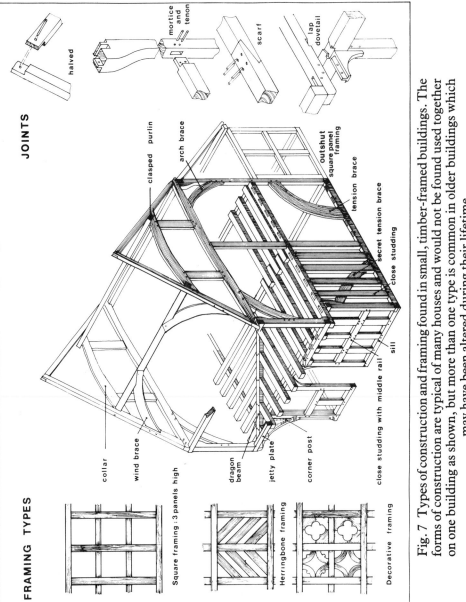

JOINTS

halved

mortice and tenon

scarf

lap dovetail

FRAMING TYPES

Square framing : 3 panels high

Herringbone framing

Decorative framing

collar

wind brace

dragon beam

jetty plate

corner post

close studding with middle rail

clasped purlin

arch brace

outshut square panel framing

tension brace

secret tension brace

close studding

sill

Fig. 7 Types of construction and framing found in small, timber-framed buildings. The forms of construction are typical of many houses and would not be found used together on one building as shown, but more than one type is common in older buildings which may have been altered during their lifetime

for example going from 7 inches at Burgh Farm, Combs, to 18 inches at Hines Farm, Earl Stonham, both in eastern Suffolk.

Close-studded buildings are scattered over wide areas of the Midlands, the Welsh Marches and the northern counties where square panelling is almost non-existent, but most are to be found in the south-eastern counties spreading into East Anglia, south of Norfolk. Though the construction of these close-studded buildings, all without the middle rail, is similar throughout large areas there is evidence that a different form of infilling was originally in use north and south of the River Trent, the filling to the south being wattle and daub, while to the north, particularly in Yorkshire, stone was often used between the timber uprights.

Some scholars suggest that large panel construction preceded close studding, but since both types were obviously in use during the same period it is impossible to date accurately the beginning of any style of timber framing and to say precisely which were the first houses to be constructed in this way. Although there are probably more late fifteenth- and early sixteenth-century close-studded buildings in the south-east of England than elsewhere, it is uncertain whether the style originated in this area as examples of close-studded dwellings, earlier than the mid-fifteenth century, occur in many areas as far north as Yorkshire.

Even in the seventeenth century despite the timber shortage the close-studded house was still being erected as far north as Staffordshire, particularly in the more isolated rural areas and a form of close studding with small uprights filled in between with brick continued in Bedfordshire as late as 1815, used in some cottages in Ampthill. About the sixteenth century, close studding with a middle rail appeared in the south-eastern counties as well as in the Welsh Marches spreading through Cheshire into Lancashire but rarely elsewhere; in order to save timber the uprights were in two pieces, above and below the middle rail, being jointed into it with tenons.

Since close studding provided a rigid structure there was no need for cross members, or bracing at the corners, as in the case of the larger framed panels. These, often 6 or 7 feet square, were also in common use from some time before the fifteenth century, but there were local variations in this type of building. Simple large square panels were used in buildings from Oxfordshire down to the south coast, with a few in Kent and Sussex, but most are found in Wales, Herefordshire, Worcestershire, especially around the Severn and Avon valleys, and also Shropshire and Cheshire. The only districts in southern England without such buildings are the stone districts of the Cotswolds and the uplands of Northamptonshire. Most of the large framed buildings in these areas are two panels high but buildings of three panels are not uncommon in the upper Severn Valley and the west Midlands, though rarely seen further north than Lancashire, or in the south-western counties. This type occurs in two distinct regions, and as well as the counties mentioned is found in the eastern counties of Kent, Sussex, Cambridge, Suffolk and Norfolk, probably mostly in Essex where the frame is often concealed behind external plastering.

Because of the weak structural nature of such large panels almost all were braced in one form or another, the patterns becoming more complicated as the buildings became larger. The commoner types of infilling are shown in Figure 7, the difference being that in the earlier buildings all parts of the frame are structural and help to keep the building rigid. In later examples the complicated infilling is often non-structural being largely applied as ornament giving very little additional strength to the house. Judging from the few surviving examples some of these patterns were rarely used and many houses in Kent and Sussex have no bracing at all even when the panels are quite large, but the other designs are found in fairly well-defined regions. Often a single example may be found outside its normal district, possibly built at a later date as the pattern travelled into other counties, and after the mid-sixteenth century this kind of framing became rare in many areas. But the evidence of surviving buildings indicates that large framing was normally used on the smaller homes of the less wealthy yeomen families.

In large framing the bracing is of a simple type using straight or curved timbers of a fairly large section taking the forms shown in Figure 7. Variations in patterns of bracing are usually confined to particular districts, and among the older buildings are rarely found elsewhere.

Straight braces can be found in buildings all over central England as far north as Lancashire and Yorkshire, and frequently in the counties of the lower Severn Valley. This is the most common type except for arch bracing which is found in Wales and its borders from Herefordshire to Cheshire, and extending over the west Midlands through Oxfordshire and to the south coast. These types are rare in the south-eastern counties and Essex where tension, or a combination of tension and arch bracing was widely used, particularly to stabilize the corners of a building.

The other two types of bracing used with large panels, the St Andrew's Cross and panelled braces, tended in the later buildings to become non-structural decorative features. St Andrew's Cross bracing is common in the counties south of Oxfordshire but it also occurred in some of the larger timber-framed buildings of Cheshire and Lancashire. While parallel diagonal bracing was less commonly used it was developed in the West Riding in the late fifteenth century, emerging a century later elsewhere in Yorkshire as a herring-bone pattern.

The older, small framed buildings are all located in the West Country spreading to other areas after the middle of the fifteenth century. Most of these small houses and cottages have plain panels, normally from 2 feet 6 inches to 3 feet square, rather than the decorated panels which became fashionable afterwards, but rarely used before about 1575, and although there were many variations these designs can be grouped into the main types shown in Figure 7. The later designs were more common in the west as more timber was available there for a longer period than in the east where the absence of large oaks and changes in fashion brought stone and brick into use at an earlier date than elsewhere. By the end of the sixteenth century ornamental panelling became general, the most popular form being an arrangement of short curved braces forming circles in the square panels. Wavy braces were also fairly commonplace, with a more restricted use in the north and west Midlands of short heavy braces which form star shapes. Most of the buildings with decorated panels lie in the counties along the Welsh border from the Severn Valley as far north as Lancashire, extending into Wales, a few examples remaining in south-eastern England and elsewhere.

The easily recognizable herring-bone pattern is also well distributed throughout the Welsh Marches, Cheshire, south Lancashire and Yorkshire and across the north Midlands. It occurs also in Worcestershire, Warwickshire and Staffordshire, as far east as Cambridgeshire and west to Taunton. Little Moreton Hall in Cheshire dating from 1559, an outstanding example of this style, is one of the most complete Tudor timber-framed buildings existing, and one of the earliest examples of a method of bracing rarely seen before about 1570.

The last type is close panelling, using smaller panels than those found in other forms of framing, a type of construction first recorded in the West Country during the early part of the sixteenth century when local timber supplies were disappearing. Whatever the type of panelling used, a timber-framed house formed a complete structural unit, even when the panels were not filled in. It must also be realized that the use of framed walls as the main structure of the house largely depended on providing a properly stiffened roof to prevent the building being overturned by the wind. As this type of house became larger, and particularly taller, this tendency to overturn in violent gales was counteracted by the use of elaborate bracing in both the walls and roof.

In its simplest form the roof consists of pairs of rafters, having the ends fixed by pegs to the wall-plate and the tops fixed together either by pegs or simple joints. The rafters were usually 2 feet or so apart, and each pair was commonly called a "couple". In later buildings these were joined together at the top by a horizontal ridge piece which kept the couples upright and also increased the stability of the structure. As roof-coverings became heavier the loads tended to push the ends of the couples outwards along with the wall-plate, causing the external walls to bulge and in extreme cases to collapse. This was resisted by placing horizontal tie-beams, and collars, across the couples as was done in the case of cruck houses. But as the span increased with the building of larger houses the roof structure tended to sag, and although prevention lay to some extent in using larger timbers, the shortage of suitable trees made this increasingly difficult. As the sizes of the individual timbers decreased, extra rigidity was given by various kinds of struts fixed between the tie-beam at the base of the roof and the rafters, and from this developed the idea of using a number of more massive principal couples with smaller ones between. From this evolved the simple roof trusses familiar today, and as far as can be established the first truss which developed had a single central upright between the lower tie-beam and the top of the couple rafters.

This type, still known as the king-post truss, was widely used in the fifteenth and sixteenth century and later examples had additional struts to brace the upright as well as giving further support to the rafters carrying the heavier roof coverings. (*See* Figure 8.) In succeeding centuries many variations grew from these simple beginnings, and in 1969 Professor R. A. Cordingley classified the main types, simplifying recognition on site. This study, *British Historical Roof Types*, was published by the Ancient Monuments Society and is an essential work of reference for the study of roof trusses which may be found in older buildings.

The basic construction of nearly seventy-five truss types and variations are described, many of which developed because of specific needs, or changes in fashion, and the types commonly found in smaller houses and cottages are those shown in the diagram. These are collar, scissor, crown- and queen-post trusses, with many variations depending on the positions of the purlins and whether these are placed over the principal truss members or tenoned into their sides. There are also many other more complicated types such as arched, braced, hammer-beam and double hammer-beam trusses which were originally used with open roofs although in later periods some of these were hidden by plaster ceilings inserted when changes were being made to the interiors of such buildings. These trusses are rarely found in the smaller houses except in districts with a long tradition of timber-framed building.

All timber-framed structures depend on the joints for stability and to make even the simplest of these required a lot of skill from the carpenters who used tools having a great resemblance to those still in use; for example both the plane and chisel were in general use as early as the twelfth century. Such was the size, and weight, of the timbers used for this type of building that over the centuries it became the practice for the carpenter to cut the wood to size, and shape the joints, in his own yard rather than on the actual site of the house. The timbers were shaped over

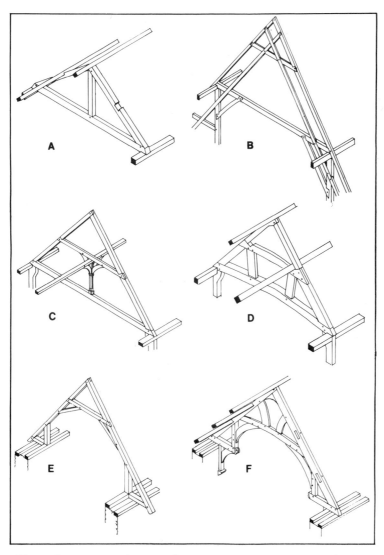

Fig. 8 Common roof trusses found in all kinds of houses: A. king-post with through notched purlins; B. early parallel rafter truss; C. crown-post roof truss with collar purlin; D. queen-post roof with clasped purlins; E. wagon-trussed rafter roof; F. hammer-beam truss with butt purlins. This last is only found in the larger and more important houses and then usually in a modified form

a saw-pit by workmen at the top and bottom of the pit using long two-handled saws, the joints then being shaped with the adze or with a narrow chisel-ended mortising axe. The framework was at first temporarily assembled in the builder's yard with all the joints marked ready for permanent erection on the site. All the main members were mortised and tenoned, or joined in other ways, while still on the ground, with loose pegs inserted to keep the timbers fixed in place. The joints were then numbered with a system normally based on Roman numerals using a combination of I, V and X. Four was usually IIII rather than IV, and IX became VIIII, although the figures were not always used the correct way up but in positions convenient to the pieces forming that particular joint.

The framework was then taken to pieces and carted, often quite long distances to the site before being re-erected using permanent wooden pegs. Usually these were oversize being driven into holes made with an auger slightly off centre to each other so that the pegs when hammered into place tended to pull the joints tightly together. So large and heavy were many of these timber-framed buildings that the setting up or the rearing of the framework called for extra labour and medieval records describe the payment of wages to such workmen, while at the completion of the work a feast was usually held to celebrate the event – a custom still surviving in our own time in the topping-out ceremonies which are held when the roof level of a tall building is reached.

After the framework was completed the panels were filled in with wattle and daub, or brickwork, the roof tiled and the chimney-stack built, so it can be seen that it was quite simple to erect a small two-room cottage once the framework was made. This resulted in the tradition that if a cottage could be erected, and a fire lit on the hearth, on common land during the hours of darkness it could not be moved by the owner of the land, usually the lord of the manor.

It is certain that as early as 1589 the practice of building cottages on small pieces of common land was becoming widespread due to the increasing population, as an Act of that year tried to stop the erection of "great numbers of cottages which are daily more and more increased in many parts of the Realm". This was because the occupiers might become a burden on the parish and to avoid this the Act also stipulated that each cottage used by a farm worker should have four acres of land attached to it. These dwellings later became known as "squatters' cottages", and whatever the truth of the tradition many small cottages can still be seen at the sides of roads built on long and very narrow sites running parallel to the carriageway. Although originally this was common land, many of these cottages were no doubt built for the road man responsible for the upkeep of that particular section of the toll road.

Parsonage Row Cottages, West Tarring, Sussex, with fifteenth-century close
studding and continuous jetty

(*Above*) Mill Street, Warwick, Warwickshire. Timber-framed houses with various styles of studding, many with continuous jetties built in the sixteenth and seventeenth centuries. The three-gabled house in the centre of the group has a new front in the style popular in the nineteenth century

King's Lynn, Norfolk. Greenland Fisheries building, a Jacobean timber-framed building with oversailing upper floor, oriel windows and the remains of a second oversailing or jettied floor

The Feathers Hotel, Ludlow, Shropshire, built in 1603 at the peak of the timber tradition before the fashion gave way to brick

Ireland's Mansions, Shrewsbury, Shropshire. An Elizabethan and Jacobean timber-framed house built about 1575 by Robert Ireland a local wool merchant. A fine three-storey, seven-bay, timber-framed house with bay windows typical of the period and dormers lighting the roof spaces. The ground floor is now altered to form commercial premises

(*Below*) Clergy House, Alfriston, Sussex, built about 1350 being a Wealden house characteristic of the Weald of Kent. This was the first house to be purchased by the National Trust soon after its formation in 1896 and was then restored by the Trust who still own it

East Grinstead, Sussex. Sixteenth-century timber-framed houses in the High Street, still with the roofs covered with Horsham stone slabs

High Street, Henley-in-Arden, Warwickshire. Sixteenth-century Wealden-type house with a recessed front, the bay window being added in the last century. The Wealden house type is found in a few districts outside the South-East, but examples are scarce although some survive in towns in Warwickshire and as far north as the city of York

(*Below*) Brickwall Manor, Northiam, Sussex. Jacobean timber-framed house built between 1617 and 1633; soon afterwards brick walls were added to some parts of the house and the new work was remarkable enough at that period to warrant the name of the house which dates from that time

Collihole Farm, Chagford. A Devonshire longhouse of sixteenth-century origin with its whitewashed stone walls a common feature of the moorland areas of the West Country

A Teesdale farmhouse of the kind built at any time during the sixteenth to eighteenth centuries and in some remote areas even later

Muchelney, Somerset. The Priest's House, a late fifteenth-century house built in the local stone. In almost all cases the larger houses of this period, whether in stone or timber-framing, are by local tradition named Priest's Houses

Haunt Hill House, Weldon, Northamptonshire. Built in the local Weldon stone between 1636 and 1643

6

The Rise and Fall
of the Timber Tradition

The first timber-framed houses of the post and panel type had simple un-decorated panels of varying sizes, the strength of the building depending on the size of the timber and the type of joints used rather than on the infilling used for the panels. In these houses the walls were in one vertical plane, often with the timber running unbroken from sill to eaves, and the rigid box-like framework could stand up without infilling to the panels; in fact such a frame was always erected first with the wattle and daub infilling added later.

The framework was rarely made on the site but often in the forests where the timber was cut, and erected on site, but a house could also be moved either in sections or if small enough as a complete unit long after it had first been made. It is often thought that moving timber-framed buildings is a modern idea, these buildings often being taken to museums or rebuilt into 'new' medieval streets, but this is in fact a very long-established technique and when the owner of a timber-framed house wished to rebuild on the site the original building was not necess-arily pulled down and burnt. Early records show that in 1250 a timber-framed house in Newport, Isle of Wight, was moved on rollers to a new site; in 1316 the Hall of Llwelyn was taken down and transported by sea from Conway to Caernarvon for re-erection, and in 1432 a four-bay house built at Sherwood was purchased, taken to pieces and transported to Nottingham Castle where three weeks were spent in re-erecting it. Many other cases are known, including the removal in 1696 of a house in the Dogpole, a street in Shrewsbury, to a site near the castle to allow the Earl of Bradford to build a new stone house in its place. During the last century many large timber buildings were moved from the centres of medieval towns undergoing re-development and were re-erected else-where for continuing use as houses. Examples include Grange House, Leominster, built in 1633, which was moved to a new site in 1855 and is now the council offices, while Selly Manor House was moved to Bourn-ville Village in 1912.

Since the last war many timber-framed buildings have been disman-tled and re-erected as museum exhibits; the first museum of this type in the country was at St Fagan's, near Cardiff, but it has many successors such as the Avoncroft Museum at Bromsgrove, started in 1963, the museum at West Dean, opened in 1970, the Folk Museum at Hutton-Le

Hole, Yorkshire, and the project to reconstruct a medieval street, Spon Street, in Coventry. More recently the technique of moving buildings intact has been improved, as demonstrated in 1961 in Exeter where a three-storeyed timber-framed building, first built in the fifteenth century, was moved to a new site a hundred yards away. The most spectacular case in this country was the moving of Ballingdon Hall, near Sudbury in Suffolk, which took place in 1972. The Hall, built in 1593 by Sir Thomas Eden, was a three-storey high, timber-framed building, having three gables and canted bay windows, and the house was jacked up, placed on bogies, and pulled by tractors half a mile up a hill to a new site, which was a cheaper and more practical method than dismantling and rebuilding.

It is now generally accepted that where timber-framed houses are concerned three distinct schools of carpentry exist; the joints and framework typical of the eastern counties, that found in western England and finally variations typical only of the north, the different techniques of construction gradually migrating from east to west. The earliest timber buildings of eastern England, dating from about 1350 to the Great Rebuilding of 1640, have close studding, that is studs less than their own width apart, some panels having a middle rail particularly in the later house, together with tension bracing where the curved braces run from the sill beam to the uprights of the house, and being tenoned into uprights and sill. In such buildings the braces are rarely straight and the use of tension braces is so widespread in the south-east of the country that they are often called 'Kentish framing', always being found in the Wealden houses which are believed to have originated in Kent.

In the western counties and the Midlands, square panels are typical, often used three-high with angle bracing, where the straight braces are tenoned into the uprights, sill or cross pieces. Such braces are used where required rather than just at the corners of a house. The building of houses with upper storeys, sometimes more than two, but not with 'jetties', was common all over England before 1400 or thereabouts, but in the construction of the sill beam there are differences between the southern part of the country and the northern counties. Generally speaking south of the River Trent the uprights, even the corner posts, were mortised into a continuous sill beam placed on the ground or on a single row of stones forming a foundation.

In northern England the main uprights of a timber building, like the corner posts or uprights marking the positions of the bays, rest on a stone footing, or even on the ground itself. Between these uprights there is a plinth wall of stone, usually about 18 inches high, on which sits the sill beam tenoned into the main uprights. The sill beam is therefore not continuous and only acts as a base for the intermediate studs and infilling.

Although some plinth walls of this type might be the result of carrying out repairs to a house when the original sill beam decayed, there is enough evidence to show that most houses were actually constructed in this way. Although the southernmost extent of such houses is indeterminate there is evidence that this type of building is never found south of the River Trent.

The stability of the earlier timber houses depended on the size of the wood used, and its section, particularly in the case of the floor joists which were always of the same section in one particular house; the joists being put side by side to form an almost solid floor of timber. The length of the timber available dictated the width of the house, the joists always spanning the shortest distance running from one outside wall to another. As timber became smaller in section it was either necessary to limit the width of the house or to find some method of strengthening the joists to prevent these sagging in the centre once fixed in position in the building. (*See* Figure 9.)

At first this was done by inserting cross-beams under the centre of the floor joists and in some instances a similar beam was used as part of the outside walls, fixed between the main posts and interrupting the continuous vertical studs. These external beams, or bressummers, were in the most important houses carved with leaves, foliage, vines and sometimes animals.

By placing a large cross-beam under the floor joists it was possible to reduce the sizes of the intermediate joists, thus saving timber. The first cross-beams, and therefore the oldest in a particular house or district, had squared edges, but later these were moulded or chamfered, the style varying from one period to another, which facilitated the dating of a building, if not precisely at least to the right century. The earliest and most popular mouldings were the simple chamfers which stopped short of the main uprights and cross-beams. The earliest of these chamfer stops were quite plain but became more elaborate during the late seventeenth century, and between the two extremes various types of Gothic mouldings were in general use, found in the more important buildings rather than in the smaller houses. Mouldings prior to the fourteenth century, which represents only a small number of timber-framed houses, tend to follow similar patterns to the stone mouldings found in the churches of the same date. After this date mouldings became increasingly elaborate with deep hollows and scrolls cut out of the solid oak, while later beams with hollow chamfers, ovolo mouldings or plain chamfered occurred most frequently in the poorer houses where smaller-sized beams were used, but this decoration did not outlast the eighteenth century.

From a careful study of such beams and the way the intermediate floor

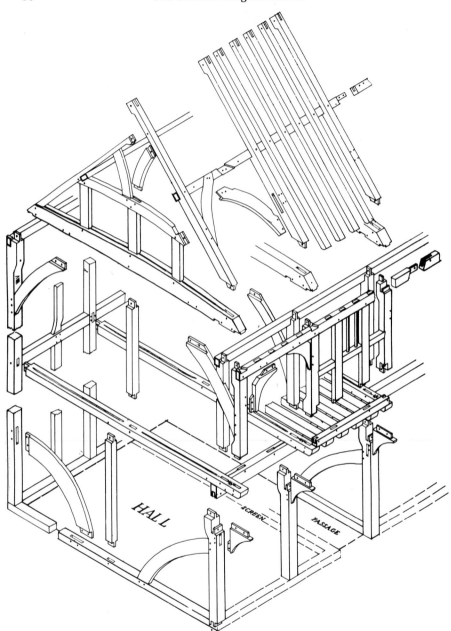

Fig. 9 Construction of a recessed front Wealden house, based on a building
which used to stand at Nos 153–5 Spon Street, Coventry (now dismantled)

joists were connected into them it is possible to date the age of a house fairly accurately and certainly more so than when mouldings alone provide the evidence. In the earliest houses the intermediate joists were tenoned into the sides of the main beam and the type of joint in common use differed from time to time, a particular joint perhaps being used for fifty years or more. The type ranged from a simple tenon joint to the more complicated seventeenth-century ones where a peg was inserted through the main beam to hold the tenon in place, after which a very inefficient joint relying largely on nails, appeared sometime in the eighteenth century.

The type of joint used provides a clue to the date of a house but not the actual date, a common misconception; it only suggests the period before which it is not likely to have been constructed. The point at which a joint first begins to appear in general use is often well established but it cannot be precisely determined when that particular joint ceased to be used throughout the whole country.

Between the years 1300 and 1700 as joints became more complicated their efficiency often declined as more and more timber was cut away to produce the elaborate housed and tenoned joints then in favour. These early types of joints are unlikely to be found in the ordinary small timber-framed house where the most frequently used joint, dating from the mid-seventeenth century, was a simple one in which the intermediate floor joists just rested in slots cut out of the top of the main beam and were pegged, or in the later examples, nailed in place. In *The Development of Carpentry*, Alec Hewett illustrates in some detail the typical ways in which the floor joists and main beams were joined, dealing with the dating of such joints more comprehensively than is possible here and this book should be studied by anyone needing further information on the subject.

It is certain that the thirteenth century saw quite elaborate joints in use, such as butted scarf joints, secret notched lap joints or lap dovetails. Once fitted together it is difficult to identify a particular joint, so that the casual observer is often unaware of the complicated nature of the joint, particularly in larger timber-framed buildings.

Early fourteenth-century timber-framed houses had certain features peculiar to the period, and wind braces were first used in simple framed roofs, although more than necessary were introduced due to the lack of knowledge about wind forces. There was no elaborate external diagonal bracing in the buildings, which were simple rectangular shapes using close studding for the main walls, although simple braces were used at the corners. Later in the century the lavish use of pairs of wind braces was abandoned for single convex braces and the problems in obtaining long enough timbers for building encouraged the development of scarf joints so that shorter timbers could be joined together, as the box-frame type of construction then in use required floor joists to run the full width of the building.

When using timber-construction methods of the period, long timbers were needed to run in one piece from the sill to eaves level allowing the cross members to be tenoned into the uprights, the whole framework being held together by tightly pegged joints. The use of shorter timbers meant that each storey was independent of the others and the entire rather unstable structure held together solely by the joints. Reducing the sizes of joists introduced a problem concerning floors as these became rather weak, since at that period the timbers were laid flat rather than on edge, and when walked on tended to sag in the centre. The difficulty of framing up the upper floors was partly solved by setting the walls of each storey out beyond those of the floor below; the weight of the upright wall resting on the 'jettied-out' floor joists counteracted the weight of people in the building and stiffened the structure considerably.

This style of building was known on the Continent before the idea first developed in this country; where it first appeared is uncertain although among the earliest examples are some cottages in Goodramgate in York built about 1320. These buildings predated those built in London in 1342 when the building contract stated that the two upper storeys of the house should be jettied. At first the jettied walls of the two-storey houses were set only slightly in front of the ground floor walls giving a slight overhang, a feature which, enduring for several centuries, may be seen on many of the small surviving seventeenth-century houses. (*See* Figure 9.)

Much more elaborate jettied town houses were built to comply with fashion during the fifteenth and sixteenth centuries. In eastern England, as early as the 1370s, all classes of buildings had the popular jetties, and their use extended as far north as York, and west to Hereford, but rarely beyond.

The projection of the jetties varied from a few inches to over 2 feet in more elaborate houses, but in the fifteenth century averaged between 1 foot 9 inches and 2 feet. However it should be remembered that the majority of the timber-framed buildings are not jettied; the most elaborate date from the fifteenth to the seventeenth centuries and most survivors are in the centres of medieval towns or are among the large timber-framed manor-houses built in the rural areas of Shropshire and Cheshire.

Although jetties enabled smaller floor joists to be used, some experts suggest that this form of construction originated as a means of obtaining more space in a house by projecting out above head height over the street in front; the space gained could be considerable as a two-foot projection might increase the area of the building by twenty per cent. The rain from the roof is also thrown clear of the walls below thus keeping the lower part of the building drier.

The wall to be jettied out was framed up as a separate section of the building and supported on or by the projecting ends of the joists of the floor below and pegged to them to prevent movement. Two methods of fixing jetties were commonly employed; the first applied to the simplest houses where the ends of the floor joists project and can be seen with the lowest beam of the upper wall pegged to the top of them. In other more important and larger buildings, the bottom beam of the upper wall was mortised on to the front of the joists concealing them from view.

Only in humbler houses were the exposed ends of the projecting joists left in their rough-hewn condition, but in the more important dwellings these joists were decorated or moulded to enhance their appearance. Even when the ends of the joists were concealed by the bottom of the upper wall, the under side of the floor joists as well as the base of the walls were often decorated with various carvings.

As the floor joists spanned the shortest distance across a building, jetties could at first be constructed only at the front and back of a house, and the longer the buildings the more impressive the jettied upper floor would appear. This tended to restrict the numbers of jetties with long street frontages, which were owned by the richer merchants, as it was common practice for medieval houses to be placed end on to the street to enable more houses to be crammed along the streets inside the city walls. It was possible to achieve a continuous jettied front along a whole street, each house lining up with its neighbour, but this required a high degree of control not always possible in a medieval borough. Usually, however, the jetty formed the front of a single house and the continuous jetty house, with rooms laid out along the street frontage, became quite common by the seventeenth century; examples can still be seen in many smaller medieval market towns such as Henley-in-Arden, Warwickshire.

The nature of the construction meant that these houses were always two-storey buildings, among the first type to develop in this way, and could not be adapted from an older house divided up by inserting a floor in an open hall type of house, a frequent practice about this period. In continuous jetty houses the principal rooms were always on the first floor and open to the roof, at least in the early period of such houses, and there were usually three rooms with a chimney between two of them.

As the jettied joists projected further and became smaller in size, brackets were often inserted under the jettied timbers, and mortised into the uprights of the ground floor walls at the other end. Many brackets were curved and highly decorated perhaps with plaster-work between the timbers or even hiding them as in many houses in Cheshire.

An essential feature of a jetty is that the floor joists must run outwards from the building at right angles to the external walls to support the upper walls, and in the earliest houses this was possible only on the two opposite sides of a house.

As jetties were confined to the more important houses they soon became a prestige symbol; only wealthy merchants with houses on free-standing sites could have jetties on four sides of the building rather than just on the street elevation. This was achieved by inserting cross-beams at floor level and reversing the direction of some of the joists which were housed or jointed into this beam, and at right angles to the others in the building so that it was possible to project the floor joists on all four sides to support jetties all round the house. At the corners where two jetties met at right angles the problem of supporting them was solved by intro-ducing a diagonal beam into which the floor joists were framed at right angles to each other. This beam, later known as a dragon-beam, pro-jected from the house's corner post which was enlarged at the top, often by curved brackets, to help support it, and these parts of the building were often decorated with elaborate carving.

The origin of the name "dragon" is uncertain and it may be a corrup-tion of the word "diagonal". Since the original names for the compon-ents of timber-framing lapsed in the eighteenth century when timber building ceased, many of the present-day names probably came into use only with the nineteenth-century revival of interest in old timber-framed houses.

Many two-storey timber-framed houses with jettied fronts have been so altered since they were built that their original shape is often difficult to recognize because the lower wall, at ground level, has decayed due to contact with the earth and at a later period been rebuilt. In most cases the timber wall has been replaced by a stone or brick wall built out under the front edge of the original jetty, thus concealing the original projection of the first floor. Many timber-framed houses have been altered in this way but a close examination of the internal framework will often reveal notches in the front beams where the uprights of the original wall have been removed, thus making it possible to recognize the true form of the house.

During the sixteenth century a new cross-section began to be used for the timber framing; previously all the timbers were square in section, perhaps 9 × 9 inches being the most common, but afterwards timber became rectangular in section and somewhat smaller. In Shropshire and Cheshire during the fifteenth and sixteenth centuries this type of house was most frequently built with the framework of the jettied walls fastened to the face of the projecting joists. In the following century a simpler form was used in which the jetties were placed on top of the over-sailing joists, the ends of which were hidden by a covered fascia board while curved pieces placed under the jetties formed a coved support; a method commonly seen on the larger Cheshire houses.

In all such houses, no matter how important, the staircases were small and placed in projecting wings or outshuts at the rear; it was impossible to cut large openings in the timber floors without causing the jetties to collapse and for the same reason central fireplaces and chimneys also presented difficulties.

Among the most renowned jettied timber-framed buildings are The Feathers Inn, Ludlow, Ireland's Mansions, Shrewsbury, both jettied at the front, Paycocke's House, Coggeshall, a two-storey house with a continuous jetty along its street front, and Little Moreton Hall, which has jetties on all sides with the typical Cheshire coved undersides concealing the projecting floor joists. Medieval town buildings with jetties are usually confined to older towns, but inevitably these buildings have been altered by later developments such as the addition of modern shop windows at ground-floor level.

The projection of jetties also encouraged the development of oriel windows, mostly rectangular in shape, the top of which was formed by the projecting jetty above, into which the window mullions were mortised. Earlier types of mullions, although square in section, were set at an angle in the frame so that an edge, rather than a side, faced the front. Later the mullions were set square so that fixing them into the frames was easier, likewise the fitting of the glass. Although oriel windows were used on houses without jetties, it was the development of the projecting upper floors which obviously enhanced the use of such windows, protected by the floors above.

As larger staircases became fashionable from the Elizabethan period onwards, the lower floor of a house was often built in stone or brick with the upper floors of timber; to accommodate these staircases in a wholly timber-framed building presented structural problems difficult to solve in any other way. Although any timber-framed houses with large staircases tend to be the box-frame type where the external walls have no over-sailing upper storeys, examples are known of jettied houses in cities like Exeter and Oxford having large internal staircases or fireplaces which are generally no earlier than the late sixteenth century.

Since a timber-framed building is tied together by its structural members all acting in equilibrium, any alterations to allow the construction of a staircase tended to make the framework slightly more unstable. Also the higher the building the more difficult it was to prevent the walls from leaning outwards, pushed by the thrust of the roof rafters carrying the thatch or tile covering. These were merely fixed by pegs to the timber beam at the top of the timber framework, and the walls were restrained from movement by tie-beams placed across the building. Movement was also inhibited by the sheer weight of the timber framework, but as the size of the beams was reduced, from the fifteenth century onwards, more efficient roof trusses were evolved to prevent the building moving.

Before the sixteenth century, crown-post trusses were widely used in east and south-east England and, as shown in Figure 8, the crown-post is placed centrally on the tie-beam forming the base of the truss, and set at intervals along the roof usually where the bays occurred. The crown-post supports a horizontal beam running the full length of the roof which in its turn gives additional support to the upper collar-beam of the truss. The central post often has curved braces springing from the top to give further support to the beam above; where this truss was exposed as part of an open roof the main post was often carved, but in poorer houses a simple square upright was used.

During the sixteenth century this type of roof was superseded by simpler forms of construction, the most widespread employing large or principal rafters set where the bays occurred and tenoned into a horizontal tie-beam forming a simple trussed roof. In some roofs the principal rafters were joined by purlins running the full length of the roof and pegged to each main rafter. Another form was the clasped purlin roof and although earlier examples of this roof are known most were constructed between the seventeenth and nineteenth centuries. The principal rafters were placed with their tops in line with the other smaller intermediate rafters while the purlin was housed into a notch cut on the underside of the main rafters. The purlins were also supported by either a horizontal collar-beam and vertical strut or a curved brace tenoned into the tie-beam forming the base of the truss. (*See* Figure 8.)

Later on, independent trusses were used which, erected separately from the rest of the roof, were held in position by the purlins which supported the rafters, all of the same size. The first to come into widespread use was the king-post truss, in general use during the eighteenth and nineteenth centuries although a few earlier examples are known. It had a central post, the king-post, running from the tie-beam at the base to support the ridge of the roof, now a board, unlike earlier roofs where the pairs of rafters were simply pegged together at the ridge. From the base of the central post two sloping struts supported the sides of the truss on which rested the purlins. This truss and the queen-post type which later replaced it are shown in Figure 8.

The queen-post truss, used in a few medieval houses, particularly in East Anglia, later became the most frequently used truss of the seventeenth century; unlike the king-post type there was no central post at each truss position so that the roof space could be converted into living accommodation. In the queen-post type two vertical posts supported the side purlins, one either side of the roof, standing on the base tie-beam and kept apart at the top by a cross-tie on which stood a vertical post holding the ridge in position. In many of the large-span roofs this horizontal tie was above head height allowing space for rooms under the truss ties, to that the accommodation extended the full length of the roof and in many cases became servants' sleeping quarters. A feature of the later trusses was the tension joints at the base of the queen or king-post trusses strengthened by using metal straps instead of tenon joints, and during the nineteenth century, straps and bolts replaced the older conventional timber joints, being cheaper to make.

In the medieval roofs, open to the ridge, trusses were elaborately carved and often were objects of great beauty, but as standards of comfort improved, rooms became smaller and warmer. Ceilings were eventually inserted below the level of the roof trusses and from the early sixteenth century such plastered ceilings were elaborately decorated until Georgian fashion demanded plainer ceilings with cornices just round the edge. The development of such ceilings coincided with the replacement of oak by softwood as the timber used for roof trusses and being hidden from view they became less decorative, and the plain functional roof of today evolved.

Throughout the medieval period the layout of timber houses, especially in towns, followed an almost identical plan of houses usually three bays long, the length being one and a half times the span. Houses were either parallel with or at right angles to the street and various layouts were developed to utilize the limited street frontage available in the congested conditions.

Houses built parallel with the street were either extended along the frontage or, to save land, shortened by building rooms at the back, giving a double-depth house with two parallel ranges of rooms. Many of these houses had three storeys jettied out over the street with living accommodation over the shops in the front ground-floor rooms. The most expensive, and rarest, houses had rooms and outbuildings grouped round a courtyard reached by an entrance from the street, usually under the first floor of the house. Similar buildings have survived in use until this day as inns, much easier to find than houses of the same style, which occupied such large sites that during the nineteenth century many were demolished to make way for great commercial buildings. The standard type of town house would have the narrow gable end facing the street with the main building extending along the site at right angles to the street frontage, so that the houses filled almost all the site and represented an economical use of space in the crowded towns of medieval England. Many remained almost intact until the eighteenth and nineteenth centuries when these town centres underwent redevelopment for the first time since they were laid out. Few timber-framed houses surviving in town centres have remained unaltered; many are concealed behind later fronts, and even in rural areas an unaltered timber-framed house is a rarity.

Although more land was available in country areas this had little influence on the design of houses and the layouts resembled those found in the towns with one exception, the Wealden house. This is the only distinctive regional timber-framed house-type native to this country, originating in the Weald of Kent and the adjacent parts of Surrey and east Sussex and almost one thousand of these houses are known to have survived in this quite small area. Many were originally isolated farmhouses but similar houses found in towns and villages in the South-East were once occupied by the wealthier merchants and shop-keepers. When first named 'Wealden' such houses were thought to be restricted to the Weald areas of the south, but recent research has revealed a few houses of this distinctive type as far north as York.

Away from the South-East another group has been identified in the Midlands, the majority in the Spon Street medieval-street restoration scheme in Coventry and a few in Warwick. There may be other examples in the Midlands awaiting discovery but almost all the Wealden houses in towns have been transformed in the way to be described later, making identification very difficult without a close examination of the internal timber framing, where this survives.

This type of house is also known as the 'recessed front' or 'Kentish Yeoman's house', the latter name being rather misleading as no documentary evidence exists suggesting that such houses were used only by yeomen; neither do the majority of these houses survive exclusively in the Weald area, but to the east of Maidstone and in Surrey and Sussex. In most of these houses the central recessed part of the building was a single-bay hall but examples with two bays are known representing the maximum width of the hall which was the core of the building. This hall, originally open to the roof, was flanked at either end by slightly projecting two-storey wings, containing a solar and other living rooms, each a bay wide, making a house of three or four bays, while the first floors of the wings were jettied out at the front of the house. The central recess, one or two bays in width, was formed by carrying the roof of the jettied wings straight across the intervening gap making a wide projecting overhang supported at the side by curved braces running parallel with the front of the house. It is these braces, with the central recess, and also the fact that the roof had hips at either end, rather than the gable ends of other timber-framed houses, which gave the Wealden house its distinctive appearance. However in a village or town where the Wealden house formed a part of a street, the ends of the roof had gables to line up with adjacent houses.

Although the external appearance was fairly uniform in style, the best examples all being close studded, the internal layout varied with the varying numbers of bays. The most common design was either a single- or double-bay hall with two-storeyed wings, sometimes with an additional service bay, or a traditional cross passage which might be part of the hall or in a separate bay, and in this case the two side wings might be of unequal widths.

The earliest date of such houses is uncertain but they were certainly built in the fourteenth century and the largest date from the late fifteenth or early sixteenth centuries. Perhaps the chief regional difference between the Wealden houses lay in the construction of the jetties, the commonest type having the jetty to the front of the two side wings, forming the rooms over the parlour and service areas. Examples survive with the jetties also down the sides of these side wings, while a rare kind of Wealden house, limited to three survivors, all in Kent, is the double type. In this the side wings are jettied out at the front, the rear, and down the sides, so that there is a central recess on both the front and rear elevations.

Many surviving urban Wealden houses suffered the same treatment as other jettied houses by having a new front wall built under the original projecting jetties. This new wall built up to eaves level allowed the front of the hall to be removed, providing a straight frontage, which increased the floor area. This often coincided with the current changes in fashion and therefore most altered Wealden houses have stone or brick fronts with Queen Anne casements, or Georgian sash-windows. Such changes also occurred when the original hall was split up by the insertion of an upper floor, forming two storeys lining up with those in the side wings. These alterations are obvious only when the remains of the original timber frame can be examined inside the house, probably during repair work necessitating the removal of some of the plaster covering to the walls, so that the identification of many houses of this type is very difficult.

Wealden houses, like most other timber-framed houses, are popularly described as 'black and white' buildings, but colouring them black and white was a Victorian fashion not based on any historical evidence. Investigations have now established that such houses were originally limewashed externally and some of the larger buildings were painted in bright colours, almost crude by present-day standards. Traces of orange, red and gold colouring have been found on buildings such as the White Hart Inn, Newark, built about 1400. The treatment was varied, and in the eastern counties the oak was left in its natural state or limewashed, while in Cheshire and the Midlands the framework was often blackened with mixtures of bullocks' blood and red ochre which produced a matt surface on both the timber and plaster infill. But it is questionable whether many so-called 'black and white' buildings were this colour before the last century since a permanent black colour was unobtainable until tar or pitch distilled from coal were produced in large quantities. The materials previously available, lamp-black and charcoal, were not durable enough to protect the timber or withstand the ravages of the weather, therefore it may be assumed that while the infill panels were often coloured, the oak was left to weather naturally and only when inferior timbers began to be used was it necessary to protect the surface by some form of painting or by concealing the whole framework under a coating of plaster. This signals the approaching end of the timber-building tradition which had spanned several centuries, ultimately ceasing during the eighteenth century.

Following the appearance of these final examples of large and elaborate timber-framed houses there was a steady rejection of the use of timber for building by the wealthier classes for numerous reasons. The prime reason was the possible danger of fire in built-up areas, followed by the modish preference for brick or stone and a modified classical style leading eventually to the Georgian style with its sash-windows, which ousted the older timber-framed houses and their small medieval casements. Probably the choice of these styles and fashionable materials by the Royal Family and Court induced others less affluent to follow their lead.

Another obvious reason for the decline was that the seventeenth century suffered an ever increasing shortage of the largest timber required for their construction. The mature oaks having been used up, the material available to poorer people was the timber from smaller trees and thinnings from pollarded trees. As a result the framework of smaller cottages was of inferior timber which was inevitably supplanted by cheaper and more plentiful brick.

7

The Fashion for Stone – the Tudor Period and Later

If any building material reveals the geology of the district it is stone and a glance at the older local houses will always provide the evidence. Therefore, before looking at the development of stone buildings it should be realized that although the stone found in this country varies greatly in colour and texture there are as few as four main classes of stone available to the local builder. These stones are found in quite clearly defined areas and until the construction of canals, and later the railways, simplified the transport of such materials it was rare for the smaller dwellings to have been built of anything but the local stone. Where this was not available other forms of building, such as timber and cob, lingered on until brick became more plentiful and cheap enough for the poorer people to use.

The stones suitable for building fall into the following groups: limestone, sandstone, granite and slate, and in their absence stones picked up on the surface of the fields were used, the most obvious example being flint. The limestone districts stretch along clearly defined escarpments from the Mendips, through the Cotswolds to the uplands of south Yorkshire. Isolated pockets of usable stone are also found in the south-eastern counties as well as in Derbyshire and further north in parts of Cumbria. It is alongside the Cotswold escarpment that the majority of limestone buildings occur in places as well known as the Barringtons, Bourton on the Water, Broadway, Burford, Chipping Campden, Cirencester, Northleach, the Slaughters and Stow-on-the-Wold.

In spite of slight colour variations in the stones, these buildings, particularly in the Cotswolds, form harmonious groups. This is not so obvious in the sandstone areas which are situated as widely apart as Sussex, South Wales and Cumbria, with the main sources of sandstone being in the Peak District and along the Pennine Ridge. Sandstone is the typical building material of the Peak and the Yorkshire Dales.

Slates and granites found in comparatively isolated and widely separated areas in the Lake District, North Wales and Cornwall give the villages of those remoter districts their own distinctive appearance. In other areas, such as East Anglia and parts of south-eastern England, the only building stones are chalk, rarely used in large blocks due to its soft character, and flint found either at or just below ground level.

Stone had been used since Roman times but the cost and the difficulty of cutting meant that it was scarcely used, before the fifteenth century,

79

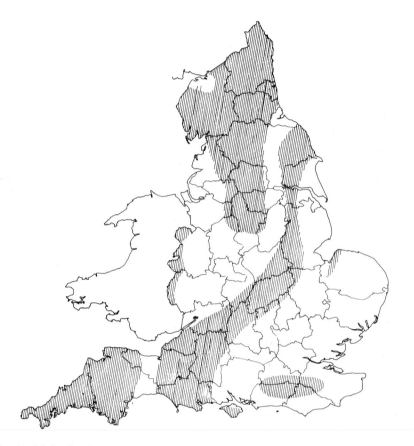

Fig. 10 Main districts where traditional stone houses and cottages are still to be found

for anything but castles, bridges, palaces, churches and abbeys. Before then stone houses were rare and the few surviving buildings, now called "King John's" or "Jews'" Houses were dealt with in a previous chapter. The early flourishing of stone in England was in the Cotswolds where the prosperity resulting from the wool trade allowed the easily available local stone to be used for houses from quite an early period. The wool merchants had for the first time enough wealth to pay for new structures, churches as well as houses, long before many other parts of the country and well before the Tudor period, long regarded as the start of the stone-building era.

Tudor society was one in which "men desired not only to be rich but to be richer than other men", wrote the Victorian, John Stuart Mill, and this greater prosperity showed in the "Great Rebuilding" as it is now described by modern historians. Professor W.G. Hoskins, the first so to name the period, considers it in some detail in his book *Provincial England*, pointing out how the rebuilding of rural England took place roughly between the reign of Elizabeth I and the Civil War, that is from 1570 to 1640, though judging from examples of dated buildings the most prolific period was from 1575 to 1625, a mere fifty years. It was during this time of increasing wealth and population that the towns, as well as the smaller rural communities, expanded as never before. The prosperity, resulting from increased sheep farming and better husbandry on the more fertile soils, meant that for the first time small landholders had enough money to rebuild the poorer houses, many of which were built of cob, replacing them with more permanent dwellings numerous in the smaller hamlets throughout medieval England. It should not be assumed that stone, where it was easily available, was always used, but many dwellings were built of this material freely used for the first time.

In some areas, for example the Welsh Borders, the timber-framed building tradition continued and many of the larger timber-framed houses of this region date from that period. In such places timber was succeeded by brick so that no rebuilding in stone took place during the seventeenth century and sometimes the owner, in order to save money, would leave the original medieval timber building hidden behind the new front elevation of stone or encase the whole timber structure in stone walls. In the Lake District, and northern England, the rebuilding occurred rather later and most of the new houses in the four northern counties were built during the eighteenth and nineteenth century, therefore many of the humbler cob buildings were never replaced, some surviving well into the present century.

Traditionally, farmworkers and their families had been housed in the same buildings as their employers, living as a community. But as farmers grew wealthier they desired more privacy and began to house their labourers in small separate cottages. These were built either in isolated places on the farmstead or, in the more prosperous parts of England, grouped together to form hamlets. Such small hamlets increased in numbers until later and more drastic changes in farming practices caused many of these to disappear in their turn, leaving a mere name on a map, today only recalled as a deserted medieval village site.

Later, still more cottages vanished with the Parliamentary Enclosures of the seventeenth and eighteenth centuries to be replaced by new dwellings in the neighbouring villages, and many of the small stone cottages to be seen, particularly in districts lacking easily available local stone, are no older than the late seventeenth century and even later. Exceptions may be found in the Cotswolds and Yorkshire Dales, districts which have a very long tradition of stone building, but these are comparatively few in number. These changes established what is now the pattern of small stone houses clustered in villages with the slightly larger manor-house standing in the centre or on the edge of the settlement, perhaps grouped with the church. This should not disguise the fact that in the early Middle Ages there were many more stone houses isolated in the centre of farmsteads worked by yeoman farmers.

Many of these houses have now gone leaving only traces of a moated manor-house site. It is uncertain why the tradition of surrounding such houses with water should persist after the defensive purpose of moats had ceased. At the time of building, moats could have provided materials such as clay for bricks, this being the reason for the original excavations. Most moats have now been filled in, leaving only slight undulations on the surface of fields even if the house which the moat surrounded has survived.

The number of moated stone manor-houses greatly exceeds former estimates; recently the Moated Manor-House Research Group has located at least 2,000 of them in Britain and probably many more await discovery. It may never be known how many of these house sites were also associated with the small stone quarries which were worked in areas where stone was available near the surface. Many of these quarries opened during the late Elizabethan period, sometimes just to provide the stone for a single house or a small group in a nearby village, and although now filled in, traces of past workings can be seen in districts such as the Cotswolds. Evidence also remains in field names including the obvious Stone Quarry Ground, Stone Acre Meadow, Stonebed, Stonelands, Stone Pit Close, to Stoney Nap found near Upper Slaughter and Stony Wong, at Askham, meaning land with stony soil from which stone was excavated.

The first yeomen's houses were of cob until in the fifteenth century timber-framing became widely used even where stone was easy to find. It should not be assumed that stone was invariably used in districts now referred to as stone areas, for in such places oak was always used where there was enough of it. Not until late in the next century did small stone houses begin to appear in southern and western England where the material was easy to quarry and split into suitable-sized blocks. About the middle of the seventeenth century houses now accepted as the traditional Cotswold type began to appear following the belt of limestone country from Dorset to Lincoln and into a few areas of south Yorkshire. Many such small buildings can still be seen in villages in the Cotswolds, Oxfordshire, Rutland and Northamptonshire all dating from the late sixteenth and early seventeenth centuries.

This rebuilding did not greatly affect northern England until well after the Restoration, at least a century after the small stone houses of the south-western counties. In fact by the end of the seventeenth century the scarcity of timber made stone a more attractive proposition for building and when during the same period Celia Fiennes was visiting Northamptonshire she was able to write, "here we are neare the quarrys of stone and the houses are built of stone as in Gloucestershire".

Yeomen and their families had lived formerly in small one-room cottages built of cob, or with a light timber frame on a rubble base, while the interior was open to the under side of the thatch-covered roof. So poorly built and flimsy were these sixteenth-century cottages that, as far as is known, none has survived. Any sixteenth-century houses remaining, and these are comparatively few, were originally husbandmen's farmhouses. Stone always formed the foundations of timber-framed buildings but it continued to be more costly than other materials, at least up to the eighteenth century, so stone houses have always been for richer people. Labourers' stone cottages appeared much later and most of those seen today probably date from no earlier than the seventeenth and succeeding centuries.

Eric Mercer in his book *English Vernacular Houses*, describes in some detail the changes which took place in the planning of houses following the sixteenth century, and it is clear that by a hundred years later two-room houses were standard throughout rural areas. Three-room houses started to appear in south-eastern England not long afterwards, but houses of four rooms were rare before 1600 even in the more prosperous parts of the southern counties. By the second half of the seventeenth century this type became fairly common as far afield as Oxfordshire and Northamptonshire where dated examples from 1660 onwards can be seen. In the northern counties progress was much slower and another century elapsed before similar houses appeared in Lancashire. Up to the late seventeenth century the biggest influence on the layout of the smaller rural houses was probably the position of the farm buildings in relation to the living quarters. Due to the value of the husbandman's stock and the frequently unsettled situation in some of the more isolated parts of the country, adequate protection had to be provided for his cattle. Traditionally this meant that the farmer's family and his stock were housed under the same roof, from which evolved a house type now generally called a longhouse from its long and relatively narrow rectangular shape. Originally it was a single-storey building throughout (*see* Figure 11), but later two-storeyed types were developed.

As well as the longhouse two other traditional patterns developed among smaller dwellings built before this period, the 'through passage plan' and the 'undivided house', as it is often called, where the layout was not divided by the passage running from back to front of the house.

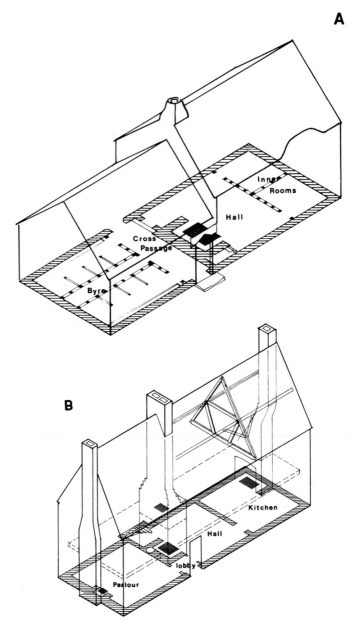

Fig. 11 Typical house-plan types used in all kinds of houses from the sixteenth to nineteenth centuries and even later in some remoter districts; A. modified longhouse type; B. three-bay, baffle-entry house; C. seventeenth-century stone-built house; D. nineteenth-century cottage.

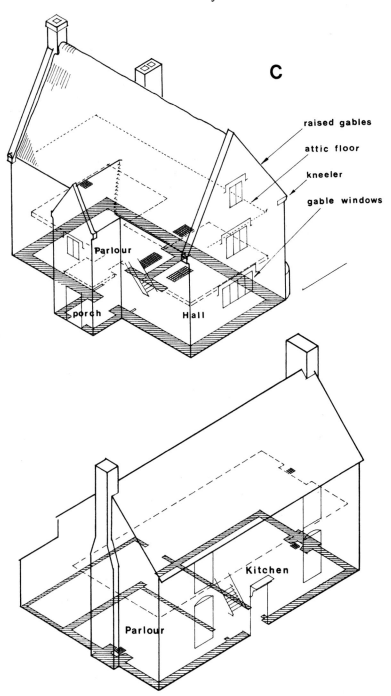

C

raised gables

attic floor

kneeler

gable windows

Parlour

porch

Hall

Kitchen

Parlour

Although regional variations did appear these basic layouts remained in common use up to at least the eighteenth century and were used in most houses in rural areas, whether constructed of cob, timber-framing, stone or brick. Although the description of these traditional layouts is included in the chapter on stone buildings it could apply equally to the sections dealing with timber-framed or brick houses, or cottages, built before the earlier part of the eighteenth century.

The fully developed longhouse was of one storey, sometimes with a loft in the roof space, evolving later into two-storey dwellings. The ground floor had an inner room reached through the outer room, or hall, the main living-room containing the fireplace. Behind this was a passage running through the dwelling dividing the living quarters from the cattle shelter. The history of this type of building in rural areas extends over a long period; in the north of England it was built of turf as long ago as the ninth century and in the south was common in the twelfth century. Some of the oldest longhouses were on the fringes of Dartmoor and Exmoor where the harsh winters made it necessary to keep cattle under cover, but many of these earlier buildings have now been altered; the byre became additional living quarters or disappeared as changes in farming led to the erection of farm buildings some distance from the farmhouses, especially when these were rebuilt during the Parliamentary Enclosures.

Earlier longhouses varied slightly in plan before acquiring a standardized and conventional layout like those built in the northern counties, from the seventeenth century onwards. The later northern longhouses are larger than those in southern England and almost all these houses have an inner room as well as a hall, a kitchen, with the fireplace always backing onto the passage, and another room added as a pantry. The northern houses are almost always one-and-a-half or two-storeys high and in some of the later houses the byre has been replaced by a storage barn. Many still survive with sash-windows replacing the original windows to conform to the fashion of the eighteenth century. In southern longhouses, staircases to the upper floors were often built in shallow turrets projecting from the rear walls; later houses had projecting wings to accommodate larger staircases and extra rooms following extensions, or alterations, from the seventeenth century onwards.

In the remoter areas of Dartmoor, Central Wales and Cumberland, the one distinguishing feature for all longhouses was a single entrance for men and beasts, all being housed under one continuous roof. Regional variations are however found in the Peak district and parts of Yorkshire, where there is usually a separate entrance for cattle though the houses are longhouses in every other respect. So although houses with through passages became quite common not every dwelling with such a plan was originally a longhouse as in many cases the third room, adjacent to the passage, formed part of the living quarters. For this reason it is quite often difficult to distinguish between the two types of house particularly when the byre is no longer used for cattle and has become additional living accommodation. Perhaps the one feature which could reveal the difference would be the width of the passage itself. The longhouse required a much wider passage for cattle to get to the byre than would be needed if not used for this purpose. Forming a structural feature difficult to alter, the passage would remain the same width long after changes in the rest of the house, so a wide passage might indicate that originally the building had been a longhouse at one stage in its history. In Devon and Somerset, for example, the passage is often 6 to 7 feet in width, much wider than elsewhere in England.

The later farmhouses, whether timber-framed or stone-built, had a passage dividing the kitchen from the rooms occupied by the farmer's family which allowed labourers to get to the kitchen for meals. The passage layout developed in different places quite independently of the longhouse, starting with the old open hall type place where the partition separating the entrance from the fireplace was a wooden screen. In the dining-halls of the great Elizabethan mansions this became an elaborate feature. In the humbler houses, like so many items, it originated in the homes of the wealthy and gradually descending the social scale it was adapted by the yeomen to improve their houses. In these cases the access passage was not invariably behind the chimney-stack as in the longhouse and the position of the flue showed variations between the northern and the southern parts of the country. Until brick became more plentiful, stone was essential for the construction of fire-proof chimneys, so the houses in districts where stone was available developed this feature before most other places.

Up to the Georgian period, smaller houses in all parts of the country consisted of three rooms; the hall, parlour and kitchen with a cross passage dividing this room from the other two. The service rooms, or kitchen, were in the case of farmhouses always near the farmyard and the parlour away from this where possible. In some earlier houses of this type the walls between the rooms were timber-framed to save stone which was used only for the stack and external walls, often 2 feet thick. From the Tudor period onward, upper rooms were often inserted in the medieval open hall houses, dividing them and so disguising the original plan that today many of these houses are difficult to detect in their present form without a detailed examination of their structure. New houses also began to have two floors, the upper one lit by dormer windows set in the roof, starting a design which became popular from that time onward. At a later date the dormer windows were framed in small gables created by continuing the main walls upwards where such windows were needed.

Sixteenth-century changes in farming methods meant that more labourers lived in separate cottages rather than in the farmhouse as before, and through-passage dwellings declined in usefulness and popularity, particularly in the south which felt the changes long before the north. As a result there developed a house type where the main entrance was either into a lobby or directly into a living-room and not into a passage dividing the dwelling into two as was common in the past. The chimney was built between the two main rooms, usually the parlour and kitchen, providing a hearth in each of them and the house was entered by a door opposite the end of the stack. This led into a small lobby formed out of the space between the side of the flue and the outside wall of the house on the side away from the prevailing wind. From the lobby, giving access from the outside, doors led to the main rooms while a third unheated room was reached through the parlour. In single-storey dwellings this room was used for sleeping but later a simple winding staircase was placed in the space at the other end of the stack providing access to the upper storey or loft space in the roof (*see* Figure 11).

The entrance could lead directly into one of the living-rooms but generally a lobby was used and from the sixteenth century onwards this simple layout was common to all districts and to all sizes of houses, regardless of variations in building materials. The undivided plan layout was first found in the larger houses of southern England and East Anglia, becoming widely used in the seventeenth-century stone houses of Yorkshire and throughout the east Midlands extending to the western districts of Cambridgeshire. During the following century the design was applied to the small, poorly built cottages in the north where cob was used rather than stone, a fact which emphasizes the contrast between housing conditions in northern and southern England already apparent by the end of the Middle Ages.

Eventually more accommodation for kitchens and dairies was provided in extensions, or outshuts, built on to the rear of small houses. Many, but not all, outshuts formed part of the original building and in the seventeenth century these became quite common resulting in L-shaped houses, although due to the low eaves level of the roof these extra rooms were very low and inconvenient. Sometimes the outshuts ran the full length of the building especially where the front house was two-storeyed, a pattern which increased in the north with the increasing use of stone for building. But progress was slower in Northumberland and along the Scottish border where, except for the Bastel houses, there were no stone houses before the eighteenth century, most dated examples being from the second quarter of the nineteenth century.

The need for more privacy and accommodation for particular purposes, such as bedrooms, increased the number of smaller rooms in a house. Previously the high cost of fuel meant that yeomen could not afford more than one hearth, but by the early nineteenth century cheaper and more easily available supplies of coal permitted the use of separate fireplaces to heat the rooms of quite modest houses. Another factor was the discovery of cheaper methods of producing glass, enabling ordinary people to glaze their cottages, which was previously impossible. To build stone chimneys with more than one flue would have resulted in very large stacks in the centre of a house so that additional hearths were often built on to the gable-end walls, although there were regional variations; in the east Midlands, for example, hearths were often placed back to back on both sides of internal partition walls. These stacks were quite solid looking and simple in outline with flat copings at the top, and not until much later were chimney-pots in general use. It was later possible to make the special bricks necessary to build the elaborately ornamental chimneys, which first appeared during the Tudor period, similar designs being rarely achievable in stone.

So began the first symmetrical layouts, with a central entrance flanked by the living-room and parlour, and service rooms in outshuts at the rear of the house, reached through the two main rooms which formed the house itself. From these buildings developed the double-depth, or double-pile houses usually approximately square on plan with two rooms on each side of the entrance lobby or passage; later often widening out to become a hall, while in the two-storey house the hall contained the staircase unless it was in a projecting wing behind. In houses of this period all the rooms on a particular floor were the same height, a common layout for the larger houses built before the seventeenth century in towns as well as country districts. Additional rooms were often provided in single or double-storey extensions to the sides or rear, and by the eighteenth century the design of the smaller houses imitated the earlier and grander dwellings, although variations such as T- and L-shaped plans became commonly used in many parts of the country.

The walls of stone houses are load-bearing, and in the simple rectangular houses the loads of the floor and roof-covering were transferred to the gable walls by long beams, or purlins, spanning the length of the house. Where possible the size of the timber required was reduced by intermediate support, provided by taking the partition walls up to the roof level and making these load-bearing and thicker than might normally be required. Later these intermediate walls were replaced by simple roof trusses spanning between the front and rear walls to take some of the roof load of the purlins, the trusses being very heavy to take the weight of the roof-covering, at this period heavy stone slabs.

The use of double-depth houses presented roofing problems, solved in some earlier examples by using two parallel short-span roofs, while another solution, common in the east Midlands, was to use one long roof with two short ones at right angles covering the rear part of the house. But no satisfactory way of covering a double-depth house with a series of roof trusses spanning from back to front was found until well into the eighteenth century when imports of softwood from the Baltic ports provided a supply of cheaper timber. This encouraged the development of shallow pitch roof trusses capable of covering a wide span without becoming too steep, but this in turn also involved the use of lighter roof-coverings. (*See* Figure 12.)

Although this evolution over several centuries resulted in a number of distinct types of house plans, nevertheless the dwellings did not fit precisely into clearly defined groups as described in the outline of the development of early stone houses. The process of simplification required the omission of many regional variations and it should not be assumed, for example, that all through-passage houses are older than double-depth buildings. The actual situation is much more confused, different layouts being used simultaneously in various parts of the country and some remained in fashion much later in areas where a particular type of house was favoured.

Since, in the Middle Ages, cutting stone by hand was tedious and expensive all the older buildings were of pieces of rubble; varying sizes, irregular in shape, or roughly squared if this could be done easily. It was an economical way of building as all the pieces of stone were usable and much could be picked up on the surface or easily dug up so that quarrying was unnecessary. (*See* Figure 13.) The stones were at first laid in a random way bound together with lime mortar, or even mud, making the rubble into a solid mass, but afterwards they were roughly levelled up to form courses up to 18 inches in height. Later the stones were roughly squared up so that they were laid in regular courses not exceeding 9 inches or so in height, with the walls often strengthened by placing large stones across the full thickness. In some districts these were known as 'throughs', and often projected beyond the external faces of the building, particularly in Yorkshire, but in domestic buildings it was more usual to cut these off level with the face of the wall. In northern districts it was quite common, up to the mid-nineteenth century, for cottage walls to consist of an inner and outer leaf of rubble, the middle cavity being filled in with mud poured in while wet and left to dry out, forming a solid mass.

In many earlier buildings the walls were often constructed without mortar although earth mixed with water was used to bind the stones together. Later, various types of mortar were experimented with and in 1641 a writer described a method of making mortar using clay, lime and cow dung, a mixture which may have been in use since Roman times. In

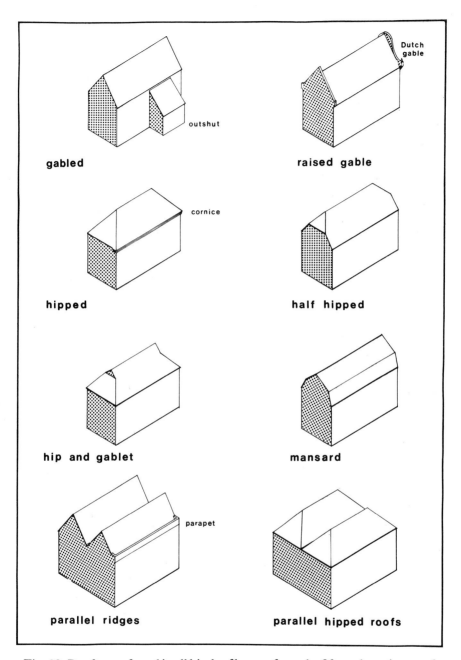

Fig. 12 Roof types found in all kinds of houses from the fifteenth to nineteenth centuries and in some cases still used

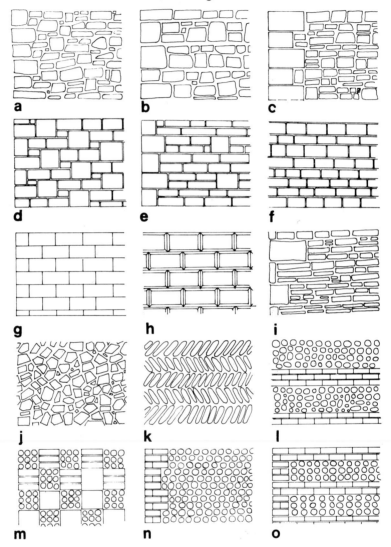

Fig. 13 Stone walling types: a. random rubble; b. coursed random rubble; c. coursed random rubble with ashlar quoins at corners and around openings; d. squared uncoursed or snecked rubble; e. squared rubble built into courses; f. regular coursed rubble; g. ashlar walling; h. rusticated jointed stonework; i. Lake District masonry with slate as the material for the main walls and granite or similar hard stones at corners; j. polygonal walling or Kentish rag-stone work; k. diagonal cobbles; l. pebbles with brick lacing courses to reinforce the walling; m. chequer-pattern flint walling with brick or stone chequer patterning; n. flint walling with brick quoins at corners; o. flint walling with brick quoins and brick lacing course

some cases small pieces of stone, or flint, were inserted in the mortar joints before these had hardened to give additional strength or help level the stones up into courses, a practice lasting at least until the last century and in some localities even longer.

The use of rubble presented difficulties at the corners of a building, as well as at window and door openings, a problem unknown in the early circular huts. Eventually the use of worked stone, used as quoins at the corners, or around openings, helped to solve the problem of obtaining the straight lines essential to rectangular buildings. However the external faces forming the walls were usually thick and if worked stone was used this was exposed on the front and back, if this was not to be plastered over, with the middle always filled in with rubble or irregular pieces of ashlar.

At the same time enormous stones were used in many old cottages for both the foundations and walls up to the lowest window-sill; above this level smaller stones were used. Such large stones were not squared up more than absolutely necessary, especially in the south-west and north-west where the local granites and millstone grits were hard to cut. As early as A.D. 684 Bede states that walls of large undressed stones were used for the monastery and other buildings at Farne Island. Some scholars suggest that the smaller the number of joints in such walls, the older the building but there is no definite evidence to support the theory.

Before the Industrial Revolution, which introduced mechanized cutting methods, the problems of quarrying and working stone restricted the size of blocks available for building and their distribution even though the rough shaping of the stone was done at the quarry to reduce the weight to be moved. For the smaller houses, especially those not on the estates of the wealthy landowners, local stone was always used and it was only for very large and important buildings that stone was transported any distance.

As methods of cutting stone improved, the quarries in the prosperous areas of southern England provided cheaper ashlar which then became more commonly used for the external facings of all houses but those of the poorest labourers. Being expensive, ashlar was beyond their reach and they continued to build in rubble, although it was increasingly used with worked stone quoins at the corners as well as around door and window openings. The rough, rubble walls were gradually abandoned and by the seventeenth century most of the houses owned by the wealthier people were of ashlar, the finest examples of which still survive in the towns and villages of the Cotswolds and the fringes of the Mendips, also along the limestone ridges of southern England. In the more remote, and therefore poorer areas small buildings were increasingly built of roughly squared rubble, whose surfaces were not worked as smoothly as ashlar, the stone being laid in slightly irregular courses, absolutely level ones only being possible with worked stone.

The characteristics of the local stone determine the size of blocks which vary from district to district resulting in distinct differences between buildings found in different geological regions. The oolites probably provide the largest blocks and the most important variety, Portland stone, can be obtained in pieces between 10 and 15 feet long and up to 5 feet in width and height. This stone was used from the seventeenth century onwards for important public buildings, particularly those found in London. As a result the only small houses built of it would be in the neighbourhood of the quarry at Portland Bill and even these would probably be largely of pieces of stone left over after cutting the larger blocks.

Most limestones come in comparatively small blocks, the smallest being used for the minor dwellings commonly seen today. Millstone grit, sandstones and granite can all be obtained in large blocks and some of these were frequently used for the construction of small houses in both northern and south-western England.

Slates tend to be brittle, and easily split, so that the pieces used for houses are usually quite small, often the waste left over from cutting roofing slates, although specially cut blocks may be found in some of the more prosperous areas where slate forms the local stone. Chalk, found in southern England, is so friable that it is not normally used for buildings, other than perhaps small farm buildings, and eastern England's only local stone, flint, takes the form of large pebbles widely used for buildings in that region.

One feature which distinguishes houses of one period from those of another is the style of the windows. In the earliest stone houses windows were quite small and squat because the sizes of the available stones limited the sizes of the openings which were divided by mullions put in to help support the lintel carrying the weight of the wall above. Most stone could be obtained in blocks suitable for building houses but it was more difficult to find the longer pieces required for spanning openings or forming upright window mullions or door jambs. Frequently these had to be brought from far distant quarries so increasing the cost that until quite early in the seventeenth century windows were low in height, reducing the length of the upright mullions. The windows were fairly long in contrast to their height having a series of openings divided by vertical stone, or more rarely wooden, mullions. (*See* Figure 14.) These windows ranged in length from the normal two, or three, lights to as many as five in a group, protected by wooden shutters or left open to the weather, until glass became available on a wider scale to enable leaded lights to be fixed. These were restricted in size due to the small hand-

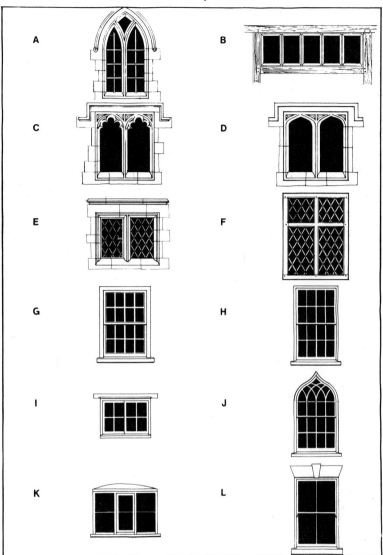

Fig. 14 Window types, all drawn to the same scale: A. medieval stone; B. medieval timber; C. Tudor; D. Elizabethan; E. seventeenth-century stone; F. late seventeenth-century timber cross window; G.early eighteenth-century timber; H. late eighteenth-century timber, in both cases these are sash-type windows; I.Yorkshire sliding sash-window. Although named a Yorkshire window this type is found in many parts of the country particularly from the early nineteenth century; J. Regency 'Gothick' window, usually in the form of a sash-window; K.Victorian cottage casement window; L.Victorian sliding sash-window with its typical large panes of glass and few glazing bars

made pieces of glass which could be produced and so opening casements were rare.

By the Tudor period this type of window was becoming a feature of many of the stone houses being built by prosperous landowners and merchants. Since cutting fine mouldings was at that time difficult and expensive, most mullions had only simple mouldings cut into the stonework if indeed any were used. Such was the conservatism of the stonemasons that on smaller houses the shape of the moulded mullions continued almost unchanged until well into the last century, complicating the precise dating of some buildings without additional evidence.

In the more fashionable houses of the early seventeenth century lintels over windows were carved in the form of what is now called the Tudor arch which, unlike the more pointed Gothic arch, could be carved out of a single block of stone. These shallow arches spanned the whole of the two-, or three-light window but rarely was it possible to bridge over anything but a small window in this way. Longer windows were usually spanned by lintels formed of smaller stones supported at the joints by load-bearing upright mullions.

Above the windows of later houses was a simple hood label, or drip-moulding, throwing the rain clear of the building, often achieved by projecting the whole lintel beyond the face of the wall. In the earlier houses this drip-moulding was straight but in the later 'Cotswold' type houses the drips had turned down ends, sometimes forming triangular spaces in the corners which might be decorated with simple carvings.

In the limestone areas of Northamptonshire, and Rutland, these drip-stones are normally quite straight with no turn down at the ends and the windows often have oak lintels and mullions in contrast to the stone ones found elsewhere. Drip moulds did however appear on houses throughout the country except for the poorer dwellings, particularly those found in the rural northern counties, which were built of granite or the local millstone grit hard to cut into any kind of mouldings. In later houses this drip mould ran right across the main elevation as a decorative feature or string course just above the level of the windows or marking the level of the upper floor.

In the north, where climatic conditions were more severe and local stone harder to work, this type of window survived well into the nineteenth century before being replaced by sash-windows, which required larger openings to be cut into the original walls. In the southern counties, narrow and squat windows became unfashionable late in the medieval period giving way to larger rectangular openings divided into four almost equal sections by the insertion of vertical and horizontal members of stone; later oak was used particularly in places where stone was hard to find. The leaded lights, at first made with diamond-shaped panes, were

Blisworth, Northamptonshire. A house of the seventeenth-century 'Great Rebuilding' period, extended later by an extra bay. The thatched roof and banded stonework are characteristic of the area

Yardley Hastings, Northamptonshire. A three-chimney house with the main door opposite the central stack. In local stone such houses are typical of the seventeenth to nineteenth centuries in Northamptonshire and north Buckinghamshire. The machine-made pantiles of the roof are continuing a tradition of pantiling used in the area in the past, although these tiles are modern

Priest's House, Brafield-on-the-Green, Northamptonshire. A medieval house disguised under later stone walls, probably in the seventeenth century and extended later

Lyddington, Wiltshire. Eighteenth-century village house built in the purple stonework of that restricted locality

Ilmington, Warwickshire. Houses of Edgehill stone, examples of those built during the seventeenth and eighteenth centuries on the fringes of the Cotswolds towards the east

Arlington Row, Bibury, Gloucestershire. Cotswold stone cottages with stone slabs on the roof

Knowlson Farm, Barkisland, Yorkshire. A seventeenth-century farmhouse with stone walls typical of the upland areas of northern England

King's Lynn, Norfolk. Brick houses of the sixteenth century with steeply pitched tiled roofs, that to the left of the group still retaining the old local style pantiles

John Smith's Hospital, Canterbury, Kent. A group of brick almshouses with curved gable walls, built in 1657

A seventeenth-century Kent house with Dutch-style gables to the roof

Old cottages, Skirmett, Buckinghamshire. Brick cottages typical of any time between the seventeenth and nineteenth centuries

High House, Dunster, Somerset. Fourteenth-century timber-framed house, rare in that district, concealed by later tile-hanging, probably in the seventeenth century

Totnes, Devonshire. Slate-hung houses common in the area and rarely found outside south-western England, except in the late nineteenth century when sometimes used in areas where slate was quarried

Lamberhurst, Kent. Weather-boarding characteristic of the countryside of south-east England

Old Cloth Hall, Biddenden, Kent. Tile-hanging as found all over south-eastern England

Weather-boarding and balloon framing, houses typical of eastern England. This example being found as far west as Hunsdon in Hertfordshire, which is quite unusual in traditional buildings

fixed directly into grooves formed in the surrounding stonework, any opening lights being in the lower parts of the window. The opening lights were of simple iron frames supported on pivots knocked into the joints of the jambs allowing the window to swing open when required. In the remoter parts of northern England, as well as in Wales, some of the original window openings have survived complete with the iron-framed casements, although frequently these have been replaced by modern metal windows. Even when the original glazing has been replaced it is often possible to recognize old window openings by the grooves into which the original leaded lights were fixed.

Although the size and proportion of Jacobean windows are similar to Tudor, the position of the horizontal transom is different, being no longer in the centre of the opening but only a third of the way down. The leaded lights tend to have rectangular panes rather than diamond-shaped ones with wooden frames gradually replacing iron. During the Georgian period many Jacobean houses were altered by inserting sash-windows in the same openings as the original windows, the proportions of the two types almost always being identical.

Window openings required straight edges and were from early times outlined in ashlar though the rest of the walls were rubble. These surrounds showed regional variations according to the type of stone available but one design was widely used from the seventeenth century onwards. In this case the jambs were formed on a series of alternating long and short stones repeating a pattern commonly used at the quoins of a building. However not until the late eighteenth century, when the development of stone-cutting saws made ashlar possible on a large scale, were complicated mouldings produced.

During the periods when the style of stone houses changed, thatch had become unpopular, being a fire hazard and having a limited life, and other materials began to provide roof coverings. First came oak shingles which in the Middle Ages were widely used even on churches as large as Salisbury Cathedral, first roofed in this way. Later stone slabs began to be used, but as far as is known the Saxons did not use stone slabs in this way possibly because their buildings were often too flimsy to take the heavy weight. Although its use declined during this period stone had been widely used by the Romans; at Ditchley in Oxfordshire a villa had Stonesfield slabs, while at Chedworth in the Cotswolds the roofing slabs came from the locality and also the Forest of Dean. After the departure of the Romans, stone was rarely used in this way before the thirteenth century, even in the Cotswolds, but records show slabs were being used for roofs in medieval towns from the fourteenth century onwards, largely to prevent the spread of fire.

During the following centuries the use of stone on roofs was confined to the areas where it was traditionally used for building and as slabs are obtainable only from stone which is fissile and also easy to cut this limits the quarries supplying it. Though numerous, many were short-lived and small, serving a small area. The prosperous larger quarries were fewer and depended on a plentiful supply of long-lasting stone easy to split into suitable-sized pieces for roofing. Even when stone was quarried on a large scale, production costs restricted the use of slabs to large important buildings; for this reason, even in "stone districts", many dwellings changed their roof coverings straight from thatch to grey Welsh slates, or clay tiles, of various patterns and colours, never being stone-covered.

As slabs will last for several centuries many surviving stone roofs will be original but others will have been repaired, or totally renewed, with second-hand materials taken from long since demolished buildings which had similar roofs. It must therefore be remembered that the covering is not necessarily original, unless the evidence suggests that this is so and since slabs were often transported some distance the material is not always from the local quarry as might be assumed.

Slabs are perhaps the heaviest form of roof-covering ever in common use, and their weight governed the size of slabs it was practical to use. Heavy roof trusses were required and, as in the case of thatch, due to the large-sized timbers used in the roof it is often possible to identify the original covering long after its replacement by a much lighter material such as Welsh slates.

Traditionally, stone-covered roofs were of two types, thick heavy slabs of sandstone, millstone grit or granite, and thinner slabs of limestone, each used in its native locality. Whatever the type, the method of fixing was broadly similar throughout the country. The stones were held down by an oak peg, or animal bone, driven into each individual slab allowing it to be hung or tied over the laths which, due to the weight, were larger and more irregularly shaped than the standard type now in use; these in their turn were pegged or nailed to the rafters. The Romans used iron nails for this purpose; in the medieval period oak pegs were preferred and at the same time the slabs were often fixed to wattle panels laid over the rafters instead of laths. In all these roofs the rafters were very large because of the weight involved, the Cotswold limestone being the lightest and weighing about a ton for every hundred square feet of roof-covering. Purbeck slabs, first used by the Romans, weighed one and a quarter tons for the same area and Horsham stone was heavier still.

The slabs were laid in diminishing courses, the largest at the bottom with the top corners of each piece rounded off to reduce the weight. The names given to these graduated courses, at least in the Cotswolds, are

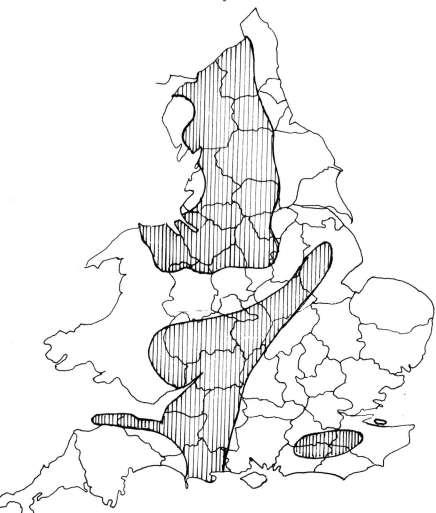

Fig. 15 Districts where stone slabs were traditionally used as roof coverings. (Based on Brunskill)

picturesque survivals, in many cases of unknown origin. Starting from the bottom, the slabs were known as undereaves or cussoms, eaves, follows, long sixteens, long fifteens, long fourteens, long thirteens, long twelves, short twelves, long elevens, long wibbuts, short wibbuts, long nines, short nines, long bachelors, short bachelors, long becks, middle becks, short becks, movities, long cuttings, short cuttings, long pricks, middle pricks, short pricks, and stone cress or ridge tile.

The slabs were often laid on a bed of hay, straw, heather or moss before being fixed to the laths; in the seventeenth and eighteenth century the mossing of roofs was quite common and the task of a special tradesman. The practice became obsolete in the following century when the under-side of the roof was usually torched, or coated, with a mixture of mortar and animal hair, or just in some places clay. This treatment was to keep out the weather and in northern counties the whole roof was often white-washed externally for the same reason. On the earliest buildings the ridge was covered with turf or thatch, a practice superseded eventually by the use of pieces of solid stone carved into a V shape. Later, clay tiles were used with ornamental cresting which varied according to the manu-facturer or the district. Since oak pegs could not hold the heaviest slabs these had to be laid on roofs with low pitches, in the south averaging about forty-five degrees and in the more severe weather conditions of the northern counties, thirty degrees or even lower. In such situations indi-vidual slabs might be as wide as 4 feet and up to 3 inches thick to prevent the rain getting through the roof. Smaller, thinner slabs had to be laid to pitches not less than forty-five degrees, the average being between fifty and fifty-five degrees although pitches up to sixty-five degrees are known, but these are exceptional.

At first these simple rectangular stone houses were gable-ended but later hip roofs became widely used which were simple to cover with materials other than thatch. As double-depth houses became fashion-able they needed to have roofs capable of covering a wide span without being too steep, impossible with stone slabs. To make such roofs water-tight a lighter material was needed, and clay tiles helped to fill this need. But most houses were covered with grey Welsh slates increasingly used during the eighteenth century, allowing pitches as low as thirty to thirty-five degrees to be constructed. With larger slates even shallower pitches were possible, in sharp contrast to the steep pitches required for stone slabs, thus changing completely the appearance of the ordinary small house or cottage.

The thick, heavy slabs of millstone grit are found in the Peak District on both sides of the Pennines and in Yorkshire and Northumberland, while sandstone from the coal measures was commonly used in the Ross-endale area of Lancashire. Sandstone provided thinner slabs and such roof-coverings occur among the old red sandstone districts of Hereford-shire and Shropshire. The sandstone quarry at Duston, in Northamp-tonshire, provided material for many roofs in that area while the Kerridge district, near Macclesfield, supplied grey-coloured millstone grit for roofing in north-eastern Cheshire. In southern England, the heavy dark-brown slabs from Horsham covered many old houses in Kent, Sussex and Surrey. Among the heaviest slabs were those from Purbeck, found on many old buildings in south-western England, particularly in the Corfe Castle and Blandford districts.

The smaller, thinner limestone slabs are chiefly used in the Cotswolds as well as over wide areas of the country where limestone is available; the largest of these Cotswold slabs are usually 16 inches by 24, being just over 1 inch thick, but slabs up to 30 inches long by 56 wide are known. The smallest slabs are however as small as 4 to 6 inches wide and half an inch thick. Houses roofed in this way can still be seen in parts of Sussex, Surrey and as far west as Dorset, stretching along the upland ridges into Oxfordshire and Northamptonshire, including the old county of Rutland. This type of slab was also used along the Welsh borders as well as in northern England where the heavy type of slabs were also in use.

The names of many of the quarries supplying roofing slabs became household words and among the best known were those at Stonesfield, four miles west of the Oxfordshire village of Woodstock. The commercial working of these quarries is recorded from at least the seventeenth century until their closure in 1909, during which time they produced vast quantities of both floor and roofing slabs, the latter often being 2 feet by 3 in size although not as heavy as the Cotswold variety. It is, however, known that this stone was used long before then, though on a smaller scale; Roman slabs from this source had four, five or six pointed sides in contrast to the rectangular slabs of later periods.

Other important sources were the quarries at Collyweston and Easton, in Northamptonshire, and Clipsham, in Rutland, and slabs from this district were used in Stamford, Lincolnshire, as well as on many important buildings in Oxford. The stone at Collyweston was obtained from shallow workings, but in most other cases the workings were very deep, as at Naunton quarry where, during the peak of its prosperity in the last century, up to 30,000 slabs a week were produced by about a hundred men.

Further west, Eyford, near Stow-on-the-Wold, and Kyneton Thorns, both in Gloucestershire and quarries in the Forest of Dean were also in production from the seventeenth century onwards, while slabs from the quarry at Slaughter were used in Oxfordshire as early as 1452.

8

The Spread of Brick

Brickmaking has a long history, the first in this country being made by the Romans, and burnt bricks, as opposed to the sun-dried variety, were in general use well before the first century A.D. The first burnt-clay products were roofing tiles, and the first bricks to be made resembled thick tiles rather than modern bricks. The sizes of Roman bricks varied considerably; $12 \times 6 \times 1\frac{1}{4}$ inches are typical, $18 \times 12 \times 1\frac{1}{2}$ inches not uncommon, and many are square with the thickness varying from 1 inch to a rarely found 2 inches. These sizes enabled the bricks to be well burnt in a wood-fired clamp which was the chief reason for their durability. Archaeological excavations in this country show that walls of Roman buildings were either of flint or stone rubble masonry with two or three rows of bricks going through the wall to tie the stones together every few feet of the height, or two skins of brick around a core of hardened lime and earth, a crude form of concrete.

As far as is known brickmaking ceased when the Romans left the country and no evidence has yet been discovered to show that any were made during the Saxon period. The Saxons, however, did use Roman bricks in substantial numbers, as did the Normans, and these can be seen in such places as Colchester Castle where the Norman walls built of flint incorporate Roman brick, on the same site as the surviving Roman work.

Until quite recently many scholars favoured the theory, first put forward by some eighteenth-century antiquaries, that in this country brickmaking ceased after the departure of the Romans and was not revived until late in the Middle Ages whilst any brick buildings erected before then used materials imported from the Lowlands, perhaps as ballast in ships returning to the east-coast ports. Since most of the oldest brick buildings were in eastern England no one seriously disputed this theory until 1972 when *Brick building in England from the Middle Ages to 1550* was published. This proved that most previous ideas were largely incorrect and it is due to Miss Wight's research that our knowledge of early medieval brickwork has undergone revision. It is now accepted that, with the help of Flemish craftsmen, brickmaking was revived as early as the twelfth century, at first only to supply bricks for "royal works" or ecclesiastical buildings, chiefly bishops' palaces like the famous Hampton Court.

At that time bricks were never used for yeomen's houses and such small buildings were not common until the eighteenth century, although before this, brick was widely used for chimney-stacks on both stone and timber-framed buildings; also from the fifteenth century onwards, it was used to replace the original wattle and daub in many such timber dwelling houses. From the thirteenth century and even earlier, vast quantities of bricks were brought from Europe for use by the Crown and in 1278 the Exchequer Records show that 202,500 were brought from Ypres for work on the Tower of London, while as late as 1365, 7,000 were also imported for work on the Palace of Westminster.

According to surviving records the first bricks made on a large scale were those in the populated eastern counties where good building stone was not available and near the ports where the Flemish immigrants lived, these people having the knowledge to make such bricks from the local clay. It is now believed that the oldest bricks in this country, apart from those made by the Romans, are those used to strengthen the flint walls of the Abbot's Lodging at Little Coggeshall Abbey, in Essex, dating from about 1190 and made on the site.

The bricks at Coggeshall were of the type now known as the "great brick", a sixteenth-century term for the large, dark-red medieval bricks between 15 and 20 inches long, the ones at Coggeshall being 13 × 6 × 2 inches thick. Such bricks were in common use until the early part of the sixteenth century, particularly in East Anglia, although from the thirteenth century these were gradually replaced by smaller bricks. Even so, the change was slow and as late as the eighteenth century great bricks sized 12 × 6 × 2 inches were being used in Kent and Sussex probably due to the tax on bricks then in force. As Miss Wight says, "size is no real guide to the date of bricks. Date is better deduced from texture, from the ways in which the bricks are used, and to what extent they are shaped for dressings and ornament. Sizes may be interesting, just because of their variety, sometimes prompted by functional reasons, and because of their aesthetic effect." It is evident that one must know more about bricks than the mere size before a building can be dated with any accuracy; texture and colour as well as general appearance may often be more reliable than size.

When looking at documentary evidence for early brickwork it is as well to remember that the word "brick" only came into general use during the fifteenth century, the previous word being "waltyle" or wall tile. Also no small brick houses surviving to the present century will contain brickwork before 1450 as such work is rare, only sixty-six examples being known in the whole country. The surviving earliest brick buildings are mostly church towers or porches as well as the detached gatehouses of great mansions, now largely rebuilt in later styles or demolished in this century. Even when brick buildings of an early date survive in predominantly stone districts these are the castles and mansions built by royalty or rich noblemen. In such cases the brick often had to be transported long distances, thus being expensive to use, with the result that large buildings of this new and foreign-looking material impressed the onlooker with the power and wealth of the owner. This was particularly so in the Tudor period when Henry VIII and Wolsey, who could have used stone, built numerous palaces in brick, the most famous being St James's Palace and Hampton Court, so that when it was seen that brick was good enough for the king the material was used more and more by people wanting to imitate their betters.

But about two centuries earlier brick-faced houses had begun to appear in some of the medieval towns of eastern and southern England as a measure to prevent fire, and almost certainly to meet this need bricks were imported by the Hanseatic League. As a result brick buildings began to replace the old timber ones in those districts rather earlier than in the rest of the country. Hull, founded in 1290, was one of the main centres of the League in England and surviving records show that from 1303 until at least 1433 this port had a municipal brickworks, the first town to do so, although nearby Beverley, then larger than Hull, was also making bricks on a large scale about the same period. Beverley Minster contains brickwork dating from between 1308 and 1335, the bricks being $10\frac{1}{2} \times 5\frac{1}{2} \times 2$ inches, the same size as those used a century later, in 1409, to construct the North Bar which involved the use of 125,000 bricks. These bricks were slightly different in size from those made by the municipal works at Hull and used in 1315 to construct Holy Trinity Church which was rendered over in the eighteenth century and uncovered a century later; this church is possibly the oldest wholly brick building in this country.

Most of these bricks were $9\frac{3}{4} \times 4\frac{3}{4} \times 2\frac{1}{8}$ inches while those in the town walls, finished in 1321, were $11 \times 5\frac{1}{2} \times 2$ inches. Hull was undoubtedly the first wholly brick town in England by the early fourteenth century and by then was certainly selling large numbers of bricks to other places in eastern England. The problem was fuel as at that time, according to the Town Chamberlain's records, at least 84,000 small trees and shrubs were needed to produce 35,000 bricks. This meant that production could not expand to any large extent until imported coal became easier to obtain, restricting the large-scale manufacture of bricks to districts around ports or towns near navigable rivers.

The early brickmakers had to use shallow, easily obtainable deposits of clay wherever these were available, the first sources perhaps being the banks of large rivers where the clay was usually exposed on the surface. Such was the demand for bricks, and in some districts the difficulty of finding clay, that an Act of 1548 stated that brickmakers were to be left to do their work undisturbed – which was not popular as clay was often taken from common land, disturbing the grazing rights of ordinary yeomen. At this period the production of bricks was a short-lived affair, a kiln being normally worked for a few seasons until the clay ran out, or constructed on site to produce bricks for a single large house, often from the clay dug out of the moat, as at Hurstmonceux, before being closed down.

Such was the growth of brickmaking that by the eighteenth and early nineteenth centuries hundreds of towns and villages maintained small brickworks and there were also many itinerant brickmakers working for a short period in one place before moving on. A survey done by industrial archaeologists in 1970 located brickworks operating during the nineteenth and early twentieth centuries in a hundred towns and villages in Northamptonshire, and many of the larger places like Northampton, Wellingborough and Kettering had several works operating at the same time. This pattern is typical of many counties, but now a name on a map alone may indicate that the site was used for brickmaking; such names as Brick Close, Snaith, and Brick Garth, Rawcliffe, both in the West Riding of Yorkshire; Brickhill Butts at Southwell, Brickkiln field at Bishop's Stortford, Brickkiln Hoppet, Magdalen Laver in Essex, and, in Hampton Lucy, Warwickshire, The Brickle meaning "land on which bricks were made".

The word brick is derived from the French *brique* used as early as 1264, but it was not in general use in this country until well after the Middle Ages, while a 1548 Act of Parliament, during the reign of Elizabeth I, concerns "the art or occupation of a brick maker, bricklayer and tiler", the term bricklayer being first used in 1530 during the building of Hampton Court Palace. The Tylers' and Brickmakers' Company was founded in 1557, during the reign of Elizabeth I and was followed by a Charter of Incorporation in 1571.

Until the invention of brickmaking machinery in the nineteenth century all bricks were hand-made, varying, however slightly, in size, colour and texture from one area to another and even from one clay deposit to another a few fields away. Apart from the type of fuel, the methods used hardly changed for many centuries, the process being a seasonal one, as before being fired the hand-moulded bricks had to be dried in the open air, possible only during the summer. This was realized as early as 1477 in the reign of Edward IV when a statute for tile-making, similar in almost every respect to brickmaking, laid down standards for their manufacture.

The clay was dug during the winter (according to the 1477 statute this had to be done before 1st November) and the heaps turned over from time to time so that the frost broke up the clay, making it more workable. The statute also stated that this had to be done by 1st February, and during the following months the clay had to be wrought to remove all stones and other impurities. After this the clay was mixed with sufficient water to form a malleable dough-like substance and left for at least two months to cure the material, the piles being protected from the rain by temporary roofs placed over them. Enough material had to be produced during the winter months to allow a continuous supply of bricks for firing during the summer, and yet not allow the clay to dry out by being left too long before being moulded. This process was necessary, as if the clay was not broken up into fine grains, or pulverized correctly the finished bricks would break up when eventually used for building. The bricks were individually moulded by throwing a "clot" of clay into a mould with sufficient force to fill it. Originally the mould consisted of a wooden box without a top which was placed on a flat surface, such as a bench, during the moulding process. Later the base of the mould was made separate, being known as the stock, which enabled the moulded brick to be removed more easily than with the first box-like moulds. To prevent the clay adhering, the mould was either dipped in water before use or sand was dusted over the surfaces, these two processes being termed respectively "slop-moulding" and "sand-moulding". The excess clay was cut off the top of the mould using a piece of wood, called the "strike", or with some wire attached to two handles, producing a smooth surface to the brick. In sand-moulding the bricks were stacked, for up to a month, to allow them to dry, this being done either in sheds or in the open air, with straw to protect them from the weather. These bricks were usually stacked on edge in a herring-bone pattern and the sheds were commonly known as "hacks" or "hacksteads", i.e. a raised place. Slop- or sand-moulded bricks were dried individually for a few days to prevent distortion when stacked before firing. During the fifteenth century slop-moulding declined in popularity although used in some rural areas up to the last century. Sand-moulding was the method generally used, as the sand left on the surface of the brick formed a rough glaze when fired and this finish is still in common use, though with machine-made bricks.

Another method of making bricks, known as "place bricks", was in use about the same time and was done by rolling out the clay on a layer of straw and cutting out the bricks by hand rather than moulding them. These bricks were, as a result, irregular in size and shape, making bonding uneven while the straw was burnt away during the firing leaving the marks showing on the surfaces. The Cow Tower, erected in the fourteenth century as part of the city defences of Norwich, and several East Anglian churches, have place bricks in their walls, but no examples are known of such bricks being used in small domestic buildings of that period or later, although this type of brick was made until well into the eighteenth century.

Apart from the few towns which had permanent brickworks most bricks were made on the building site or as near as possible to it to avoid transporting the finished product. Almost every district in Lowland England had clay earth suitable for making bricks, produced by itinerant brickmakers or by farm workers during periods when their occupation made this possible and using small pockets of local clay until this was exhausted. The bricks were burnt in temporary clamps, or heaps, used for firing only, and because of the difficulties in firing, bricks of varying quality and colour were produced. There were many irregularly shaped, or wasted, bricks due to underfiring or overfiring, a problem largely avoided in later years by the use of permanent kilns. The method of erecting the clamp varied from one brickmaker to another and in Tudor times these were generally round and of earth; a clamp was used as a measure of the number of bricks in the Exchequer Records of Henry VIII's reign.

The most commonly used type was just stacks of unburnt bricks, the outside covered with clay applied as mud and left to dry, forming a hard skin, similar clamps being in use during the Roman period. Inside the clamp, between the bricks, were layers of small trees and brushwood, the commonest fuel, which was fired from outside, burning according to the direction of the wind. Making such bricks was a hard slow process but the numbers produced in this way should not be underestimated and records show that in 1561 at Loseley such a clamp contained no less than 120,000 bricks, but this had to be fired twice, first with a hundred tons of fuel, followed by an extra sixty tons as the bricks had not been well fired.

One of the earliest descriptions of brickmaking is in a letter written in 1683 by J. Houghton to the Sheriff of Bristol and quoted in Nathaniel Lloyd's *History of English Brickwork* first published in 1925. After explaining how bricks were made he states that a moulder, or brickmaker, helped by a temperer, who prepared the clay, and a boy who carried the bricks, could make 2,000 bricks in a summer's day of about fourteen or fifteen hours. Without assistance the output would be about a thousand, the rate of pay being 4s. per hundred bricks.

Houghton then describes the kiln used:

When we begin a new brick ground, for want of burnt bricks we are first to build a kiln with raw bricks, which the heat of the fire by degrees burns, and this will last three or four years; but afterwards we make it with burnt bricks and we choose for it a dry ground or make it so by making dreyns round it. This kiln we build two bricks and a half thick, sixteen bricks long from inside to inside and about fourteen or fifteen feet high; at the bottom we make two arches three foot high. . . .

Small fires were lighted in each arch and gradually increased until the bricks became red hot throughout the kiln, firing taking about three days. The bricks sold for about 14s a thousand, the price for making and burning was 7s. a thousand and the wood used as fuel cost 3s. for every thousand bricks.

By the middle of the seventeenth century, as the population increased, there was an increasing demand for bricks for building so that methods of production gradually became more efficient, especially when the use of coal as fuel became widespread. As production increased, less reliance had to be placed on small, local, clay deposits, and temporary clamps for burning, so that deeper and more plentiful deposits of clay were used as long as the pits could be excavated by hand. As a result many hundreds of small brickworks became established on more or less permanent sites, allowing the use of purpose-built kilns.

The type used hardly varied from its first introduction until the middle of the nineteenth century, and in the smaller brickworks, until well into the present century. The kiln known as the Scotch, or updraught type, was in its simplest form two parallel walls between 6 and 12 feet apart and between 20 and 30 feet long, the height being normally 10 feet. In later kilns these walls tapered from several feet thick at the base to about one at the top to allow arched fire openings to be built at the bottom. The space between the walls was filled with bricks to be burned between twenty and thirty thousand being packed in such a way that the hot gases could spread up between them. The kiln was closed by building up the end-walls, or "wickets", with broken or defective bricks plastered over with brick dust and wet clay. The top was also covered with a layer of broken, or underburnt, bricks, from previous firings. Along the base of the outside walls were a series of arched fire holes where the coal for firing the bricks was burnt.

These kilns would be fired very slowly for three days, to dry out gradually the charge of bricks, after which the full heat would be put on to burn the bricks thoroughly before blocking the fire holes and allowing the kiln to cool down. Although costing very little to build, these kilns were rather inefficient as the temperature distribution was extremely poor, a lot of heat being wasted in warming up the kiln and afterwards having to let it and the contents cool down before removing the burnt bricks. In this process considerable heat was lost through the poorly constructed roof resulting in large numbers of badly burnt bricks varying greatly in colour and size. To cut down heat losses later kilns had permanent roofs of brick arches but the faults were not really eradicated until the down-draught kiln was developed in the middle of the nineteenth century. In this kiln the hot gases passed downwards through the bricks being burnt instead of upwards, although the construction of both types was very similar. The real difference was the screen walls which were placed inside the kiln, around the fire holes, and these deflected the heat upwards to the arched roof. The hot gases were then turned downwards through the bricks being burnt, the cool gases passing out of the kiln, through a chequerwork floor of fire bricks, into horizontal flues leading to a chimney. The screen walls were also perforated to allow some of the gases to pass directly from the fire holes into the lower part of the kiln, giving a more even temperature distribution throughout the kiln, which usually held from thirty to forty thousand bricks at one time. A later, and more successful type of down-draught kiln was circular with a shallow, domed roof of brick arches with the fire holes set radially round the circumference. Although more expensive this kiln created a good even temperature throughout the charge reducing both the numbers of badly burnt bricks, and operating losses.

These kilns were the only types in use until the introduction of the Hoffman continuous kiln in 1859, together with efficient brickmaking machinery made the large-scale manufacture of bricks possible and gradually replaced the older hand-made bricks; a development considered in more detail in another chapter.

The raw material for all bricks is clay, which geologically speaking is broken-down rock, and it is the varying composition of this which results in the differences found in the finished products; great variations in colour can occur in bricks made in one district due to slight changes in the chemical composition of local clay deposits. As with rocks, clays are found at varying depths but only the shallow superficial clays were used for medieval bricks and at this period no bricks were made from the deep-lying, and older, carboniferous shales, the Keuper marls and Jurassic clays which are used for nearly all modern bricks. This partly accounts for the differences in appearance between medieval bricks and those made after the middle of the last century though this is not so obvious in East Anglia, a region where up to modern times the superficial clays were still being used, as this was the only available source. This is what gives the bricks of eastern England their own distinctive appearance unlike any found elsewhere.

Pure clay is almost white, but this is rarely found, and most clays are grey, brown, reddish, and less frequently dark blue, consisting of varying proportions of oxides of iron and aluminium as well as compounds formed by these metals with silica. It is these chemical and other impurities in the clay, together with the conditions of firing, which create differences in appearance and if there is vegetable matter in the clay then the inside of the bricks will be dark and underburnt as was often the case with early bricks.

Due to the iron oxide most clays turn red on firing and if air supplying the necessary oxygen is present, this change takes place at about 900°C, the lower the temperature the lighter the bricks. Above this temperature the bricks normally become a dark red or brown and sometimes even purple, the colour depending on the position in the kiln so that the bricks were never evenly coloured throughout. On the other hand restricting the supply of air entering the kiln produced purple or dark-blue bricks, the density of the colour depending on the clay being used; the dark-blue bricks typical of the Victorian period were obtained from Staffordshire clays. Since it was impossible to produce high temperatures the bricks from medieval clamps are rarely dark red, except by accident, but are a light red, or "salmon" colour typical of the lower temperatures, while pale pink underfired material of poor durability was not uncommon and in some cases even used in the walls of early medieval brick buildings.

Although most parishes could provide clays suitable for brickmaking it was impossible to use all clays successfully because of such impurities as water-soluble salts, which caused white staining to form on the finished bricks. It was soon found that some brick earths could be used direct from the pits and eventually the larger brickworks tended to develop in these areas. These clays had the right plasticity for the material to hold its shape, and although the earliest brickmakers would perhaps not have known the reason, the best bricks were those made from a mixture of clay and sand, or clay and chalk, known in some areas as "malm", which by 1850 had become a term to describe the best building bricks, pale yellow in colour. In most cases it was found necessary to add something to the clay to help the bricks keep their shape and avoid undue shrinkage when they were being fired. From an early period the potters realized the value of adding sand to the clay and this was soon copied by the brickmakers who added materials ranging from sand in the medieval period, to ashes from burnt household waste in the Victorian era.

Being dug from different geological strata the clay produced bricks which reveal the chemical composition of the original material so that early hand-moulded bricks varied in colour and had slightly irregular shapes which are easily recognizable, unlike the precise, evenly coloured, machine-made bricks commonly used from the middle of the last century. The colours were so different that hand-made bricks varied from district to district, and whereas before the Industrial Revolution red bricks were generally used in most areas, other colours were also widely used where suitable clay was available. Because of the high cost of transport, whether by water or road, bricks were rarely carted more than a few miles from where they were made and thus no bricks were used over a wide area of the country; the real changes in patterns of distribution started with the development of canals, later followed by the railways. So unless the external walls have been rendered it is possible to recognize the older small buildings in a particular district because these are built of bricks made of clay found in the immediate locality.

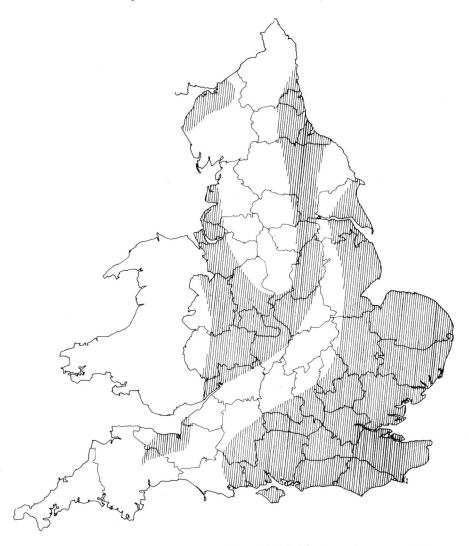

Fig. 16 Main districts where traditional brick houses and cottages still predominate

Before the eighteenth century, brick was only used for the larger houses, except for the building of chimneys, and only in East Anglia where no stone was available was brick used for small houses, but by the

Georgian period it was being used country-wide in this way. Many of the small houses still lining most village streets date from this period, and particularly in districts where stone was easy to find, the rubble was picked up from the ground and used without any further labour or cutting. On the other hand the making of bricks required a skill not easily acquired in the earlier periods by poorer yeomen, besides incurring the expenditure of a large amount of money before any bricks were ready for use. The earlier bricks, therefore, being expensive were originally used for ornamental dressings, or to bond together the rubble walls of stone buildings. In East Anglia bricks were almost always used to bond together walls formed of flint or to form decorative panels on such buildings. To make the bricks show up from the flints or stonework they had to be as bright a red as possible, not always possible in areas where the natural clay contained a large amount of lime. In these districts, from at least the sixteenth century, and probably long before, brickmakers found it was possible to brighten the colour by adding red ochre to the clay and in 1504 a mixture of ochre, the "offalles" from glovers' leather and ale was used for this purpose during the building of the manor-house at Collyweston.

Before the eighteenth century, lighter coloured red bricks were made of clays containing a high percentage of lime although after this period it was found possible to add lime or salt to other clays to produce similar bricks which were then very fashionable. Until this was done the only clays suitable for making light bricks were the Jurassic clays of east and south-eastern England, which were near enough to the surface and easily accessible. From these clays cream, or "white", bricks were made in East Anglia, throughout the counties of Cambridge, Essex, Bedford and Huntingdon and also in parts of Kent. The colour was produced by using clays containing a high proportion of chalk and these became known as "gaults", a name possibly akin to the old Huntingdon word for digging, "gaulting", but it is uncertain where the term originated.

Actually these light bricks are rarely white but more usually pale yellow or buff. The gault clays found in Cambridgeshire, and some parts of Kent, produced very pale bricks while the pale pink or yellow types from some parts of Essex contained more lime than was usually found elsewhere. Other gault bricks, made from clay containing phosphates, were coloured blue, mauve, grey or black and these were widely used for diaper decoration in early brickwork.

Other types were the yellow bricks of the Thames Estuary, the reds of the Midlands, particularly common in Warwickshire, and the purple bricks of east Dorset. Silver-grey bricks were traditional in south Oxfordshire spreading further south throughout Hampshire and Sussex. Similar grey bricks became so desirable during the Georgian period that red bricks were given a thin facing of grey by adding salt to the coating of sand used for moulding before the bricks were fired. Later types, common during the nineteenth century, were the white bricks of the Severn Valley, made of white clay containing much silica but almost no iron, and the very hard dark-blue bricks developed for use by the railway engineers of the Victorian period, and made from the clays found in the coalfields of south Staffordshire and other coal-mining areas such as County Durham.

Among the best-known local bricks were the yellow-brown stocks marked with patches of black or dark blue where not burnt properly, used in all the new domestic building developments in the eighteenth and nineteenth centuries, no matter for what type of occupier. These bricks were originally well made, moulded on a stock, and in the Georgian period the name meant the method of moulding rather than the type or colour; the word now refers to the yellow-brown bricks produced from clays on both sides of the Thames Estuary and known as London Stocks. Stocks could be any colour, the name distinguishing them from "place" bricks, which were cheap underburnt red bricks never used for facing brickwork in the Georgian period, or afterwards.

Although colours differed considerably, sizes, apart from the "Great Brick", rarely used after 1300 (except in East Anglia), remained almost the same from the reign of Elizabeth I to the present day. Variations in size rarely exceeded a few inches and evidence indicates that there was a tendency to use one size of brick in a particular building rather than a common size throughout the whole country, although similar-sized bricks might be used for building in the same district or work for the same owner. There were exceptions and when John Morton, Archbishop of Canterbury, built Lambeth Palace in the 1480s the bricks used measured $10 \times 5 \times 2\frac{1}{2}$ inches but at the same time he also built a palace at Croydon where he used bricks sized $9\frac{1}{4} \times 4\frac{3}{4} \times 1\frac{3}{4}$ inches, the two buildings less than ten miles apart.

During the thirteenth century and fourteenth century the sizes of imported Flemish bricks, which were later copied by English brickmakers, were between 8 and $9\frac{3}{4}$ inches long, $3\frac{3}{4}$ to $4\frac{3}{4}$ inches wide and $1\frac{1}{2}$ to $2\frac{1}{2}$ inches thick, but even then several sizes were in common use, some as large as $12 \times 6 \times 1\frac{3}{4}$ inches. That no sizes were really standard is evident from the fact that in the part of Hampton Court Palace built by Cardinal Wolsey, between 1514 and 1529, the bricks made on the site were $9\frac{1}{4} \times 4 \times 2$ inches. A few years later, between 1529 and 1539, King Henry VIII completed the Tudor part of the building with bricks sized $10 \times 4 \times 2\frac{1}{2}$ inches, some made on the site and others some distance away.

In all cases the width of the brick is governed by the size of the human hand; the measurement which has changed least is the half-girth plus the thickness, as these are the important dimensions when it comes to picking up a brick. As all bricks have to be picked up and laid in course by a bricklayer any large and inconvenient sizes must have had a very limited use, though in the sixteenth century "Great Bricks" were still in use in East Anglia, sometimes in the same buildings as the usual 9-inch long brick.

Any variations in particular sizes of bricks probably resulted from undue shrinkage during burning and some of the medieval boroughs attempted to regulate local brick sizes, an example of this being recorded in the 1425 Quarter Sessions Records at Colchester where it was ruled that a model "fourme" should be kept at the Moot Hall for brickmakers to copy when working in that locality. Not long afterwards, in 1477, Edward IV attempted, with little success, to standardize the sizes of bricks at $8\frac{1}{2} \times 4 \times 4$ inches, but because of local variations building contracts of the period usually specified the size of the bricks to be used; for example an agreement, dated 1505, for the building of Little Saxham Hall, in Suffolk, gave the brick sizes as $10 \times 5 \times 2$ inches.

Many sizes were used until in the Elizabethan period a rough standardization took place when, in 1571, the standard brick was fixed at $9 \times 4\frac{1}{2} \times 2$ inches, slightly smaller than the early Tudor bricks generally used. This size was known as the Standard or Statute Brick to distinguish it from the "Great Brick". The 1571 standard fixed the size until the Brick Tax of 1794 encouraged the use of a slightly larger brick as this new tax was based on the number of bricks rather than the dimensions. The tax was abolished in the mid-nineteenth century when the introduction of mechanical brickmaking standardized the brick at $9 \times 4\frac{1}{2} \times 3$ inches or $2\frac{7}{8}$ inches. It is these bricks which are used in most small country cottages or houses, and as such buildings are rarely earlier than the eighteenth century it is unlikely that they would contain large medieval bricks, these being found in the larger houses, defence works or church buildings of eastern England.

During the early medieval period it was impossible, due to the inadequacies of the clamps or temporary kilns, to produce consistently standard-sized bricks as these were often distorted by being fired at uneven temperatures. This makes early brickwork invariably haphazard and uneven, the bricks originally being used to tie together and strengthen stone rubble walls or to build rough brickwork for defensive and other structures, but never at this period for small domestic buildings. The mortar joints were necessarily very wide to help correct some of the irregularities in the sizes of the bricks used in these old walls which contained a lot of straight vertical joints, tending to weaken the structure.

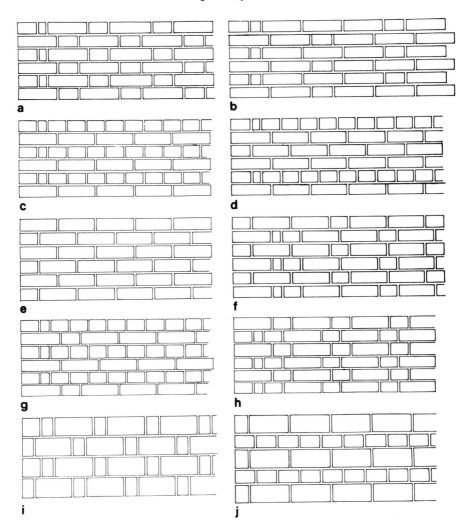

Fig. 17 Brick bonding types, representative of the many bonds found in all sizes and types of houses; a. Flemish bond; b. Flemish Garden Wall bond; c. English bond; d. English Garden Wall bond; e. stretcher bond; f. monk, York or flying bond; g. English Cross bond, with each alternate course of stretchers being moved over to give a stepped effect to the brickwork; h. Dutch bond, a variation of Flemish bond; i. rat-trap; j. Dearne's bond, with alternate rows of bricks being used on edge. Bricks on edge give a 4½-inch course rather than the traditional 2½-/to 3-inch and thus more walling can be built with less bricks, but the strength is much reduced.

Once kilns working at even temperatures were developed it was possible to make regular-sized undistorted bricks, the length normally being twice the width. Such bricks could be laid in straight, level courses with an even thickness of mortar between, forming the joints. From quite an early date it became possible to avoid straight vertical joints in brick walls by developing a bond which entailed moving the bricks slightly in each course so that joints did not occur one over the other. The first recognizable bond, still being used today in many buildings, was formed by laying alternate courses of stretchers (the long sides of the bricks showing) and headers (the ends showing). This became known as the English bond although it is not known when such a bond was first used. One of the earliest examples of a complete building using this type was Tattershall Castle, in Lincolnshire, erected about 1450. (*See* Figure 17 for details of this and other types of brick bonds mentioned below).

9

More About Bricks,
Tiles and Chimneys

Before the seventeenth century many walls, especially in smaller buildings, had no definite bonding, particularly where the brickwork was to
be concealed by stone facings or rendering. English bond was regularly
used during the pre-Elizabethan period and by the mid-sixteenth
century it was being used for all large brick buildings. It was employed
until the seventeenth and eighteenth centuries when it was replaced by
more fashionable Flemish bond, typical of the buildings of the period; in
this case headers and stretchers were laid alternately in each course.
Although Flemish bond was commonly used in the reign of Queen
Anne, a few rare examples occurred as early as the sixteenth century; for
instance Woodham Walter Church in Essex, dating from 1563, contains
brickwork with this bonding. Flemish bond, though rarely used in Flanders from which it is named, was widely used elsewhere as it was cheaper
when special facing bricks were being used, because there is a greater
proportion of stretchers. It was used for the more important and fashionable buildings of the Stuart and Georgian periods, such as Kew Palace in
1631, especially as the walls of such seventeenth-century buildings were
thicker than those of today. There are instances of Flemish bond being
used for the important front elevations and English bond at the rear
where it would not be seen.

Flemish bond began to appear in small dwellings from the eighteenth
century onwards, in some areas almost displacing English bond, while
later bonds developed as variations of the two original types, the first
probably being English Garden Wall bond – three or five courses of stretchers to one of headers. Judging from the number of surviving examples
this was the most popular bond for the smaller buildings of northern and
central England.

The similarly named Flemish Garden Wall bond was three stretchers
followed by one header in each course; the headers are placed vertically
over each other alternately with the stretchers. This bond was used
throughout southern England and as a result is often known as Sussex
bond, but it rarely appeared in Georgian buildings as the number of stretchers in a row created problems when placing sash-windows symmetrically, considered an essential feature of such houses. Another bond,
largely used in the south-eastern counties, is a slight variation of English
bond known as English Cross bond; in this the second brick of the alter-

nate stretcher courses is a header.

The building of structures with header bond, showing only headers on the surfaces gives very strong walls; straight walls using this bond have three-quarter bricks to start alternate courses. Rare before the eighteenth century, it became commonly used then for small houses or cottages in south-eastern England, taking advantage of the large numbers of bricks with blue-grey headers produced by burning the clay in the wood-fired kilns of the district, when coal was scarce and expensive to transport. In many Sussex villages such houses have red bricks outlining the door and window openings contrasting with the blue-grey headers forming the main walls.

Perhaps the simplest bond, stretcher bond, is the only bond capable of being used for half-brick walls, 4½ inches thick, the thinnest wall possible when using a standard brick, and was commonly used for all the humbler dwellings from the eighteenth century onwards, when brick was used for the new buildings required to house the increasing population. Stretcher bond was used for replacing decaying wattle and daub in the panels of old timber-framed buildings and also in the panels of new houses of this type built during the seventeenth century. The modern wall, using two skins of stretcher-bond brickwork with a cavity between, now used for all present-day housing, only dates from late in the last century and its development is described elsewhere.

Bricks cannot be used without some kind of mortar to bed them in and originally mud was used for this purpose, but being so soft it crumbled away until it was realized that the mixture could be hardened by adding lime. This was first done by the Romans when mortar was, according to Vitruvius, made of two measures of sand to one of lime, but the secret was lost until its rediscovery in the medieval period, since when the proportions have varied only slightly. The soft mortar has often been washed out of the joints of any surviving medieval brickwork.

Joints were then half an inch to 1 inch wide, they became thinner in the seventeenth century when better bricks were available. The width of the joints affects a building's appearance. Joints were usually finished flush with the face of the brickwork. This applied up to the present period when recessed joints began to increase in popularity. Another popular joint was 'flush and rodded', a flush joint with a central groove giving a slight shadow line. The rod compressed the weak lime mortar making it more watertight. Mortar, cheaper than bricks in the medieval period, often formed as much as a quarter of the wall surface in contrast with one-sixth after the Restoration. The colour of the mortar depends on the sand used, which may be varied or have colouring matter added to make the joints match, or contrast, with the bricks being used. The lime mortar used in old brickwork can easily be recognized and may indicate the age of a wall, but this is not a reliable guide without other evidence as many buildings may require repointing every few decades. Portland cement which largely replaced the lime in mortar from the 1850s onwards, gives a hard grey-looking joint unlike the soft effect of the older pointing and this is now generally used for all building work.

Although in the thirteenth century brick had been used for the building of complete palaces and large mansions it was rarely used for small dwellings until the eighteenth century when its durability and ease of handling proved it suitable for building fire-proof chimneys. It was for these that brick was first used as part of smaller dwellings to help prevent the spread of fire damaging thatch-covered roofs. The larger buildings, whether castles, palaces, or timber-framed mansions, had chimneys from as early as the twelfth century; in the Norman castles these were built into the walls forming part of the actual structure, while by the middle of the following century some of the larger stone houses had cylindrical chimneys of stone with open tops or vents to let out the smoke. Many of these chimneys were also covered with pottery louvres, or finials, forming part of the roof covering, and these were often moulded into the shape of human figures; examples of medieval chimney-pots recovered from archaeological excavations can be seen in museums at Lewes, Salisbury and Winchester and in the City of London Museum. Of the thirty-six examples known, two dozen come from Sussex, a few from London and the rest are rarely found north of Oxford but are spread over southern England, indicating that the earliest chimney-pots were developed there from the twelfth or thirteenth century, tending during the later medieval period to resemble the shape of present-day pots.

These early clay chimney-pots, conical and tapering towards the top, mainly had straight sides; others were bellied out in the centre or were cylindrical. By present-day standards the pots were originally quite small, obviously made by potters in imitation of cooking pots, being 5 inches high and 4½ inches wide at the base tapering to half that size at the top. The more usual sizes were 10 to 15 inches high and 8 to 10 inches diameter at the base tapering to 4 to 5 inches at the top.

In East Anglia, due to the shortage of timber and stone, most mansions were built of brick and had chimneys of the same material as early as 1450. From the fifteenth century onwards the use of brick for chimneys became country-wide but smaller houses seldom had any type of stack before Tudor times. The smoke probably escaped through a hole in the roof or through a simple chimney of wicker or clay or one framed up out of timber beams filled in with wattle and daub; such features were hardly fire-proof but examples survived on many of the farmhouses of mid-Wales or isolated parts of Cumbria. In other areas of the country also wattle and clay stacks survived until well into the eighteenth century; even in 1719 people in Suffolk were being fined for their clay chimneys. The lack of simple fire-proof stacks on the yeomen's houses contrasted with the large chimneys of the Tudor mansions. These had elaborately decorated stacks of almost every shape, including octagons, hexagons, circles, squares and even spirals, all made of specially moulded or cut bricks. Other stacks were decorated with floral designs carved out of the brickwork or rubbed down to produce raised patterns. These large stacks, several feet high and often clustered together in groups, formed an important feature of the overall design of the house, whose character would be greatly altered if they were missing.

Original Tudor chimneys in their turn gave way to the simpler stacks of the Stuart houses and during the sixteenth and seventeenth centuries many brick chimneys were built projecting outside the external walls of the older timber-framed houses. It was also during this period that many such houses had extra floors inserted and during this process many massive brick chimneys were built in the centre of the original house, helping to support the new floors. These stacks often contained a large recessed fireplace, the ingle-nook, and it was from this period that these became widely used, continuing to be built even during this century. In all early chimneys the flues were very large and exceeded fourteen inches by nine inches, considered by J.W. Hiort in his *Practical Treatise on the Construction of Chimneys*, dated 1826, to be the minimum suitable for flues to be cleaned by boys, many Tudor flues being several times this size.

Since brickwork is more durable and fire-proof than stone it was also used for building chimneys on to the older stone buildings even in areas where stone was easily obtained. From the seventeenth century onwards, smaller dwellings always had simple plain chimneys, square or rectangular, often with stepped or buttressed sections where the stack reduced in size as the height increased. It was recognized from an early date that chimneys had to be taken well above the roof covering to avoid fire damage and in 1621 courts at Clare, in Suffolk, ruled that every chimney to be erected should be built of brick "above the roofe of the house fower feete and a halfe upon the paine for every such offence to be hereafter committed the summe of VL [£5]". The more imposing stacks often had a number of projecting string courses and a simple coping of stone or brick at the top; large clay or terracotta chimney-pots beloved of the Victorians were not generally used until the Industrial Revolution made coal more available for domestic use.

There is little modern literature about the historical development of chimneys; perhaps the only book covering the whole history was *Chimney Pots and Stacks* written by Valentine Fletcher in 1968, easily accessible to any who require a detailed study of the subject. The author relates that in England the word chimney originally meant a fireplace; no precise date can be given for its first use in the modern sense although it was used thus by both Chaucer and Shakespeare. The book also illustrates with diagrams and names several hundred types of clay chimney-pots widely used during the nineteenth and twentieth centuries, enabling the identification of windguards, bishops, hood tops, crown tops, fluted beehives, horned can, and many others.

By the seventeenth century it had been discovered that flues could be made smaller and grouped to form plain compact rectangular stacks so that from this time onwards the sizes of chimneys and fireplace openings resembled more closely those of today. Provided that flues were large and straight a good draught was created, keeping the fire going, but in order to conform to the new housing types of the Georgian period flues had to be reduced in size, becoming as small as 9 by 9 inches and often having numerous bends to allow stacks to be placed symmetrically at roof level. To lengthen the flues and create the necessary draught, chimney-pots became widely used during the eighteenth century and by the following one, several hundred types of pots were developed giving a distinctive look to Victorian rooflines. The largest of the pots were the "tall boys", often as high as 7 feet 6 inches, made in parts of Leicestershire and in Nuneaton in Warwickshire.

About the time of the appearance of the first brick chimney-stacks, bricks were also used to form low walls under the sill beams of timber-framed dwellings, aiding preservation by preventing the beams from being in constant contact with the wet ground. From this it was but a short step to erecting complete buildings in brick, and this was first used where stone was not available although later, because of its cheapness, brick was often preferred even in areas where stone was plentiful.

An essential difference between houses built of the two materials was that the walls of cob or stone houses were always much thicker than those of brick, stone walls being well over a foot thick and in the oldest structures perhaps 4 feet. The earliest medieval brick walls were often as thick as those of stone as the builders had not appreciated the strength of brick and the heavy loads it could stand before collapsing. Over the centuries increasing experience has led to a reduction in the thickness of brick walls, thus saving bricks which were originally expensive to make. Before the early seventeenth century, brick walls, even for single-storey buildings, were never less than one and a half bricks (14 inches) thick and gable walls, which supported the roof purlins, even thicker, but declining standards often reduced the thickness of walls to the detriment of their stability. It became necessary therefore under various Acts of Parliament, to draw up specific regulations governing the thickness of the brick walls to be used for houses particularly in the City of London, and these are discussed in a following chapter. But despite regulations, the walls were often likely to be only one brick, 9 inches thick, and on the upper floors this was often reduced to half a brick, 4½ inches in thickness. Half-brick walls were certainly used for the external walls of almost all small rural cottages to be occupied by the poorer workmen; this was done until the late nineteenth century, creating problems for the present generation wishing to save such dwellings as thin walls of this type are no longer permitted for habitable dwellings under the modern public health Acts.

During the eighteenth and nineteenth centuries many builders believed that brickwork was not stable without additional strengthening which they imagined was obtained by inserting bonding timbers into the brick walls. Until at least the Victorian period it was the practice where there were irregularities in the sub-soil under a building to place one or more lines of timber balks along the centre of the footings and build the brick walls up on them. Smaller bond timbers were also placed at various heights in the walls, these being isolated, at random intervals, and not joined up to each other as in a timber-framed building. These timbers, concealed under the internal plasterwork, decayed after many years, leaving holes and often weakening the walls to the point of collapse. Brick chimneys were also commonly built on timber foundations with bonding timbers inserted into the flue walls, later creating a fire hazard often unsuspected by the owner of the building.

As towns suffered the ravages of rapidly spreading fires among thatched buildings, other roof-coverings came into use including clay tiles which, as far as is known, were made some time before bricks became common. As with bricks, the Romans made the first roofing tiles which were about the same size as Roman bricks but much thinner; as was the case with bricks, the art of making tiles disappeared after the departure of the Romans. Tiles began to be made again during the twelfth century and were at first copies, in clay, of the wooden shingles then in general use. The William Fitzstephen Assize of 1189 was made to prevent the spread of fire in London and clay tiles were among the permissible roofing materials suggesting that by this date tiles were being produced in quantities at least in southern England. By the early fourteenth century tile-making was flourishing in the eastern and south-eastern counties and so the larger houses in these areas frequently had tiled roofs but there are few contemporary references to tiles being used similarly in the western parts of the country. There appears to have been neither tile-making nor brickmaking in these areas until several centuries later and during the Middle Ages almost the only known western tile-making centre was Bridgwater in Somerset, at that time a port

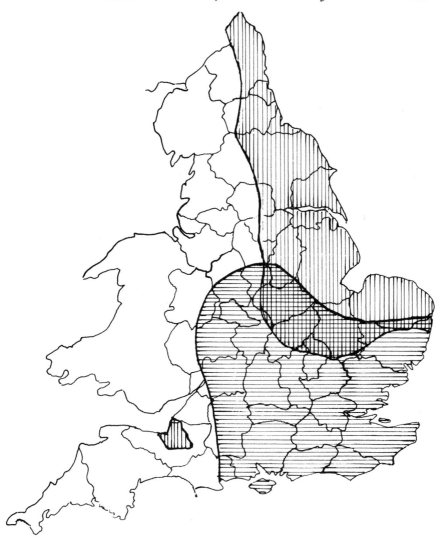

Fig. 18 Districts where pantiles and plain tiles were traditionally used. Pantiles were used in eastern England and the Bridgwater area in Somerset. (Based on Brunskill)

accessible from Flanders, where such tiles were in common use.

There is a distinct connection between brick and tile-making as tiles were usually made in the same places as bricks although finer clays were necessary for successful tile-making. Until special kilns were developed during the Industrial Revolution, tiles were burnt in the same kilns and at the same time as bricks. The tiles needing higher temperatures were put in the centre of the kiln surrounded by the bricks which required slightly lower temperatures for their manufacture.

Therefore the colours of roofing tiles vary as for bricks, the majority being shades of red but the gault clays of Cambridgeshire gave light-yellow or dun-coloured tiles typical of the area and still in evidence on many old buildings. Other places produced dark-brown or blue tiles and most of the colours match the colours of the local bricks at least up to the early years of the last century when the dark-coloured tiles made in Staffordshire and Shropshire, spread to almost every part of the country slowly replacing local types as the smaller tile works closed. Nowadays the principal areas for making roofing tiles are where the tradition was well established before the nineteenth century, for example parts of Staffordshire, Leicestershire, Berkshire, Barton-on-Humber, and Bridgwater in Somerset. This last town, where tiles have been made since the sixteenth century, was almost the only source of supply in the west of England at that time.

The statute of 1477 laid down the size of plain tiles as $10\frac{1}{2} \times 6\frac{1}{2} \times \frac{5}{8}$ inches and as late as 1722, during the reign of George I, the same sizes were reaffirmed by Act of Parliament, while today the standard size is $9\frac{1}{2} \times 5\frac{3}{4} \times \frac{1}{2}$ inches or still approximately 10×6 inches. The 1477 statute was, however, not very successful; because of the wood-fired kilns then in use it was difficult to avoid distorted tiles, similar problems arising when burning bricks, and local variations became inevitable. For example, tiles in Kent were commonly 9×6 inches, in Sussex $9 \times 6\frac{3}{4}$ inches and in Leicestershire as large as 11×7 inches. These early tiles were all of the plain type fixed like stone slabs, either by a peg pushed through a hole in the tile allowing it to be hung over the lath or tied with straw in the same way; the use of nails for the fixing, although common in the Roman period, was not generally adopted until with the early Industrial Revolution nails became easier to make. Later tiles had one or two nibs projecting from the top edge allowing the tile to be hung over the lath, a method of fixing still used. Nibs were not in general use until the seventeenth century, when better kilns enabled more regularly shaped tiles to be made, but some earlier examples are known to have been made in Lincolnshire; these, dating from the fourteenth century, are uncommon and not used on smaller buildings of that period.

Before Tudor times tiles were used infrequently in western counties, but the ease of fixing encouraged their use on a wider scale even where stone was the local building material. So stone houses often had tiled roofs long before brick became common for buildings in the same district, and long before tiles or bricks were made in the locality, as tiles – lighter than bricks – were easily transportable for considerable distances.

By using clay tiles instead of stone slabs roof timbers could be smaller, an important factor during the post-Reformation timber shortage. It was also possible to lay tiles at pitches as low as forty degrees and still have a watertight roof, and this had an influence on the design and internal layout of the smaller houses.

It was eventually found possible to keep a tiled roof watertight by double lapping the plain tiles, that is lapping each tile over part of each of the two tiles below it and staggering the tiles in each alternate row, like the bonding in a brick wall. This succeeded only when the development of better kilns led to increased production of regularly shaped tiles. On earlier roofs, when irregularly shaped, distorted tiles sometimes had to be used, the lapping was inefficient and the rain was kept out by bedding the tiles in moss, straw or mortar. Few old roofs now survive with the original tiles intact as the roof-covering often needs renewing and many older houses have had completely new roofs since they were first constructed, sometimes more than once in their lifetime.

Plain tiles only were commonly used in England until comparatively late in the seventeenth century when single-lap tiles began to appear, known as pantiles, which remained watertight even when only one tile overlapped the lower ones. This was achieved by various types of curved tiles and it was not until modern times that interlocking concrete tiles enabled flat single-lap tiles to be made watertight. The history of single-lap tiles is uncertain but pantiles were first imported into the east-coast ports from Flanders where they were in common use, and were used on buildings such as barns, rather than houses. It is known that crudely shaped pantiles were made in Norfolk for roofing farm buildings, being bedded in the same way as the earliest plain tiles; in some places in the Fen district such tiles were laid on bundles of reeds to keep out the weather.

The first home-produced pantiles were probably not made successfully until about 1700, although it is known that Charles II granted a patent for making pantiles in 1663. To satisfy seventeenth-century fashions, quantities were imported, gradually being replaced by the locally made tiles which, like tile-hanging, became generally associated with Georgian buildings. Some of the old pantiles still existing, mostly on farm buildings, are of Dutch origin being in places having trade connections with Holland. Pantiles are rarely found on the older buildings of south and east England where plain tiles were preferred.

At first, bricks were used in the same way as stone so that there was little difference in the appearance of the smaller houses over large areas of the country; frequently one material was substituted for the other depending on the locality. During Tudor times poorer people tended to imitate, on a smaller scale, the houses of the wealthy, particularly that of the lord of the manor who owned the land on which the new house was to stand, so fashion had some influence on the appearance of the many new small houses then appearing. These "Tudor-style" houses required the use of four centred arches over the door and windows, comparatively simple to carve in stone but more difficult to form in brick. It was eventually found possible to reproduce such features as moulded mullions and transomes, dripstones and arches over windows in brick roughly cut to shape by a brick axe and then rubbed smooth, but this was slow and expensive work. Many of the brick houses, therefore, had stone quoins at the corners as well as arches, jambs and mullions to the doors and windows in the same material, the lighter stone contrasting with the red brick walls, a decorative feature which continued well into the nineteenth century although the original window styles had altered beyond all recognition.

Later improvements in brickmaking along with the smallness of the units permitted the achievement of certain effects impossible in stone until efficient stone-cutting saws were introduced during the eighteenth century. Clay bricks could be moulded and burnt into special shapes which although too expensive for smaller buildings could be used for decorative purposes on more important buildings. Such features often survived in a much-changed form on the smaller houses of the following centuries as simple, projecting string courses, marking the floor levels, and oversailing bricks at the eaves; these were either of simply moulded bricks or corbelled dentil courses of alternately projecting and recessed header bricks.

Pantiles were imported into London and east-coast ports up to Scotland, these traditional roof coverings are now being replaced by modern concrete tiles. Before the nineteenth century pantiles were rarely found in the Midlands or the West Country, except in Bridgwater, where the skill developed through trading connections with Flanders. Such tiles were commonly used in London from the seventeenth century onwards until the advent of cheap Welsh slates.

Another type, the Roman or Spanish tile, was made in several places including Bridgwater from the reign of George I, later becoming widely used on the buildings of the Regency period. These tiles, usable at pitches of between thirty and thirty-five degrees, much lower than plain tiles, are of two types of tapering half-round tile, one concave and the other convex, which are laid alternately overlapping each other at the edges; courses not being staggered as are other tiles. Based on the original kind used by the Romans in many parts of Europe, they were traditionally produced in various shades of red and when first reintroduced an Act of Parliament regulated their size as $13\frac{1}{2} \times 9\frac{1}{4} \times \frac{3}{4}$ inches thick, but the modern size is slightly larger, 16 long $\times$ 14 inches wide. They became popular during the years after the Great War, and were made with bright-coloured glazed finishes on top of the clay, including the blue and green tiles still roofing many pre-war houses and bungalows.

During and after the Georgian period, tiles were used, apart from covering roofs, for covering walls, tile-hanging being most common in southern England, particularly in Kent and Sussex. Ordinary roof tiles, as well as slates, were used and this fashion became widespread.

Between the twelfth and sixteenth centuries the brickmakers, and often the potters, also produced large amounts of baked clay floor tiles, usually 6 inches square and of various shades of red with printed or inlaid patterns in contrasting coloured clays, the most common being yellow. Though such tiles were common in ecclesiastical buildings up to the sixteenth century, they were not used in domestic buildings where even in the better houses ground floors were of earth, a practice still followed in the case of the smaller nineteenth-century buildings. In areas providing suitable stone slabs these were often used not only for the ground floor, being laid directly on the earth, but also for the upper floor if large enough timber beams could be found to support the heavy weight, a practice lasting through the Georgian period even for sizeable town houses. Other types of materials were also used; the best-quality houses had boarded floors, which in the older houses were sometimes laid loose to allow their removal if the occupier moved house. The earliest floors were of oak or elm boards but as timber became increasingly difficult to obtain, softwood came into general use reserving the hardwoods for structural beams and joists. Until well into the last century such floorboards were laid with butt joints, as the modern tongued and grooved joints did not appear before that time.

Another commonly used material was plaster, mainly found in the Midlands, in buildings of all periods from the reign of Elizabeth I to the early years of Queen Victoria. The best material was gypsum, coming from the east Midlands, which was used as early as 1556 for floors in Hardwick Hall. Lime was also used, mixed with clay or crushed burnt bricks, laid on straw or reeds placed across the supporting floor joists, and allowed to harden into a layer usually 2 inches thick. So hard did these floors become that today the material is often mistaken for a crude type of concrete, but such constructions can be recognized by the reeds underneath or, if these have rotted away, the pattern will still show on the bottom of the hardened plaster; the same will apply if straw was used instead of reeds.

Among the most easily recognizable features of the earlier brick buildings, and unknown on stone buildings, are the patterned brickwork and elaborate gables either at the ends of buildings or over dormer windows. Both these features tended to lose popularity when the simple Georgian style began to pervade the country, but in somewhat debased forms these designs were revived by the Victorians and Edwardians.

Patterned brickwork was introduced from the Low Countries some time early in the fifteenth century, originally being simple diaper patterns using the overburnt darker headers to form the design, contrasting with the lighter red bricks of the walls. All-over patterns of this type were widely used during Henry VIII's reign and almost all the large brick mansions then being built in southern England have some of this pattern incorporated in the main elevations. The designs became increasingly complicated until such brickwork became unfashionable when classical and Italian designs were favoured for the new mansions of the Stuart period, Tudor buildings often being demolished to make way for them.

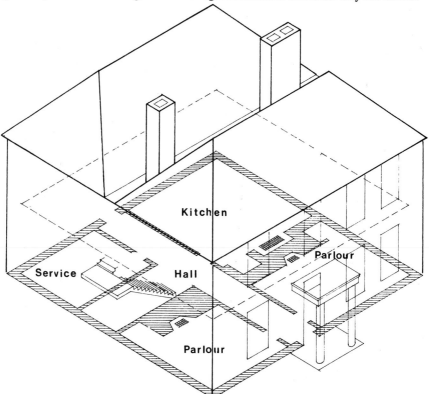

Fig. 19 A double pile house-plan typical of that introduced after the Restoration and which became so popular that it was in use throughout the nineteenth century

During the Georgian and Regency periods the commonest pattern was an all-over chequer, or diaper, pattern made possible by the general use of Flemish bond, the pattern usually being formed by blue or grey headers with red stretchers. Many examples of this type of brickwork can still be seen in south-eastern England, especially the Sussex villages bordering the Downs.

Originally the gable walls were taken just above the tiles to form low sloping walls, which usually involved cutting the bricks to provide a smooth base for the brick or stone coping. A particular feature of the brick houses of eastern England was the filling-in of the resulting triangles with tumbled brickwork where the bricks were laid at right angles to the slope of the roof to provide the base for the coping stones. This brickwork is a distinguishing feature of many houses from Kent to Lincolnshire built from the seventeenth to nineteenth centuries. Later the gable walls were raised well above the roof-covering to form crow-stepped gables, followed in turn by the Dutch gable formed by a series of curves, typical of the houses of the Jacobean period. Such gables still exist in many towns in the eastern counties where Flemish immigrants had settled, bringing the style from the Low Countries.

Similar gables were commonly used over the dormer windows first appearing in the Elizabethan period when the roof space provided additional living space. Unlike the houses of the Stuart period, when small separate dormer windows appeared as part of the roof, those in the earlier houses were formed by carrying up the wall to form gabled dormers, the upper floors often being only half in the roof space; such windows were often used both in the small stone houses of the limestone areas and in the eastern counties' brick houses.

So these simple brick and stone houses remained the standard pattern, with slight regional variations until, the whole appearance of all sizes, and types, of houses was drastically altered by the events following the Fire of London. This resulted in the appearance of the standard Georgian-style brick and stone houses throughout the country and it is probable that nearly a million of this type of house still remain in use.

10

Southern England

The next four chapters indicate how regional characteristics of the English countryside, and local materials, influence the design of houses and cottages. The landscape varies with the region, and from district to district within that region depending on the underlying geological features, supplying different local building materials which used to determine the type of dwelling found in each district. The words "used to" are intentional as this was the situation before the railway era for it was rail transport, far more extensive than canals, which speeded the country-wide distribution of mass-produced bricks and slates and led to the inevitable closure of hundreds of small local brickyards.

In most counties where brick clay was abundant a large number of such kilns produced distinct types of bricks and local archaeologists have discovered that during the last century there were at least one-hundred-and-forty sites in Northamptonshire where bricks had been made at some time. Nothing suggests that the situation is peculiar to Northamptonshire and where surveys have not already been done by local historians in other districts, locating such disused sites can be a useful guide to the age of the smaller dwellings built of the local brick. While the precise dating of such buildings may not be possible, a rough idea of their age may be gained if other features fail to provide a clue. The best place to look for likely sites could be old estate maps and early editions of the Ordnance Survey maps which give possible clues which can be followed up on the ground, although most abandoned clay pits are filled and returned to agricultural use.

The documentation of such brickworks is frequently non-existent since these clay pits often had a limited existence, only producing enough bricks for a small group of houses, and the only hint of their whereabouts may be in the field names of the locality; the "place-name" volumes of the county are an essential guide as well as older farm workers who may remember bricks being made in the locality. In contrast, stone quarries were worked for much longer, although now largely filled in, and documentary evidence is more plentiful, but as the stone was normally worked for local buildings over a very long period, precise dating of a house is more difficult.

The first of these chapters deals with the south of England, from Kent to Cornwall, covering a wide range of geological conditions and varying landscapes, largely man-made. This part of the country, especially in the

South-East, was the earliest inhabited part of England and contains a wide variety of old houses built in various materials with many of the earliest dwellings replaced by later houses on the same sites as the people in the region became more settled and prosperous.

Because this book deals with the development of the smaller house it has to omit the background history and development of a particular district which is at least as important as its buildings. In fact its building types often cannot be explained without a knowledge of local history much of which can be found in books about villages such as the Village Series published by Robert Hale Ltd.

The region covers the Weald of Kent, Sussex and Surrey and the farming landscape of south-eastern England, the once well-wooded chalk hills of the Downs, the remote uplands of Salisbury Plain with the low-lying valleys in between the Quantocks and Mendips, as well as the coastal plain of Hampshire. Finally there is the exceptional variety of the scenery of the West Country where the landscape ranges from the sub-tropical coastal strip to the flat moors of Dartmoor and Exmoor with their granite outcrops, some of the oldest rock formations in England. All these changes are reflected in the types of houses found throughout southern England, a diversity not found elsewhere in the country and which can only be fully appreciated by visiting the area to explore its many towns and villages.

The first dwellings in the region were of clay or chalk, what is now called "cob", and were originally used throughout the region although the surviving buildings of this long tradition are now grouped in one or two definite areas towards the south-west. These are represented by the clay and straw cottages of the New Forest, the chalk cob of Hampshire used for buildings on Salisbury Plain even until the 1920s, and the large number of such dwellings still remaining in Devon and Cornwall, although few of these are over two hundred years old. In spite of a long tradition this type of building is now rarely found as far east as Kent but this does not prove that such cottages never existed, since in this long-inhabited and prosperous part of the country small cob dwellings would long ago have been replaced by more permanent and fashionable houses of timber and brick.

The place to search for earth houses is Devon where the characteristic building material of the county is cob, itself a Devon word for a mixture of clay and straw used for building, which obviously indicates the widespread use of the material in that county. This is perhaps due to the remoteness of some areas particularly near or on Dartmoor. The cob used is a mixture of shillet, a local shaly clay, cow dung and straw used to form walls never less than 2 feet thick, and the houses have the rounded corners easy to form in such material. Earlier cottages were built directly onto the earth and later buildings almost always had a low stone plinth wall below the cob walls to keep the base dry. The colour of the cob varies according to the clay used; where chalk is present, in the north of the country, the walls are whiter than when the darker buff clay of the southern districts is used, and always colour-washed in varying light colours still typical of the south-western counties.

Most of the surviving cob houses and cottages in the West Country are of the eighteenth and early nineteenth centuries and there are typical examples in such villages are Dunsford, East Budleigh, Iddesleigh and Whimple; the largest cob building in Devon, and probably in the country, is the sixteenth-century manor-house at Hayes Barton. The ease and cheapness of making cob from local clays meant it served its purpose for a very long time and it is known to have been used to extend earlier houses. The almshouses in Cheriton Fitzpaine, first founded in 1594, have original lower walls of stone with cob forming the first floor above, as also have a group of fishermen's cottages at Bantham, near Kingsbridge, in Devon. Other villages with cob cottages are Broad Clyst, Broadhembury, a Saxon nucleated village on the slopes of Blackdown Top and the settlements of the South Hams district. Cob and thatched-roof cottages may be found in the villages of Otterton, Colaton Raleigh, Branscombe and Newton Poppleford, near Sidmouth.

Further west in Cornwall the clob, a local variation of the name, was usually made of two parts of clay used with small pieces of "shilf", or broken slate, the natural stone of the area, bound together with straw. In many small Cornish villages cob cottages, originally thatched, are often now covered with slates, and are usually one-and-a-half storeys high with roofs sloping down almost to ground level to cover outshuts, or extensions, at the rear. A typical feature in Cornwall and Devon, whether the cottages are cob or stone, is the round-ended oven which projects from the front wall of the older buildings and the large tapering chimney, a type not found elsewhere in this country. Thatched cottages, very few in number compared to Devon, may be seen at Coverack, Crantock, St. Mawes, and Veryan, the cottages mostly being of local stone rather than cob.

Invariably local people tend to use whatever material is available and so heather was substituted for straw in many of the cob cottages of Dorset. The walls had a whiter appearance as the local earth was frequently a chalky mud containing lime which had a hardening effect. In fact the more lime present in the clay, the harder the walls, particularly with the cob buildings of the Salisbury Plain area of the neighbouring county, where chalk and lime occur in large quantities in the Wiltshire clays.

Dorset villages are full of cob cottages, especially in the picturesque group of villages known as the Winterbornes – Abbas, Came, Clenston, Farringdon, Herringston, Houghton, Kingston, Monkton, Muston, St Martin, Steepleton, Tomson, Whitechurch and Zelston, all prefixed by the name Winterborne.

The biggest group of cob cottages in the county is at Milton Abbas, a village built by the first Earl of Dorchester between 1771 and 1790 to replace a medieval market town which stood near his house. The village street is lined by two rows of semi-detached thatched houses all one-and-a-half storeys high, with a room back and front on each floor, the houses keeping their original outside appearance except for an occasional bay window in place of the casement. The doll's-house-like dwellings extend in an unbroken line except for the church in the centre facing the alms-house, with single chestnut trees between each pair of houses, some still the original ones planted in the eighteenth century.

In the villages of south and west Somerset and the neighbouring counties of Wiltshire and Hampshire, the later cob houses are of chalk, mud and straw placed between shutters and allowed to dry out and harden, while in the New Forest area another form of construction was used, the rammed earth or *pisé*, uncommon elsewhere in this country.

In Devon, Dorset and Somerset, cob walls often concealed cruck frames, and some older cottages may be seen with the gable wall filled in with stone and brick above the cob wall. These gables were originally filled in with rendering on oak laths rather than cob, a flimsy infilling often replaced later by other materials.

East of Salisbury Plain, cob cottages, or even cob farm buildings, become rarer until in Kent this type of construction becomes an item of special interest rather than the local timber, the normal building material until replaced by brick from the eighteenth century onwards. But with cob went thatch, until in more recent times it was replaced by the local clay tiles or later still by grey Welsh slates, and where such changes have taken place the roof has often had to be altered to accommodate the new covering and the roof timbers lifted to alter the pitch. Where this has been done, probably during the last century or more recently, the change is sometimes revealed when a different material, such as brick, has been used to fill gaps in the original walls either at the eaves or along the gables.

The south-eastern corner of England, particularly the Weald of Kent and the surrounding chalk downlands were once covered by dense oak woods and this abundance of timber supplied many purposes besides building, and the cleared areas became agricultural land. From Saxon times the Weald was the centre of a thriving iron industry whose furnaces were fired with charcoal made nearby which continued until in the seventeenth century the supply of timber became practically exhausted, necessitating the search for coal, and later the use of coke. The only remaining industry was weaving, carried on by craftsmen from the Continent who settled in such towns as Cranbrook and Tenterden.

Thriving industries, and the plentiful timber, meant that the merchants, farmers and yeomen of the Weald were wealthy enough to replace earlier cob buildings with timber-framed houses and so Kent still contains some of the best medieval timber-framed buildings in the country. Cruck buildings were followed by timber-framed houses of all types, except perhaps the elaborate jettied houses typical of the Welsh border counties, and the timber houses still seen throughout Kent, Surrey and Sussex were the first to develop in this country, other districts slowly adopting the different styles of framing.

The first houses were close studded with the uprights barely their own width apart, while later houses had the framework placed on stone or brick plinth walls or, in exceptional cases, the whole ground floor built of one of these materials with timber only at the first-floor level. By the seventeenth century, widely spaced framing with brick infilling was in general use east of Salisbury Plain, beyond which most smaller houses were by then being built in stone.

Many medieval timber-framed houses were altered later to take a central chimney and the hall divided by the insertion of a floor, but as well as box-framed houses there is also in the South-East the only distinctly regional type of timber-framed house, the Wealden house, described in Chapter 6. Large numbers of this jettied house survive in the Weald areas of Kent, Surrey and Sussex, some dating from the fifteenth century but the majority are about two centuries later. A few unaltered examples still exist such as The Old Shop at Bignor in Sussex, built in the fifteenth century, but in many the addition of new brick walls across the front conceal the original façade.

Dwellings with exposed frames may be seen in Biddenden, Chiddingstone, Chilham, Cranbrook, Goudhurst and Tenterden as well as in the more rural areas where there are many good half-timbered farmhouses or such fine buildings as the early sixteenth-century Priest's House at Smallhythe. Very few are in anything like their original condition having undergone restoration or extension to provide extra living accommodation.

Surrey also has numerous timber-framed yeomen's houses, again much altered, the remnant of those demolished to make way for recent developments on the fringes of the ever-expanding urban area of London. In Sussex, slightly more removed from London, almost every small town and village has timber-framed houses except along the coast where the soil and the houses built on it were of poorer quality.

Fine examples may still be seen in Winchelsea, Rye, Crowhurst,

Petworth, Horsham, and tucked away among groups of farms in more rural areas; isolated examples also survive in the larger towns as in the High Street at East Grinstead which has a number of fine timber-framed buildings, the best of them, Clarendon House, dating from the late sixteenth century. In spite of alterations, enough of the first building usually remains to recall the original appearance of the house and the life-style of its occupants. Among a number of fine houses worth visiting in the Northiam area is the manor-house at Great Dixter, one of the largest timber-framed hall houses in southern England, fifteenth century but altered by Lutyens in 1910, and also Brickwall, a timber-framed house with a Jacobean brick north front, the new work being remarkable enough to warrant the name.

Further west, in Hampshire, for example, timber buildings become more elusive although survivors from the fifteenth century onwards remain in Chilcombe, Itchen Stoke, Tichborne and in Winchester itself. The Wiltshire villages of Horton, Wilsford and Bishops Cannings also have examples and so does Salisbury, and although the tradition was not well established in Somerset there are a few at Glastonbury.

While exposed framing is rarely used in the West Country, many older houses, especially in Hampshire and Dorset, have very fine timber roofs and trusses. A particular type of West Country roof truss commonly found in Dorset has a collar-beam supported on arched braces springing from the wall-plate and strengthened by elaborate longitudinal wind braces. Rare in Dorset is a row of jettied houses at Cerne Abbas, the village near the Cerne Giant, the prehistoric turf-cut hill figure, but this type becomes almost non-existent in Devon and Cornwall except perhaps for replicas dating from the end of the last century when timber-framing once again became fashionable.

In northern England timber buildings may be found in a state resembling their original condition but in the south the commonest alteration is obviously to the infilling of the panels. All the smaller houses built before the seventeenth century had panels of lath and plaster, as brick was often too costly, but now almost all this early infilling has been replaced by brickwork especially in the external walls; the sizes of the bricks used often indicate the date of the alteration, and the change could have taken place in Kent as early as the sixteenth century when brickmaking was going ahead. The infilling is often of very early brickwork laid as diagonal nogging but there are at present no proven cases of brick being used in this way before the seventeenth century.

The bricks, always of local origin, are brown, red and orange in the Weald while in the chalk areas of Hampshire and Wiltshire light-coloured bricks are laid alternately with layers of flints, a form of infilling usually of a later date than ordinary brickwork. The problem of finding suitable timber first became acute in Kent and Sussex and inferior woods were used so that it was essential to cover the external framework to hide the timbering and also protect it from the weather.

There were several other traditional methods, the earliest using wattle and daub, or at a later date plaster, and the whole framework and the infill panels were entirely covered, disguising the fact that the house was timber-framed. There was some pargetting also, less elaborate and rarer than similar work in East Anglia. Tiles were used no later than bricks, for wherever bricks were made so were tiles, and preceded them, being thinner, easier to produce, and requiring less burning in kilns.

The colour of the tiles is always similar to the bricks of the area giving some indication of when they were made, mass-produced, machine-made tiles appearing only in the last century. The earliest tiles, the plain $10\frac{1}{2} \times 6\frac{1}{2}$ inch type, were first made for roofing and later used as wall coverings, and have been made near Maidstone from the Roman period up to the present century so that tile-hanging has been long established in south-eastern England. Although timber-framed houses were the first to be covered in this way, most examples date from the late eighteenth century when the fashion first became widespread. At first tiles were fixed to laths attached to the outside of the timbering and later were pegged or nailed direct into the mortar joints of the brickwork itself, always being used to keep the weather from penetrating the thin timber or brick walls.

There are still many dwellings in the south-eastern counties with tile-hanging concealing the upper floor or, in some cases, the timber-framing of quite large houses, while the ground floor walls are covered with brick or weather-boarding; although houses completely covered with tiles may be seen, particularly when poor timber was being used. It should not be assumed that tiles were used at a later date only to cover up the timbers of an older house, in order to keep in fashion, for many houses had flimsy timber frames which were always meant to be covered up in one way or another. With minor variations the plain tiles were hung so that the lower 4 inches showed, forming straight courses running around the house; this method of fixing persisted until the nineteenth century when fish scale, including the recognizable half-circle or scallop type, the fish tail, the V, hammer head and other shapes were increasingly used.

Corners were a problem, requiring specially shaped tiles, or in the humbler houses timber battens were used to conceal the joints between the tiles at such points, while doors and windows were set flush with the surface of the tiled walls to avoid the awkward junctions created if windows were set back into reveals.

The oldest tile-hung houses are obviously in Kent, Surrey and Sussex.

Lewes displays very good examples of elaborately patterned tiling and also the use of black glazed tiles, but during the eighteenth and nineteenth centuries the fashion spread, especially during the Victorian period when large villas, featuring all kinds of ornamental tile-hanging, were built in such places as Bournemouth, and along the Thames Valley at Pangbourne, Maidenhead and Reading. In fact all the counties south of the Thames attracted such large villas, country retreats for the newly rich businessmen of London and other large cities, the building of the railways providing rapid communication with the capital city and giving rise to suburbia and the 'metro-land' of outer London. It is this elaborate nineteenth-century tile-hanging which is most commonly seen today, carried out in mass-produced red tiles in contrast to the smaller attractive cottages of the Weald, covered with the plain hand-made tiles slightly more irregular in shape and colour than the Victorian products.

There are a few buildings in southern England covered with the so-called "mathematical" tiles described in Chapter 14; such care being taken to make the tiles imitate brickwork that these houses often deceive even the experts. Whole buildings of quite frail timber-framing were covered with these tiles which closely resemble brick, allegedly first made to avoid paying the tax on bricks imposed in 1764, although they were in fact used as early as 1755 in Rye and elsewhere, well before the tax was introduced.

It is uncertain why these tiles were restricted to a limited area of southern England, but they were to be seen in the market-place at Marlborough as well as in Canterbury, Hythe, Rye and Tenterden, where the tiles are red, but yellow tiles occur at Belmont. Isolated examples are found as far apart as the Isle of Wight, Guildford, Croydon, Winchester, Salisbury and the Brighton district; Lewes probably has the greatest number in England but difficulty of identification suggests that other examples may be undiscovered. A particular type of black glazed mathematical facing tile was used in a few places around Brighton during the mid-Georgian period, but few houses now survive.

Slate-hanging, another type of covering, is restricted to a very small area of the West Country, and although possibly used earlier on some isolated large houses it did not become generally used until the Stuart period. It was intended to protect the house from the weather on exposed sites or for purely decorative purposes, and was often used to cover the outside and alter the appearance of earlier buildings. This was carried out at Dunster in Somerset on a fourteenth-century building known as The Nunnery, which is three storeys high, the ground floor of stone and the upper two timber-framed, the framing now hidden behind the later slate covering.

Slate-hanging did not become popular until the Georgian and

Regency periods when it was much used in the seaside towns of south Devon and Cornwall. The slates were hung on laths fixed to the walls, or fixed directly to the walls which could be of brick or local granite, and such houses still exist in Ashburton, Launceston, Liskeard, Padstow, and Topsham, mostly dating from the late eighteenth and early nineteenth centuries, the later examples using "fish scale" or tapered cut slates, or slates of contrasting colours, to form patterns or alternate courses.

Another traditional covering, weather-boarding, is mostly found on houses near the ports of Kent, those near the Medway and also the ancient ones on the south coastline, and the Sussex coast and parts of the Weald. The older weather-boarded houses in these areas are not so numerous as in East Anglia or around the Thames Estuary. The boards, especially on the later houses, were always softwood imported from Scandinavia into the east-coast ports from the early nineteenth century onwards, and this cheap and plentiful timber was liberally used in the vicinity. At first the boarding was used to cover older timber-framed houses either to hide the inferior timber then being used or because due to changes in fashion the earlier houses with exposed timber frames were considered to be out of date.

Sometimes the older houses were covered with local elm boards, but in all the earlier examples the boarding was left in its natural state or covered with black tar in contrast to the white paint popular in the nineteenth century, when in the early years brick houses were often covered with boarding, but it was also used on specially built houses having a light framework of softwood joists, later known as balloon framing. Such houses, finished with white paint, are a traditional feature of the Weald and coastal areas of Kent, most dating from the last century. Many other houses, with brick walls at ground-floor level with timber-framing and weather-boarding above to the first floor and gables, can be seen in Biddenden, Cranbrook, Smarden, Tenterden and elsewhere. These white, timber-clad houses were much favoured all over south-eastern England and some can even be found tucked away in undisturbed corners in the built-up area of London.

Before dealing with the brick and stone houses of the region the traditional roof-coverings should be considered. There were clearly defined districts where tiles, stone slabs or thatch predominated, patterns of distribution which remained unchanged for several centuries, until first disturbed in the last century by the introduction of Welsh slates and mass-produced red clay tiles, and later even more rudely disrupted by the advent of concrete tiles, first produced in 1900 but widely used from the 1930s onwards.

The earliest coverings were thatch but because of its limited life all the thatched roofs seen today are modern, although frequently replacing an earlier thatch and preserving a traditional design fixed when the house was first built a century or so ago.

Norfolk reed was the traditional covering of the buildings of East Anglia but was rarely used in southern England, although it is now appearing in districts where it was previously unknown. The original material in this region was long straw or, where available, heather, followed later by combed wheat straw, known as Dorset reed in that county, which is not reed but a specially cut wheat straw with the butt ends exposed as with true reed. In Hampshire some older houses were covered with marsh reed from the tidal coastal estuaries, and similar use was made of the reed from Romney Marsh in Kent, but land drainage made both these marshy areas suitable for cultivation so that such local reed is unobtainable.

Many houses were thatched throughout the southern counties, the largest number being in Devon, and villages worth visiting are Brendon, Dittisham, Honiton, Throwleigh and Widecombe where the thatched cottages are mostly of the local stone rather than cob, likewise the few villages in Cornwall which still have thatched buildings.

In Dorset, apart from the villages of the Piddle Valley, there are stone-built, thatch-covered cottages in Buckland Newton, Burton Bradstock and Charmouth as well as around Bridport. The Wylye Valley in Wiltshire has the two most famous villages of Castle Combe and Lacock, while in Somerset the villages of the Hams area as well as Crewkerne, Dunster, Pitney and Winsford have many thatched cottages and the tradition continued in the villages near Fordingbridge and along the River Test in Hampshire.

Eastwards in Surrey and Kent few of the older thatched buildings have survived but the situation is better in Sussex where many buildings have thatch on timber-framed or flint walls, and the famous Wealden house at Bignor is roofed with long straw.

Thatch had, and still has, a wide distribution but stone slabs are restricted to the districts around the quarries, many of which have ceased production and are being filled in. In the South-East the only major sources of roofing slabs were the sandstone quarries of the Weald areas, parts of Sussex, Kent and Surrey up to the slopes of the North Downs. Since almost all these quarries were in the Horsham district this name is now applied to these very heavy slabs which were originally on half-timbered houses with stout roof trusses whose rafters were sometimes as large as 6 × 5 inches in section. Horsham slabs become dark brown on exposure and were laid on steeply sloping roofs finished with gables rather than hips and often kept in place with mortar. Quarries near Tunbridge Wells supplied similar slabs and another source of stone, the Isle of Purbeck in Somerset, provided slabs traditionally used in the Dorchester and Sherborne areas until displaced by cheaper nineteenth-century mass-produced materials. Purbeck slabs were amongst the heaviest in the country and were originally used only on houses built of local stone, rather than cob, with massive roof trusses; these often give an indication of the original covering even if now replaced by lighter tile coverings. On exposed sites older roofs have often been waterproofed by covering them with a cement slurry which does not enhance their first appearance and in the fishing ports of Devon and Cornwall waterproofing with red lead or tar often conceals the original roof.

True slate has been used in Devon and Cornwall from the Middle Ages up to the present day and although quarried at a number of places most existing slate roofs were supplied by the vast quarry at Delabole, the main source of green slate, although five quarries still operate in Cornwall producing blue-brown slate, while the two quarries near Tavistock in Devon produce only blue-brown.

Whatever the source or colour, slate is used in all sizes up to 24 × 12 inches but smaller sizes light enough to be hung by oak pegs over roofing laths acquired the local name of "peggies". By the end of the nineteenth century few of the original quarries had survived, and Delabole now represents all that remains of an industry which once rivalled that of North Wales whose cheaper grey slate gradually displaced the local material. Now grey Welsh slates can be found throughout the southern counties and indeed all over England particularly on any house or cottage built after the seventeenth century as hipped or gable-ended roofs became commonplace.

Before cheaper transport brought about changes in the traditional distribution patterns in the last century the other main roofing material, plain clay tiles, was available only in areas where bricks were made, including a number of places in Kent, Surrey and Sussex, but the use of pantiles was rare. These were so unusual that when eighteenth-century buildings in Tunbridge Wells were erected using them they acquired the name The Pantiles by which they are still known.

In many old houses further north, tiled roofs always ended with gables but those in the Weald varied greatly. In Kent the tiled roofs, particularly on the Wealden houses, were fully hipped, and others had side or rear outshuts over which the roof came down to within a few feet of the ground. The few mansard roofs seen in parts of Kent are usually nineteenth century and untypical. The most frequently used type is the half hip, giving a part gable like the end of a traditionally thatched roof, which allowed a window to be inserted in the gable to light the roof spaces, the use of dormers being uncommon in this area. Other houses in the Canterbury and Thanet districts, and near the Medway ports, have curved gables of the Dutch type showing the influence of trade with the Low Countries, and also a wide range of tiles and bricks. The ports, and navigable rivers, enabled fuel to be carried to the brick kilns when timber became scarce, the first bricks being used to infill timber-framed buildings. Later houses were built entirely of local bricks whose varying colours give the region its special characteristics, the numbers of old brick buildings diminishing towards the east, approaching the stone-producing areas, until during the Georgian period the fashion for cheap brick made it preferable to stone.

Due to the suitable clays of the Weald the tradition of brick-making flourished from the medieval period until a short time ago in a considerable manner of small brickworks, most of which have now closed down. Kent, Sussex and Surrey have always supplied the greatest range of hand-made bricks in Southern England, one of the most typical, the red multi-coloured stock, having black burn marks where not properly fired, while flared headers, which are bricks with dark ends, were also much used.

There were brickworks at Dorking, Chaileys, Pluckley and Tonbridge, and during the last century thirty-five brick kilns in East Sussex. The one at Ashburnham was originally an estate brick kiln which operated from the fourteenth century until 1968, moving every hundred years or so to a new site, the last move being in 1840.

The older Tudor bricks usually exclusive to large houses in Kent are red, but later examples are yellow, brown or lighter reds while near the Medway can be found white, or very pale yellow gault bricks. Around Sittingbourne they tend to be yellowish brown and in north Kent, near Faversham, the reds predominate. The white bricks of Sussex contain lime, the black ones of Surrey manganese, while nearer the Thames Valley the yellow bricks contain chalk or traces of sulphur. During the eighteenth century the wood-fired kilns of Sussex produced many light-blue bricks which were widely used to make patterned brickwork along with the darker red bricks. In the eighteenth and nineteenth centuries the most widely used bricks in the south were London Stocks, distinctive yellow bricks marked with patches of black or dark blue where not burnt properly; these formed large areas of "Georgian" or "Victorian" London and other towns in south-east Kent.

Bridgwater in Somerset produced pantiles and was the other main source of red bricks very similar to those used in East Anglia. This town is full of seventeenth and eighteenth-century brick buildings with particularly fine examples along West Quay, one of the four quays in this river port.

Although bricks came into general use in the West Country later than in the Weald, brickworks were operating in parts of Dorset and Devon, and the presence of small nodules of manganese in the Devon clays resulted in speckled bricks.

As all the older buildings are in the South-East most brick buildings dating before 1450 are in Kent, Surrey and Sussex, but a rare exception, in Wiltshire, is the Manor House at Chilton Foliat mainly built in the reign of Elizabeth I although some earlier work exists. No early examples are known in Somerset, Devon or Cornwall, indicating the long-standing dependence on local stone, and as elsewhere in the country all the early brick buildings are large palaces, castles or ecclesiastical buildings so that few small farmhouses and cottages are pre-seventeenth century in date.

Apart from the timber-framed buildings of the South-East there is a regional similarity about the houses or cottages, being two-storeyed with sash-windows and hipped or gabled roofs with a variety of roof-coverings. The distinguishing factor in these seventeenth-century houses is not the style or design but the material used for the walls, either brick or stone, with the natural dividing line lying somewhere in Dorset, while cob is found west of Salisbury Plain.

In Dorset many small manor-houses are of both brick and stone and in the south-east of the county red brickwork with blue diaper patterning is common, and an unusual bond of one row of stretchers for each of headers, but most of this work is post-eighteenth century. Wiltshire brick was long used around Swindon but its increased use in this district undoubtedly dates from the time when Swindon became a railway town. The earliest brickwork in the chalk areas may be the brick dressings used in the flint houses.

Little building of any kind went on in Devon between the Restoration and the eighteenth century by which time brick had become the accepted material for small houses in spite of the great variety of local stone, and brick houses were common throughout the whole of southern England. There is no one distinctive regional type of brick building in the southern counties but the majority of the Georgian and Regency houses are in the larger cathedral or market towns and also the newly developing coastal resorts, with the "Dutch" style of the previous century in a few places in the West Country such as Great Torrington.

These Georgian houses follow a similar style but local stone was used where available, the supreme example being Bath with its terraces, crescents and squares of stone-built early Georgian houses. In the east, houses of this period are usually in brick although the Regency period preferred its brick houses covered with stucco in imitation of stone, as in the coastal resorts of Brighton, Sidmouth, Lynmouth, Torquay, Worthing and Weymouth among others.

Some developments were perhaps fortuitous since many towns of southern England suffered serious fires, for example Blandford in 1731 and Dorchester in 1713, 1725, and 1775, so that rebuilding in brick followed the lines of the London Rebuilding Acts described in Chapter 14, forcing changes on the inhabitants whose surviving timber-framed houses must have then looked rather old-fashioned. These developments, succeeded by the early nineteenth-century brick houses and later the Gothic-style houses demanded by the Victorians, can be seen on the outskirts of all the larger towns and coastal resorts, Bournemouth perhaps being the most extensively developed during this period. Brick was now so popular that brick houses were rising in the centres of cities like Salisbury where previously all building was in stone. The later buildings came in Cornwall where Truro is essentially a late Georgian town and Penzance is mainly nineteenth century.

In all the brick and stone towns of the area, especially Bristol, Dorchester, Marlborough, Salisbury and Winchester there are domestic buildings of all styles, sizes and periods, especially Georgian. Bath, the exception, remained a stone-built town up to this century, proclaiming that stone is the great natural building material of southern England and the great variations in type and colour influenced the design of houses built by the yeomen. Whether the stone is soft, and easy to cut, or hard and difficult to carve, determines the type of house to be found in the locality, as does the type of roofing material. Easily curving thatch results in low, one-and-a-half storeyed houses with rooms in the roofs, while tiles, and especially pantiles around Bridgwater, are hard to cut, so traditionally roofs end in gables. The houses of the area are a full two storeys high, with hips usually appearing only in the last century.

The building stones of the South-East are often covered by extensive deposits of chalk, but even in Kent, not normally a "stone" county, a few quarries have in the past provided the materials for houses in the district. Quarries near Bethersden supplied the sandstone of the Weald, sometimes incorrectly called "Bethersden marble", while other sources in Sussex were near Fittleworth and East Grinstead and in the vicinity of Horsham, a name often associated with this type of stone roofing. In older houses this honey-coloured stone was used in small roughly squared up pieces at the corners and around openings to form straight edges to the rough stone walls.

Slightly further east in the North Downs another sandstone, geologically different from the Wealden stone, occurred at Bargate, Gatton, Merstham and Reigate, acquiring the local name of Reigate stone.

Hard grey stone quarried in Surrey near Godalming, Huntmore and Northbrook was a type of Bargate stone also widely used in Kent where it was found in various places around Maidstone. This Kentish Ragstone, found chiefly at Borough Green, was used by the Romans in the city walls of London and for many medieval churches in the Weald area, before becoming popular for Victorian houses. It is hard to work and in a polygonal form was used in rubble walling, the irregularly shaped blocks needing wide mortar joints, a distinctive type of walling still to be seen in many small nineteenth-century houses throughout Kent and adjoining parts of Surrey and Sussex.

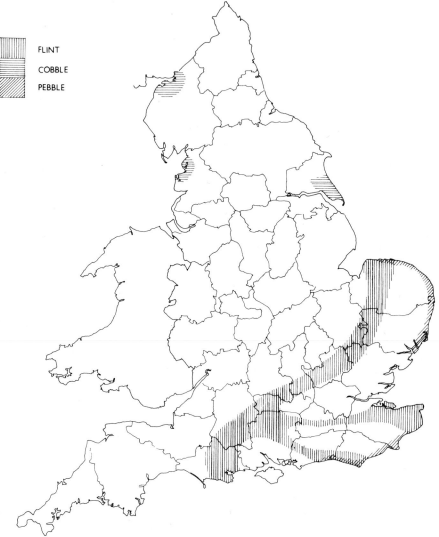

FLINT

COBBLE

PEBBLE

Fig. 20 Main districts where flint, cobble and pebble buildings still survive

Flint, found on the chalk uplands surrounding the Weald, was used

(*Above*) Clare, Suffolk. The
Ancient House, built in 1483,
and now covered with
elaborate pargetting of the
seventeenth century

Clare, Suffolk. Detail of the
pargetting on The Ancient
House

(*Above*) Cockley Cley, Norfolk. Seventeenth-century baffle entry house in flint with brick dressing and an old pantile roof

Burnham Market, Norfolk. Nineteenth-century house, similar to many found in the smaller villages, constructed of knapped flint and with brick dressings round the openings and at corners

Red Barns, a seventeenth-century Lancashire farmhouse, although typical of the uplands of north-west England

Newton Arlosh Church in Cumberland. A typical Vicar's Pele house, now forming part of a church

Houses on the north side of Long Lane, Smithfield, London. Built before the Great Fire and typical of the construction of the period. These survived long enough to be drawn by J. T. Smith in 1810 and described as "houses lately standing"

Neville's Court, City of London, destroyed 1940–1. Example of a house built in accordance with the requirements of the 1667 Building Act although the dormers are of a later date

1–7 Neards Street, London.
Houses built under the 1709
Building Act, with parapet
wall, stone cornice and
recessed windows

(*Below*) 46–49 Doughty
Street, London. Houses built
under the 1774 Building Act
with the sash-windows built
into reveals concealing most
of the surrounding frames

(*Above left*) Hampstead, London. A street of Georgian houses built in brick after the 1774 Act. (*Above right*) Abbey Street, Bath. A similar group of houses but built in the local Bath stone

North Brink, Wisbech, Cambridgeshire. A fine Georgian street with houses built in brick, much of it from the Low Countries, and with examples of such building erected in accordance with the requirements of the London Building Acts of 1709 and 1774; although at a slightly later period

8–9 North Brink, Wisbech. Detail of eighteenth-century shallow bay window, roundels in the glass are not original. Note the blank window over the door to maintain the symmetry of the front elevation for most of the houses, farms and workers' cottages built during the eighteenth and nineteenth centuries, contrasting with the older houses of the more prosperous Weald farmlands. Flints are always used with brick dressings, and provide most of the stone walls seen in the villages of the South Downs and to a lesser degree the North Downs, and this method of building extends across southern England to Salisbury Plain. Inland, flint of the chalk area is greyish in colour when the centre is exposed, but the flint from the south-coast beaches is yellowish and often used for small cottages, finished externally with a coating of tar. In slightly superior houses partly squared or knapped flints were used and although most of the flint cottages, and farm buildings, are nineteenth century the tradition is an old one, first employed by the Romans and later for the building of medieval churches throughout Sussex and East Anglia.

The chalk uplands of the southern counties cover most of Hampshire, skirting north of Salisbury, going west almost to Sherborne and north-wards across England to East Anglia. The eastern parts of Dorset and Wiltshire have many brick and flint houses, although flint may be com-bined with the local stone as well as with brick, used either in the form of square-chequer patterning or as alternative courses of flint and stone. All these buildings have dressings and quoins of brick or stone to straighten up the rough corners of the flintwork, and may be seen in the countryside north of Salisbury. In south Somerset a flint-like stone, chert nodules, is used for cottage walls particularly around Chard. These stones, slightly larger than flint, were picked up on the surface of the ground and used for building in exactly the same way as flint. Chalk itself, though obtainable, is not widely used for domestic buildings even today, being too soft for structural work, although some nineteenth-century farm buildings can be found constructed of 9-inch square blocks. A few of the poorer cot-tages in rural Wiltshire were built in the same way but always with a brick or stone plinth at the base and often rendered over externally.

The building stones of Hampshire and the eastern parts of Dorset and Wiltshire are not extensive and in the New Forest district the typical cottage was of cob, one-and-a-half storeys high, with a thatched roof coming close to the ground and rooms in the roof space lit by dormer windows. Further west the strata of the liassic limestones showing on the coast near Lyme Regis run northwards through the Cotswolds towards Yorkshire, providing along their whole length some of the country's best stones. Limestones are the most widely used of all building stones and stone from the Lyme Regis area was shipped to London as early as the twelfth century and used for work on the Tower of London. This limestone varied in colour from bluish-white to yellow and was used in cut pieces bedded in wide mortar joints to form shallow coursed walls, as many quarries only produced small pieces suitable for this type of walling.

The chief stones of Dorset included the softer brown limestones, the Portland stones and the so-called Purbeck marbles found in the Dorchester, Swanage and Corfe Castle districts. Portland stone, hard to cut, rather inaccessible and very expensive to produce, was not much used for the local houses, but was in demand during the seventeenth century when Wren used it for St Paul's and many of his other London churches and it was also specified for any public building to be erected on the Duke of Portland's London estate.

Locally the dark-grey Purbeck stone was much used for building but mainly for heavy roofing slabs, which were laid at low pitches, bedded in mortar and often covered with cement slurry. Simple roofs ended in gables to avoid the cutting necessary to form hips and if there were any dormer windows their roofs ran with the slope of the main roof rather than having independent pitched roofs.

For generations the best Wiltshire stone has come from near Chilmark, a greenish-grey stone easy to cut into smooth-faced blocks which are sometimes used locally with flint or brick to form chequer-patterned walls, typical of the older small houses. In the Vale of Pewsey the soft brown local stone is often found coloured green, hence its name "greensand", and being easy to work was used in many smaller houses from the seventeenth century onwards. Yellowish stone nodules like flint, but slightly larger, were formerly used for building in the Chard area but, unlike grey flint, are squared off and laid in regular courses with larger stones used as quoins or around openings.

Stone found on the Marlborough Downs takes the form of grey sandstone lumps, called locally Sarsens, which are found on the surface of the chalk, broken up to form small pieces and squared off before being used to form chequer-pattern or banded walls. These large blocks of stone were left lying on the surface after the rest of the soil had weathered away and as such were used in the Bronze Age to build parts of Stonehenge and Avebury, but in more recent times have been broken up for building purposes.

Much of Somerset is below sea level and though there are no massive rock formations the land rises to form the Mendips, Quantocks and the Bath Hills where the best stones are found. Bath, Doulting and Hamden Hill (or Ham Hill) limestones have been continuously quarried for many centuries, though the present-day quarries are not on exactly the same sites as in the past. The most famous stone comes from the Bath district, and was used for building the new spa town from 1728 to about 1769, with stone from Combe Down, Corsham and Box Hill. The Saxons used the latter stone to build the original church at Bradford-on-Avon as well as the famous medieval tithe barn and it was used for the weavers' houses in various streets in the town. The best stone, a dark cream colour, was lavishly used in Bath and elsewhere during the eighteenth and nineteenth centuries to build quite modest houses, and the newly invented stone-cutting saws enabled finely cut smooth ashlar to be produced cheaply enough to be used for the external walls of almost every house in the valleys nearby.

In parts of Somerset blue lias stone, often a pale grey colour, was found in thin layers and used in this way bedded in thick mortar joints. Mendip stone is greyish with red streaks, almost lavender in colour, and in contrast the quarries near Cheddar Gorge provide a pinkish stone, but near Malmesbury the stone is of poorer quality so the external rubble walls of many smaller houses are rendered over.

Other important quarries were near Shepton Mallet, Wells, Montacute and the Nadder Valley and although most of the smaller houses are not more than two centuries old, many medieval churches and manor-houses still survive. Towns like Wells, Frome and Shepton Mallet can boast fine stone buildings from the fifteenth century onwards, one recurrent feature being the two-storeyed bay windows popular in many parts of Somerset from the seventeenth century onwards.

Further west the hardness of the granites, or the grey stones of the Quantocks, made them difficult to work so that, unlike the pink sandstones of the valleys, they were not extensively used until better cutting methods were evolved in the last century. On Dartmoor and Bodmin Moor granite in large, naturally weathered, uncut blocks was picked up on the surface of the ground, and was first used in Cornwall during the fifteenth century but only for very important secular buildings and churches, of which a number still survive. Older and larger granite houses were of assorted sizes of roughly squared rubble, the later buildings were of squared granite, pale grey in the north and reddish brown in the south of the county, the walls often about 2 feet thick, the cavity being filled in with smaller stones.

Sandstone is also found south of a line from Tintagel to Torquay, and east of Exeter. It is pinkish red in colour, almost brighter than any other stone in the country; a lias stone full of shells, known as Beerstone, found near Sidmouth was not much used for smaller houses.

These varied stones all have their influence on the design of buildings serving a particular locality. In Somerset and Wiltshire the easily worked stone made it possible to build walls higher than with cob and the traditional house was of two storeys, the roof covered with stone slabs, thatch or tiles, ending in simple gables, and the chimney placed at one of the gable ends. Many chimneys may now be two-thirds of the way along the ridge due to extensions or the addition of a second floor to the low outbuildings at one end.

In Devon, houses and cottages of stone rubble or cob, originally with thatched roofs, still survive in Dunsford, Lustleigh and Cockington; brick and worked stone were used only for important houses, churches and defensive works, some stone manor-houses dating from as early as the fifteenth century. The uplands of Devon and Cornwall saw the early development of longhouses to shelter the farmer and his stock, and many remain but always altered to form a larger dwelling, the cattle being housed separately, continuing a trend which started in the late seventeenth century. Scanty, timber-made buildings of this material are rare in the south-western counties, and most of them are seventeenth century or later.

In Cornwall, early buildings in any material other than cob are rare except in the south-eastern corner of the county. Even the larger manor-houses were originally of cob, but after the sixteenth century were gradually replaced by stone and brick houses; afterwards only smaller houses were of cob or stone rubble, often rendered and colour-washed. As granite blocks were hard to work this was rarely done and the larger pieces were used at corners as quoins, forming some sort of straight edge to the walls with the smaller pieces being used in between to form the main walls. On Dartmoor, cottages and barns were commonly of dry stone picked up from the ground and laid without mortar or with mud, the walls being whitewashed to weatherproof the buildings and make them stand out in the wild moorland landscape. The nature of the granite demanded long, low single-storey buildings with additional living or storage space in the low pitched roofs and as ground-floor rooms were rarely over 6 feet high the roof came very near the ground, emphasizing the lowness of the buildings. Roofs were thatched or covered with stone slabs, and the chimney, sometimes an oven, projected from the front of the building at the side of the entrance, the stack broad-based, stepping inwards before reaching eaves level, a feature not seen elsewhere in southern England.

Very few old Cornish cottages are of agricultural origin, as most are miners' cottages, typical of the extreme western part of the county. They were built in rows, or singly, each two storeys high with one or two rooms on each floor, and date from the nineteenth century when two-thirds of the world's copper came from Cornwall.

11
Eastern England

The counties of Lincolnshire, Norfolk, Suffolk, Cambridgeshire and Essex, ranging from the Humber to the Thames, form with a few exceptions the low-lying areas of the country where the highest land does not exceed four hundred feet, and the Fenland is often below sea level. The region divides itself into three well-defined districts, the Fenlands of the north-west, the chalklands and heath of the north and eastern areas, and the fertile farmland lying to the south and east. This area, isolated by the marshes of the Fens, the forests in the south and the wet claylands of Essex, and approachable only along the line of chalk hills forming a continuation of the Chilterns in the south-west, attracted few people. But with the coming of better roads and railways in the nineteenth century and the reclamation of the Fenlands, vestiges of its original wild isolation remain only where communication is difficult during winter months. It should be remembered that although the Romans drained some areas the Fens were not drained on a large scale until the early seventeenth century when the present land pattern of the area began to take shape. For this reason most of the Fens buildings are of brick and of later date, although the rest of the region has for centuries been a prosperous agricultural area, where the past landowners made great use of the only natural building materials easily available – clay, timber and flint.

In these counties there are no major sources of stone, although the clay soil of Lincolnshire lies over beds of limestone, but building stones are quarried just outside the area in Northamptonshire and Rutland, where abundant quantities of stone are found at Weldon, Collyweston and Clipsham. In Lincolnshire itself, where the stone deposits are not so extensive, limestone has been worked at Ancaster, where the quarry was up to 30 feet deep. A similar type of stone was also worked at Ketton, near Stamford, and Lincoln Cathedral was built of local limestone, but further south towards the lowlands of the Fens, no stone except flint was available and other materials are generally used.

In the past the use of unbaked clay or cob was widespread in East Anglia and in the late eighteenth and early nineteenth centuries often took the form of various types of clay bats, or lumps, a form of block cast into a mould. After drying, these were used to build walls, the blocks being bonded like bricks and laid in courses with damp clay used as mortar. Buildings of this type are still quite common in central and south Norfolk, east and west Suffolk and south-eastern Cambridgeshire, where the local boulder clays were used. The method varied slightly with the district; in Cambridgeshire clay and chalk were mixed to form a marl which was moulded into unbaked bricks and chalk was also used in the rough cast used to cover the completed buildings. Elsewhere the blocks were known as clay lumps, in which case the clay was mixed with straw in the same way as cob, before being made into blocks.

These blocks would naturally disintegrate without protection from the weather so that the walls were covered with a layer of clay, chalk or plaster finished with sand to form a rough cast, and coloured by lime-wash or tar, the latter being normally used on the plinth to prevent water getting into the walls. Later in the nineteenth century when bricks became easily available such cottages were often covered externally by 4½ inch brick walls making them impossible to identify from the outside and such small buildings are hard for the casual observer to recognize, unless he should luckily see the covering being removed or see places where it has fallen off a dwelling in a bad state of repair. Otherwise it is hard to distinguish these cottages from those with normal brick walls rendered over either when being built or at a later date. Clay lump walls are thicker than brick, although half the thickness of traditional cob walls, and are always on a plinth of flint or brick, which is of later date than flint. These blocks were not used in this way in other parts of the country and many such cottages, mostly nineteenth century, still survive but the numbers dwindle every year as no more are being built to replace those condemned by the local authorities as being unfit or not conforming to modern building standards.

Cottages of this material still survive in some of the villages between Thetford and Diss, while Shipdham also has several good examples. For the interested visitor the Folk Museum at Cambridge has, among its interesting exhibits, an example of a clay bat removed from a local building during demolition and a good collection of gault bricks made locally over many years, often with the maker's name stamped on them, enabling some to be dated.

Although these counties are largely flat agricultural areas with few large woods this was not always so, and the present-day pine forests in parts of Norfolk and Suffolk, the largest being Thetford Chase near Norwich, are of recent origin and planted by the Forestry Commission. Certainly up to the reign of Elizabeth I the whole area contained extensive oak forests and in the smaller domestic buildings timber-framing was generally used, a tradition maintained until the arrival of brick, not commonly used until after the Restoration. The expense of stone gave the timber tradition a longer lifespan than in most other districts and it did not disappear until well into the seventeenth century.

All types of timber-framing may still be found, the earlier buildings having traditional exposed timberwork with wattle and daub infilling, and later examples with brick nogging to the panels or the whole of the framework covered with plaster. A few buildings date from the thirteenth or fourteenth centuries but most are from the period 1580 to 1640 when timber building reached its peak in this part of the country. The types of framework are those found elsewhere and the pattern of development similar to the rest of the country, but East Anglia has more examples of timber-framed buildings than anywhere else except perhaps the Welsh borders.

The oldest timber buildings are located in parts of Essex and there are many examples in such places as Colchester, Saffron Walden, Thaxted and Coggeshall. The earliest are of the "hall" type which were originally open to the roof although many have had floors inserted later, the oldest being the thirteenth-century Little Chesterford Farm, and one at Tiptofts near Wimbish, built in the following century. Most of these earlier houses had a central hall flanked by two wings whose gables faced the front, a type common in the fifteenth century, after which the upper storeys oversailed the lower. Later houses had rooms built over the hall which was then confined to the ground floor, and frequently the timber-framed ground-floor walls have been replaced by brickwork, so disguising the original building.

With a few exceptions, Essex houses built before the end of the fifteenth century are close studded with large uprights very close together and few, if any, curved corner braces, showing that timber for building was still plentiful in the area until the end of the Tudor period. Such houses are rare as most date from the seventeenth century, by which time the wattle and daub infilling had been replaced by brick, the panels being filled with brick nogging at right angles to the frame or in a herring-bone pattern. Sometimes the infilling was of laths plastered over to finish flush with the timbers rather than projecting beyond them, as often occurred in the more westerly counties. After the sixteenth century as timber became scarcer the posts got thinner and the spaces wider so that eventually it became quite common for the whole of the framework to be plastered over, concealing the inferior timber then being used for the smaller buildings, so that in the following century when softwood began to be used instead of hardwoods it became essential to cover all the timberwork to protect it from the weather. In recent times it has become fashionable to remove plasterwork from such timber buildings to expose the framework, but in many cases the timbers were never meant to be exposed as the wood was scored to form a key for the plaster; these unsightly marks, which cannot be removed, are a sure indication that originally the building was meant to be covered with plaster.

The most important timber-framed house in the region, and perhaps one of the best in the whole country, is Paycocke's House at Great Cogge-shall in Essex, built by the chief clothier of the town about 1550, which is now owned by the National Trust. The house has five bays forming a continuous façade along the street frontage, and the close-studded framework is largely original although the brick nogging only dates from about 1905. Other fine examples may be seen at Thaxted whose Guild-hall, built in 1470 by the cutlery merchants of the borough, is now one of the few medieval buildings still surviving in Essex. It was first restored in the eighteenth century, again in 1910 and a few years ago, so that today the building is very much in its original form, with its open ground floor which was originally used for trading. Other town houses of about the same date in Thaxted are in Stoney Lane and Newbiggin Street, as well as timber houses such as Park Farmhouse built in the early sixteenth century. The Priory, No. 38 Town Street, and No. 12 Watling Street are examples of older timber buildings refaced and altered in the eighteenth century; the first house originated about 1480 and the roof of this earlier house survives cased inside the later building. Many of the houses in Newbiggin Street were brought up to date in the eighteenth century when new door-cases and sash-windows were inserted into the original timber-framed buildings, others being plastered over or concealed behind other materials.

Most of the larger villages in the county possess some timber-framed buildings but many have been altered or extended at later periods, the new work often being in brick. Groups of sixteenth and seventeenth-century timber-framed houses can be seen at Aldham, and the Hall at Belchamp St Paul is an example of an L-shaped building with one wing dating from the sixteenth and the other from the seventeenth century. One is in timber-framing, and the other in brick has its original chimney-stacks, but in this case the brickwork dates from the sixteenth century and the timber frame a century later, so it must not be assumed that timber buildings are always older than brick houses in the same locality.

The market town of Saffron Walden has a magnificent parish church, one of the largest in the country and built between 1450 and 1525; it also contains a number of important timber-framed houses. A number of small houses are grouped around the church and in the High Street, but perhaps the most important building is in Bridge Street standing on the corner of Myddelton Place. It is the best medieval house in the town, having a long façade of exposed timberwork with a courtyard, and around the corner two oriel windows with carved beams and posts on the lower part of the house, which dates from about 1500. Other houses in the street are of the same period, some having overhanging upper storeys, and the Eight Bells Inn in the same street contains some very fine carved timberwork.

Colchester also has a number of timber buildings including the Red Lion Hotel, dating from about 1470; originally a private house, the building has exposed close studding and projecting upper storeys with traceried panels between some of the uprights.

Cambridgeshire has very old few old timber houses of any size as the proximity of the Fens made timber hard to obtain in sizes appropriate for such buildings and in Cambridge itself almost all medieval buildings, apart from college buildings, have disappeared or have been thoroughly altered. Some survive on the corner of Bridge Street and Northampton Street, indicating the former appearance of the medieval streets of the city but even these have been restored and much altered as part of a recent redevelopment scheme for the land at the rear. Among the few timber-framed houses in Ely is St Mary's Vicarage, known as Cromwell House due to its connection with the family of the Protector; the timber-work, at first-floor level, probably dates from some time in the four-teenth century while the ground floor walls are of stone.

In Norfolk the oldest buildings are of flint and brick and among the comparatively few timber houses are examples in Thetford, Diss, King's Lynn, where the best houses are those now forming the Green-land Fisheries Museum, and in Norwich; here, among other streets, the places to look are Elm Hill, Palace Street and Gildencroft.

In Lincolnshire the number is even smaller as in this county the oldest buildings are undoubtedly the Jews' Houses in Lincoln which are of stone, but the best timber buildings in the city are a row of much-altered sixteenth-century shops and houses forming one side of High Bridge, as part of the original High Street which was built on a bridge across the river, a medieval development unique in this country.

In Suffolk, on the other hand, there are a number of half-timbered buildings, on which the carving reached a very high standard of work-manship. Such houses can be found not only in the larger towns like Bury St Edmunds and Ipswich but in many small villages, where examples like Giffords Hall, built in 1428, Otley Hall and Alston Court, Nayland can be discovered. Numerous surviving town houses have timber-framing of all types ranging from the close studding of the fifteenth century to the widely spaced squares of the seventeenth, the later houses with the upper floors jettied out. This tradition continued here well into the seventeenth century, much later than over the rest of the country, where jetties had now been discarded in favour of timber-framing using smaller timbers jointed together to form a rectangular framework with vertical sides, and the panels filled with brick nogging.

Ipswich has several such houses largely built between 1620 and 1640, but unquestionably the best place in East Anglia for timber-framed buildings, as well as medieval buildings of all types, is Lavenham, which is among the show-places of the whole country.

In 1300 the wool trade in Lavenham was prospering and by the following century the town was one of the most important centres of the cloth trade in East Anglia, which continued until the early seventeenth century, after which the town declined. This is perhaps why its medieval buildings remained almost unaltered until the early nineteenth century when visitors began to rediscover the town, and some rebuilding in the Victorian period followed. All the houses are of two storeys, with a few single-storey dwellings, the construction being of the post and lintel type with the large members of local oak being closely spaced so that it was possible to reduce additional bracing to a minimum. The panels were usually infilled with wattle and daub or clay on elm sticks, later replaced by brick nogging.

Most houses were jettied out at first-floor level, with the upper floors being carried on the ends of the projecting floor beams, although many buildings are not now in their original condition due to the ground-floor walls being rebuilt in brick, this lining up with the ends of the beams above; internally the partitions were also of close-studded walls with elaborate king-post roof trusses. Originally, all the more important fifteenth-century buildings were ornamented with carvings of geometric or naturalistic motifs, these carvings, the best in East Anglia, being in key positions such as the first-floor supporting beams and brackets, as well as on corner posts, doors and window surrounds.

The whole town is full of timber-framed buildings of which many have recently been restored or had the original plaster covering stripped off, and only a few of the more important can be mentioned. In Lady Street, the old Wool Hall, dating from the fifteenth century and open to the roof, was incorporated into the Swan Hotel as recently as 1965. The hotel, the cellars of which date from the fourteenth century, is faced with some pargetted emblems typical of many in the town, emblems associated with the wool trade including the mitre, spur-rowel and fleur-de-lis. Nearby are the Tudor Shops and De Vere House, originally fifteenth century but now much restored with modern brick nogging to the timber frame. In the Market-Place, the Guildhall, built about 1529 by the Wool Guild, has very ornate carved posts, spandrels and friezes, with oriel windows on the ground floor and carved gable timberwork, and the surrounding streets contain many other houses with varying types of timberwork.

The inferior wood used to augment dwindling timber supplies was covered all over with plaster or pargetting, which is a typical East Anglian form of decorating; the plaster is finished off with combs to produce curved patterns or moulded into decorative shapes to conceal the effects of cracking. This technique extended from the late sixteenth century until the middle of the eighteenth, losing favour when plain plaster again became fashionable. Most of the surviving examples date from the seventeenth century when the craft was widely practised in the eastern counties but not elsewhere, and the pargetting seen on buildings today, originally sharply moulded, is now frequently weather-worn.

The incised decoration known as combed work appeared first and, being the easiest to do, was the most popular. It was done with a five-pronged wooden comb and other designs in common use were herring-bone, basket weave, cable moulded and fan-shaped. Another pattern found on humbler buildings was known as "sparrow picking", using a triangular piece of wood fitted with prongs to make small holes all over the plaster covering.

The front of the building was often divided into a series of plain rectangular panels of different sizes and either the frames were moulded or the panels filled with a variety of raised motifs or features indicating the original use of the building. Carried out in lime, sand and horsehair, the relief ornaments usually appear as panels, diamonds, squares, rect-angles, circles or ovals with initials and dates, Tudor roses, fleur-de-lis, crowns, birds, fishes and odd things such as boots or scales. Most of the pargetted buildings are in Essex, Cambridgeshire and south-western Suffolk, with fewer examples in the adjacent counties; particularly fine examples can be seen on The Garrison House in Wivenhoe, the old Sun Inn in Saffron Walden and the Ancient House or Sparrowe's House in Ipswich. This type of decoration, widely used in the seventeenth century, became unpopular a century or so later.

Eastern England's most distinctive form of timber construction is found in Essex, Cambridgeshire and the Weald of Kent, where the frames of timber houses are covered externally with weather-boarding finished with tar or paint, a style popular in the eighteenth and nine-teenth centuries although a few buildings of this type date from the seventeenth century.

In Essex and the Weald of Kent this style of building is most common-ly found near the ports into which timber was imported from Scandina-via as supplies of English oak and elm declined. This timber tradition persisted here while the rest of the country was preferring brick to timber-framed building, but a few of these buildings can be seen beyond the coastal areas of eastern England, rarely west of London, where a few examples such as Romney House, dating from 1797, and Heath End House, can be seen at Hampstead.

The boards were normally fixed horizontally on the surface of a build-ing which was not necessarily timber-framed. The original boards were of elm, infrequently of oak, fixed with pegs, but after the eighteenth century the boards were usually softwood, such as pine, nailed onto a framework made of softwood studding of a much smaller section than was normally the case in the older timber-framed houses. The weather-boarding had the lower edge chamfered and the upper edge "feathered", i.e. cut to a very thin edge, and these overlapped each other to prevent rain getting into the building. Later on, the boards were sometimes tongued and grooved or rebated into each other, rather than being over-lapped, and while tarring was generally popular in Essex, the boards were usually painted white or cream in the south-eastern counties. Certainly this was so in the Weald of Kent, but the fashion now seems to be to paint the boarding in rather brighter colours.

Weather-boarding has been known on the outside of barns since the late sixteenth century and some farm buildings of this type, still to be seen in Essex and Kent, are even older. These would be familiar to many of the Pilgrim Fathers, coming from eastern England, and as a result weather-boarded houses and farm buildings were put up in New England from the seventeenth century onwards. In England there were few domestic buildings in this style until the eighteenth century when boarding began to be used more often on the new timber-framed housing using smaller softwood joists for sections, with vertical studs made of one piece running continuously from the sill to the eaves level, with the horizontal members nailed between the uprights to keep them rigid. This method, later known as "balloon framing", was only used for the smaller domestic buildings then being put up near the ports of East Anglia and Kent; although there are a few eighteenth-century houses, most of the survivors are from the nineteenth century.

The oldest surviving stone houses in the eastern counties, the Norman manor-houses now called Jews' Houses, were built in Lincoln during the late twelfth century, and have been described in Chapter 3. These houses were of course among the more important ones of that period since expensive stone was not used for humbler houses which were first of cob, then of timber and later of brick. During the following centuries brick was used for all the large houses, but quarries in the adjacent counties of Northampton and Rutland still supplied stone for many ecclesiastical buildings. These quarries included some of the most important in the country, notably those at Ancaster, Weldon, Ketton and Barnack, most of which had been producing stone since the Middle Ages, only ceasing in the present century. The largest buildings were of course the cathedrals, those at Ely and Norwich being largely built of Barnack stone which came from quarries three miles from Stamford, while the stone for Lincoln Cathedral came from a quarry a few miles north of the city.

However, changes in fifteenth-century fashion made brick the accepted material for even the more eminent Cambridge colleges and few other places in the region had many sizeable stone buildings except for Stamford, in Lincolnshire. In this, the most important stone-built town in eastern England almost all the houses, regardless of size or type, were of stone from the seventeenth century onwards, indicating the nearness of the town to a number of quarries, most of the stone coming from Casterton or in the locality of the town. Celia Fiennes in 1697 wrote that Stamford is "as fine a built town all of stone as may be seen", and that remains true today. Stone houses of all periods and sizes, among the best in England, form the background of an exceptionally fine town centre. Many are of dressed stone but others are of rubble, hard coarse rag stone being used for the walls with dressings of better stone at corners or around openings. The earlier houses have gables, mullioned or bay windows typical of the Jacobean period, while the eighteenth-century buildings, plain and in Georgian style, are very similar in design to the contemporary brick houses.

The central part of East Anglia rests on chalk which overlies the red chalk, an impure red limestone, the exposed strata being quite clearly seen on the coastline near Cromer and Hunstanton; beds being often two or three hundred feet thick, running across eastern England from Bedfordshire. The hard, lower chalk has been used for building in the area since Roman times, while during the medieval period the larger pieces were used for carvings in Ely Cathedral and also many local churches and Cambridge college buildings. As chalk covers most of the region many of the churches and smaller houses are built of "whyte chalk" or clunch, a form of chalk pebble which could be found either on, or just below, the surface of the local fields. The name was first recorded in use as early as 1415, and in the following centuries it also meant soft chalk used for the interior of walls as a filling between the outer skins of harder stone. Traditionally the name is restricted to the lumpy chalk marl found near Cambridge and the last place the material was dug was Burwell quarry which closed in 1962; Burwell village church is a fine example of the use of this material.

Since clunch is a form of pebble it is difficult to form straight edges when using it, so houses built of it always have plinths and quoins of brick used in the same way as stone dressings are on buildings of rubble. Sometimes the brickwork is used to divide the façade of buildings into a chequer pattern with panels filled in with alternative blocks of clunch or flints, while other buildings have alternate courses of clunch and brick, for example the sixteenth-century building of Christ's College, Cambridge.

Nearer the coast where clunch is rarer, houses and cottages were often built of ordinary pebbles picked up from the sea-shore or the surface of the boulder clay in the Norfolk fields. These ordinary rounded stones less than 3 inches in diameter, in many cases just the smaller unbroken flints, were used only with great difficulty, being laid in a random way on a bedding of mortar, or clay, to form walls which are either whitewashed or more commonly rendered over after completion, although near the Norfolk coast the walls are often finished with tar. As with clunch it is difficult to form straight edges when using pebbles and so other materials have to be used for dressings, almost always brick, for if no dressings are used the corners have to be rounded. Sometimes pebbles of similar size may be laid in courses or set in diagonal and herring-bone patterns reinforced at the quoins and jambs with bricks, or with alternate brick courses as when using clunch, and buildings can also be found with rear and side walls of pebbles but a more impressive front elevation of brick. The Cromer and Blakeney districts of Norfolk, with a long tradition of building with pebbles, have examples of these attractive buildings which are constructed and survive only on the more isolated parts of the coastline.

The most distinctive and widely used building stone in East Anglia and parts of the south-eastern counties is flint, found as nodules of silica lying on the ground or the beaches of Norfolk and Suffolk where they have been washed out of the chalk cliffs. The flints, varying in size from 3 to 12 inches in diameter, have a centre of dark slate colour surrounded by a thin outer casing of whitened stone. Flints are difficult to use but for lack of other stones have been taken for building since Saxon times, although back in Neolithic times they were excavated for other purposes at what is known as Grime's Graves in Norfolk.

There are problems in using such small stones, so flints are found only in the older churches, some with Saxon towers, and not widely used in larger domestic buildings until the seventeenth-century timber shortage; most of the small houses and cottages seen today date from the last century. Even in areas where flint was plentiful brick was always used if available; larger Georgian houses were normally of brick, flint being relegated to use in tenants' or labourers' houses and farm buildings. Especially in the poorer buildings of north and east Norfolk, the rounded ends of the flints, which were laid in rough courses bedded in clay or lime mortar with very wide joints, showed as an irregular surface on the outside of the wall; this was as far as possible faced up with mortar and by setting small chips of waste flint into the joints themselves.

In other cases the nodules were "knapped" or split exposing the core of the flint, a practice common in churches after the fourteenth century but rarely in domestic buildings until several centuries later. The flints were not normally used throughout the whole wall, but usually formed an outer casing to a rubble or cob wall, and the structure, not very strong, was often tied together by using large stones, perhaps obtained from another district, to go through the walls at intervals, or by laying courses of brick at intervals.

As with clunch and pebbles, all flint buildings also have stone or brick dressings at quoins and jambs. In the more important buildings, particularly the churches, these would be limestone, but for small domestic buildings brick was always used. The bricks were also used as alternate courses, or to make chequer patterns, exactly as with clunch, so that the two types of buildings look very alike from a distance.

In later buildings, particularly the churches but rarely the small houses, the knapped flints were roughly squared up. These flints, about 4 inches square, were then used in almost the same way as brick headers to produce various overall diaper patterns with stone or brick as well as chequer-work designs similar to those developed in clunch.

These squared flints are common to the southern part of East Anglia, especially Suffolk and Essex, also parts of Kent and near the Sussex coast. Another use of flint, although not for domestic building, is too widespread not to be briefly mentioned, and that is its use for the round towers of many churches, most of which were at least 20 or more feet high. This method of using flint avoided the use of other stone for the quoins or jambs. These twelfth-century towers of unfractured flint form a prominent feature of the East Anglian landscape, five at least still surviving in Essex, forty-one in Suffolk and one hundred and nineteen in Norfolk where tradition suggests that such towers were formed as part of the defences against Danish invaders.

East Anglia possesses many houses, cottages and farm buildings in local brick, the colours always being pale due to the lack of iron in the gault clays which lie under the chalk covering almost the entire area. The older dwellings are always made of bricks from one of the numerous small brickyards which until the turn of the century could be found near every large village until mass-produced, machine-made bricks caused their closure. The influx into the western fringes of the region of these cheaper bricks of a standard pattern was particularly pronounced, as just beyond East Anglia at Fletton, near Peterborough, where the clays were particularly suitable for brickmaking there developed what was to become the country's largest brickworks, today producing a very high percentage of this country's brick supply.

The local gault clays provide the pale buff bricks, the so-called white bricks of Cambridgeshire, the Fens, Suffolk and west Norfolk. Pale yellow bricks are the most common but many varieties of pale pinks occur with some darker reds and browns in the north and west of the region, but nowhere are the locally made bricks as dark in colour as those of the Midland counties to the west. The use of white bricks for smaller houses and cottages was most prevalent in the early nineteenth century during their peak popularity before cheap transport introduced bricks from other areas, and examples of such buildings can be found in every village in the Fen district and Suffolk.

The colours of the bricks are also related to the colours of the roof tiles which, with few exceptions, are also pale. Traditionally East Anglia is the home of the pantile, introduced after the seventeenth century, although plain tiles were commonly used on the western fringe of the area where the local clays resemble those of the Midlands more than the gault clays to the east. The pantiles of the Fens were usually light buff or pink although red and brown tiles occurred elsewhere, but the most distinctive ones, exclusive to this area, have a black gazed finish and are rarely pre-nineteenth century. Pantiles were formerly mostly used in the villages of Norfolk and Essex and round the coastline of East Anglia, but not often on the older houses of the inland villages south of the Suffolk border. Two types were used, the S-shaped pantiles of Cambridgeshire and Norfolk and the flat and roll type common in Essex.

Their use influenced the shape of local buildings as due to the difficulties of cutting such tiles diagonally, hipped roofs were uncommon and most older houses have gabled ends, the walls being taken just above the roof tiles to form low parapet walls. The roof slopes are also steeper than with plain tiles, the normal pitch for pantiles being about forty degrees, but where tiles have replaced thatch on the older buildings, the pitches are between fifty and fifty-five degrees; when tiles have been laid to such slopes it is often an indication that the original roof covering was thatch. The smaller houses have rooms in the roof spaces which are lit by dormer windows covered with pantiles running in the same direction as those covering the main roof. When pantiles are used, dormer windows are not covered with independent pitched roofs forming gables, as with other houses built during the Jacobean period.

Thatched roofs are still common throughout the eastern counties, and there are probably more of them in Suffolk than in any other English county, including a large number of thatched churches, rarely seen elsewhere. Some of the houses were built in the reign of Elizabeth I, but in all cases the roof-coverings will be of recent origin; most of the buildings, however, will be no older than the seventeenth century when dormer windows started to appear. Thanks to the nearness of the Wash and the Fens, reed and sedge are more commonly used than straw, resulting in a different kind of thatching from that found in the Midlands. The roofs have much steeper pitches than are normal in other districts, and gable ends to the roofs, in contrast to the hipped roofs which are more easily formed when using thatch. The widespread use of thatch means that such houses and cottages can still be seen in many villages including Flempton, Chelsworth and Cavendish in Suffolk, Woodbastwick and

Rollesby in Norfolk and Birdbrook, Aythorpe Roding and Henham in Essex. Though thatched buildings are fewer in Lincolnshire where the tradition was not so well established, Cambridgeshire still has many thatched houses and cottages in such villages as Lode, in the Fens, Great Wilbraham, Comberton, Foxton – and Grantchester, made famous by association with Rupert Brooke.

The houses have simple sloping roofs and dormers and in the north-east, the influence of the Dutch immigrants resulted in the larger houses having crow-stepped and Dutch gables, resembling those typical of the Low Countries. Such gables originally had pantile roofs although the covering may now have been replaced by other kinds of tiles. The chimney-stacks are more often at the gable ends than in the middle of the house, and most brick-built smaller houses and cottages date from the seventeenth century or later. Examples of all types ranging from Jacobean to Georgian may be found in Boston, Bury St Edmunds, Dedham, Ipswich, Louth, Newmarket, Southwold, Spalding as well as the more obvious places like Ely, Norwich, Lincoln and Cambridge; and the North Brink at Wisbech is one of the finest Georgian streets in England.

12

The Midlands

The Midlands, consisting of Nottinghamshire, Leicestershire, Warwickshire and Worcestershire, form the central plain spanning England from the Severn Valley and the counties of Hereford and Shropshire on the borders of Wales, to Lincolnshire, bounded to the north by the Pennine foothills with the coal and iron deposits of Staffordshire, the birthplace of the Industrial Revolution. The clay deposits of the Midland plain are interrupted by upstanding masses of old rock forming the isolated peaks of the Wrekin, the Lickey Hills, the Malvern Hills, the Nuneaton Ridge and the Charnwood Forest Plateau. To the south are the Cotswolds, almost all in Gloucestershire, and the Edge Hills forming the northern edge of Oxfordshire and extending into Northamptonshire, and many of these upland ridges provide some of the best building stones in the country. Further south beyond these hills are Hertfordshire, Buckinghamshire, Bedfordshire and Berkshire, with their chalk downs and the clays of the Thames Valley.

The Midland plain itself does not nurture any particularly distinctive styles of building, but being a prosperous area always contained many fine examples of traditional building from the early medieval period onwards. Considerable numbers of these older houses and cottages have survived to the present day, especially in districts undisturbed by the rapid development of the industrial areas since the early nineteenth century. The most important regional styles are in fact found on the fringes of the area, for example the stone buildings of the Cotswolds and the timber-framed houses of the Welsh borderland.

All over the region the use of clay for walls was once commonplace, and during the nineteenth century, throughout the Black Country, miners' cottages were almost always built of clay 'lump' or blocks. Mud walls are still to be seen as boundaries to farmyards in many of the rural areas forming the common border of Northamptonshire and Leicestershire, but the cob cottages remaining throughout the Midlands are getting scarcer with increasing demolitions when they fail to come up to the standards required by the modern public health acts. To locate cob buildings requires some local knowledge, as the casual observer may see nothing unusual about these small whitewashed buildings until they are examined closely both inside and out, but at Barby in Northamptonshire a large two-storey, timber-framed and cob manor-house survived until 1978 before being demolished. Isolated cob buildings throughout the

Midlands are the remnant of a very large number which once existed but there are no large concentrations of such buildings as in Cornwall and Cumberland, and identification is often made more difficult because may have now been covered with brickwork, hiding the original construction.

Historically the most characteristic building method used in the once well-wooded Midland plain is that of the timber frame except in some stone areas, like the Cotswolds, where such timber buildings are almost unknown; this is not to say that timber was never used in these areas but its scarcity made stone preferable. Although crucks and the timber frame were in use during the same period it is probable that the oldest buildings are those using crucks, and in the Midlands most small buildings of this kind had two or three bays, being between 32 and 48 feet long, the majority having one-and-a-half storeys with a room in the roof space.

Although full crucks were once used throughout the Midlands, particularly in districts near well-established forests, the oldest buildings of this kind are in Herefordshire and almost all such buildings are no earlier than seventeenth century. The problem in identifying them is that most have been altered since they were first built, the most common alteration being the cutting off of several feet at the base of the crucks where these had decayed and supporting the remainder of the timbers on a stone or brick plinth wall. In some cases, however, crucks were originally put on plinth walls; in the Banbury area, houses with crucks, built in the sixteenth century and seventeenth century, always had these raised up on stone walls often over 2 feet thick. In other cases the buildings have been rendered over or cased in brickwork so that the crucks are no longer exposed as they were originally, but exposed crucks are easy to identify from their unmistakable shape. External crucks are still quite common in the west Midlands but there are few examples in the eastern counties where this construction was infrequently used due to the lack of suitable large trees. It is known that crucks were used in the more isolated parts of Leicestershire up to the late seventeenth century and, having come down in the social scale, they were also used with mud walls in the poorer cottages during the same period in many parts of Northamptonshire, but most surviving cruck buildings are found much further west.

Examples are known in Worcestershire, Shropshire, Staffordshire, and Warwickshire where Stoneleigh boasts seven cruck cottages, the largest number for any village in that county. Without doubt most of the cruck buildings are in Herefordshire where, according to a survey made in 1949, there were at least one hundred and forty-three still standing and although most were dwellings, there were also about thirty barns or other agricultural buildings some of which were perhaps originally cottages converted to other uses when the new brick farmhouse was put up at a later date. The largest numbers of cruck buildings can be seen around Eardisley, Dilwyn, Pembridge, Eardisland and in Weobley, where many fine timber buildings can be seen particularly in Broad Street.

Cruck houses were very narrow as it was impossible to widen the building if the crucks were used in the traditional way but a later development, the base cruck, enabled buildings to be wider with the crucks concealed inside the house. Buildings of this type are difficult to identify from outside but one that can easily be seen is The Manor House at West Bromwich, in the West Midlands, and other Worcestershire examples are The Tithe Barn at Middle Littleton and a farmhouse, The Hyde, at Stoke Bliss.

The timber tradition of East Anglia was cut off from central England by the stone areas of Northamptonshire, so the simply designed timber buildings of the east Midlands became increasingly elaborate with the progression westwards to districts of plentiful timber and it was here that timber-framed buildings were erected well into the seventeenth century, long after the rest of the country abandoned the practice. Throughout the Midlands, timber houses of this date are still quite common, but except for a few of the more important, the older ones are rarely found intact and the survivors have been altered internally as well as being robbed of such carved decorative features as barge-boards and corner posts.

From the fourteenth to sixteenth centuries, timber-framed houses had the upper floors jettied out with large panels made up of massive timbers strengthened by angle braces at the corners, although the later examples have the panels divided up by straight horizontal or vertical timbers; the use of curved short braces was a later feature. Narrow close studding and large square panels were both in use at the same time but in the Midlands the close studded houses are usually later than those with large panels, the earliest examples being in Warwickshire and Shropshire, where some houses have only the front close studded to save timber, while the slightly later close-studded houses of the border counties often have a middle rail inserted to divide up the long narrow panels.

Throughout the region there was a steady trend towards more elaborate designs and by the early seventeenth century ornamental panelling was common in all larger houses, the most decorative being the 'magpie' houses along the Welsh borders. It was these houses which formed the peak of the timber tradition, after which a decline in size and design as timber became scarcer meant that houses again had very simple and flimsy timber frames with 4 foot square panels. Timber now became unfashionable except for the building of poorer houses and it is these which are most commonly seen in the villages of the region. The typical house was three panels in height, with the frame raised on plinth walls, but often the timber was of such poor quality that the framework was frequently concealed behind plaster or brickwork, particularly after the Civil War, although such houses continued to be built until quite late in the eighteenth century.

The east Midland villages along the river valleys, or near the traditional forest areas, possess a few small timber buildings but they are hard to find in the upland areas where stone was easily available. Large timber-framed buildings are rare in Northamptonshire although in parts of Leicestershire there was a tradition of timber building. Such houses were of simple design until after the sixteenth century when the panels were often filled in with parallel diagonal struts in the west and south of the county including Hemington, Kilworth and Market Bosworth. At Shearsby there is a cottage dated 1669, which is long after brick had become commonly used elsewhere in the area.

The situation is similar in Nottinghamshire where villages near wooded areas such as Sherwood Forest contain the few surviving timber buildings which are usually much altered; elsewhere stone or brick predominates, and although there are some timber houses in Newark these cannot compare with those found in the towns farther west. In the upland areas of Northamptonshire and Oxfordshire the few surviving timber-framed houses are very small and overshadowed by the large numbers of buildings in local stone, without any large concentrations of timber houses as nearer the Welsh borders.

Once in the lowland areas of Warwickshire the position is entirely different and along the valley of the Avon, or on the fringes of the Forest of Arden, all types of timber buildings can be seen in large numbers. While not as impressive as the buildings further west these Warwickshire houses are good examples of the smaller dwellings built between the fifteenth and seventeenth centuries, although with few exceptions very much altered or heavily restored since they were first built, the panels now always filled with pale red bricks, typical of the county, or poorer brickwork covered with plaster.

In Warwickshire there are some of the most frequently visited timber-framed buildings in the whole country – the properties associated with Shakespeare. At Stratford-upon-Avon there is the fifteenth-century house which was the playwright's birthplace, the grammar school built about 1473 and the adjacent almshouses finished in 1427–8, while at Shottery is Anne Hathaway's cottage and at Wilmcote, Mary Arden's house, a fine close-studded building, both dating from the sixteenth century. To visitors these buildings represent the typical English timber-framed house, ignoring other timber houses in Stratford which do not have such important historical associations, among them Harvard House built in 1596, which was later covered with plaster so that the timber frame remained hidden for several centuries until it was uncovered again earlier this century.

Warwick also has several important timber houses including Oken's House in Castle Street, and near the West Gate, the Lord Leycester Hospital, dating from the fifteenth century, one of the finest medieval timber-framed buildings in the country. Opposite is the Elizabethan House, one of the oldest buildings in the town, and other similar buildings in the High Street have been faced with brickwork during the seventeenth and eighteenth centuries. Many smaller timber houses can also be seen in Stoneleigh, Bidford-on-Avon, Welford-on-Avon, Temple Grafton and Alcester where Malt Mill Lane contains a particularly fine range of timber-framed buildings.

Henley-in-Arden, standing in the centre of what was formerly the Forest of Arden, still has nearly a hundred timber-framed houses – the largest single group in Warwickshire. While none of these has historical associations like those in Stratford there are houses in this pleasant market town ranging in date from the fifteenth to the seventeenth centuries standing next to others built of brick when timber ceased to be fashionable, all grouped around the fine medieval parish church and the fifteenth-century guildhall. The main street, still largely unspoilt, displays every style of timber-framing except for the elaborate ornamental panelling typical of Shropshire, and among the buildings are heavy timber-framed, close-studded fifteenth- and sixteenth-century houses as well as numerous sixteenth- and seventeenth-century examples of square panelled houses, the panels always filled with local red bricks. Other timber buildings refaced with brickwork during the next two centuries stand near some whose timber frames are still exposed but altered by the later insertion of casements, sash-windows or Georgian and Victorian bay windows, all in their turn reflecting changes in fashions.

The wealth of timber buildings in the Arden area proves that an abundant supply of timber was available from the forest during the medieval period, and further north in Staffordshire ample quantities allowed most of the larger manor-houses to be timber-framed until the seventeenth century after which brick became the favoured material, using the local clays to produce high-quality bricks. Staffordshire does not have as many timber buildings as Cheshire but timber-framed cottages can be seen in Alrewas and Abbots Bromley and larger buildings in Lichfield, Stafford and Tutbury although one of the best houses is Balterley Hall O' Wood, built as late as 1750 but still using the timber-frame technique.

Worcestershire possesses many timber buildings of all kinds particularly in Bewdley, Chaddesley Corbett and Abbots Morton which has 'black and white' houses of a great variety and the largest farmhouse, started in about the fifteenth century, is at Lower Tunbridge. Other interesting buildings are Booth Hall in Evesham and the Commandery in Worcester, both fifteenth century, while Huddington Hall and Mere Hall, Hanbury, date from the following century; visitors to Avoncroft Museum of Buildings can see the Bromsgrove Merchant's House, dating from about 1475, which was moved to the museum a few years ago for restoration and re-erection.

In Herefordshire, square framing using massive timbers made an early appearance, surviving until the seventeenth century well after the timber-building tradition disappeared in the rest of the county. There are many buildings of this type in Bromyard, Dilwyn, Eardisley and of course Weobley, where some in Broad Street date from the fourteenth and fifteenth centuries. Larger buildings of importance, although not always domestic in character, include the Saracen's Head and Kyrele's House at Ross-on-Wye, the Chequer's Inn and Old Town Hall, at Leominster, Court Farm at Preston Wynne and the Feathers Hotel at Ledbury; the latter, less famous than its namesake at Ludlow, is of great interest and dates from about 1560.

Pembridge perhaps contains the most 'black and white' domestic buildings in the country and has hardly been altered during the Georgian and Victorian periods although modern buildings have enhanced the appearance of this small town. Among the terraces of timber-framed buildings are examples from the fourteenth to seventeenth centuries and of particular interest are the Market House, with its square framing, and the Greyhound Inn, a close-studded building with oversailing upper floors supported on carved brackets, both early sixteenth century in date, Bridge Cottage, fourteenth century in origin and Clear Brook House, a specially ornate three-gabled house with brick chimneys, all dating from the seventeenth century.

But in Shropshire the timber tradition surpassed any other county and many buildings still survive showing the elaborate designs popular just before the fashion changed in favour of brick. In this area houses had jettied upper floors from the time of Elizabeth I, a feature which continued long after that period, while close-set studding and square panels were both in use; later houses had panels filled in with complicated bracing, lozenges or star shapes leaving little space for the white of the traditional wattle and daub infilling.

In most villages throughout the county small timber houses can be discovered along with rather more important buildings such as the Tithe Barn at Hodnet, built about 1619, Lee Old Hall of 1594, Bishop Percy's house in Bridgnorth built about the same time and the large Elizabethan house at Dunvall, Astley Abbots. It is, however, in the centre of the medieval towns of Shrewsbury and Ludlow that most of the finest timber buildings remain, only a fraction of the original number, some being erected long after brick became compulsory in London. They are rivalled by very few others in the country in size or ornamentation and give a glimpse of the aspect of medieval London before the Great Fire.

Pre-war Shrewsbury had largely retained its medieval street pattern, and the original appearance of these streets can be appreciated in Grope Lane, a narrow alley lined by two-storey timber buildings with the upper floors jettied out over the roadway. Reference can be made to a few only of the more important domestic timber buildings in the town and Henry Tudor House, the King's Head Inn and the Abbot's House are all pre-Reformation. The latter building has jettied upper floors, a ground floor which has been altered, a first floor with its original close studding, and a second floor of large square panels, showing that both were in common use at the same time. Mytton's Mansion and the Golden Cross Inn date from the fifteenth century, Owen's Mansion from the sixteenth, but undoubtedly the grandest timber building is Ireland's Mansion, built about 1575. This building has seven bays and is three storeys high with an additional floor in the roof lit by dormer windows, the whole of the outside being of close-set studding and diagonal strutting while many of the decorative features, such as barge-boards, are still intact.

Of all Ludlow's many timber-framed buildings it is The Feathers, built in 1603, which represents the culmination of the timber tradition, and it is one of the last timber buildings of any size in the country. According to Nikolaus Pevsner, "everything of motifs that was available has been lavished on the façade. In addition, on the first floor along most of the façade runs a balcony with flat openwork balusters. Lozenge pattern on the first floor, cusped concave lozenges on the second. Three bay-windows and three gables, but the left bay and gable projecting further than the others. . . ."

Part of the limestone belt running from Dorset to Lincolnshire forms the uplands north and south of the Midland plain where stone is the natural building material, from the well-known Cotswold area north-eastwards towards the Edge Hills and the Northamptonshire escarpment, which divides the Midland plain from the south Midland counties of Berkshire, Bedfordshire, Buckinghamshire, Hertfordshire and parts of Oxfordshire. Isolated peaks stick out of the undulating plain, among them the hill at Napton in Warwickshire and Bredon Hill in Worcestershire.

The Cotswold style of building is the most famous, using the grey stone from quarries around the valleys of the Cherwell, Colne, Evenlode and the Windrush, merging with the brown marlstone of north Oxfordshire and the redder stone of Northamptonshire. The best Cotswold stone is probably that found around Burford and Chipping Camden or Broadway, where the majority of the smaller domestic buildings date from the seventeenth and eighteenth centuries; contrary to popular opinion Cotswold villages are not full of Elizabethan buildings, only houses in a style used for several centuries and hardly changed. Earlier buildings have survived, for example the churches and grander manor-houses, but the older buildings are always on the lower slopes of the hills as the hilltops were reserved for sheep which provided the wool on which the wealth of the area depended. Houses on the higher ground, like the stone walls dividing up the fields, usually came after the Enclosures of the seventeenth century or later.

Each small valley and village has a manor-house, which can still be seen at Fairford, Filkins, Lechlade, Great and Little Rissington, Painswick, Snowshill, Stanway, Temple Guiting, Upper and Lower Slaughter and Upper Swell, and Winchcombe, while Bibury has Arlington Row, perhaps the best-known row of small cottages in the Cotswolds, and now owned by the National Trust. It is a pattern first developed as long ago as the twelfth century, surviving almost intact until the start of the last war, carried on by local craftsmen using the local stone in such a way that entire towns and villages of stone buildings can be seen all over the area, from Ilmington and Moreton-in-Marsh, through Stow-on-the-Wold and Bourton-on-the-Water, along the high ground westwards to the Golden Valley around Stroud and Minchinhampton overlooking the Severn Valley and the Vale of Berkeley. Not only are the houses and cottages of the local stone but a unity is given to the landscape by the use of the stone for the walls of farm buildings and fields, so that the use of timber-framing and brick is restricted to the lower lands of Gloucestershire, stretching towards the Severn and the lower lying parts of south Warwickshire, where the Cotswolds run down to the Midland plain.

The style of Cotswold buildings has for centuries been what is popularly known as 'Elizabethan', the variations from one century to another lying in the shape of the door and window openings and the mouldings, but as masons were conservative in their outlook such features can mislead one when dating the houses unless other evidence is available. The basic shape of these dwellings was firmly established at an early date, as not only did the pattern of living change very little in such a prosperous agricultural district for hundreds of years, but also the material used dictated the style of buildings erected.

The better houses were of squared ashlar while the others were always of rubble, a cheaper material, and large blocks of stone were rarely used except for mullions to windows. The steep roof pitches were also necessary because of the stone slabs which covered them and the space created in such roofs was used for rooms lit by windows in gables taken up flush with the face of the building, rather than by the dormer windows common elsewhere, a feature of the Cotswolds first apparent in the Middle Ages. The windows always have stone mullions with lintels and dripstones over, lintels of wood being generally found on the poorer cottages, and the windows in the larger houses diminish in size as their position in the walls becomes higher, with three lights to an opening on the lower floors and two in the roof gables, which normally have parapet walls above the level of the roof-covering. Bay windows were rare except in the larger towns where the typical flat-roofed bay and door, next to one another and covered by a single roof, were often used on the smaller buildings.

It is difficult to make a limited choice of examples worthy of special attention among the numerous handsome domestic buildings, but Broadway, Chipping Camden, Cirencester, Stow-on-the-Wold and Burford attract thousands of visitors and the smaller and more secluded villages are always worth exploring as the search for fine old houses and cottages is always rewarding. To the north-east on the Edge Hills, in North Oxfordshire, there is a similar pattern although the buildings, shading to the rusty brown of the local ironstone, become simpler in outline, which is partly because in the Middle Ages this area lacked the wealth of the Cotswold woollen merchants and money was not available to construct such elaborate houses or churches. In this district, rooms in the roofs are lit by windows in small detached gables formed on the plain tiled roofs, clay tiles taking the place of stone or thatch, mullioned windows are rarer and all door or window openings have oak lintels rather than stone. While stone slates were commonly used in areas near Stonefield or Collyweston, clay tiles are more general where clay is at hand. Villages on Edge Hill are smaller and more scattered than in the Cotswolds, but Wroxton, Hornton, Farnborough and Warmington abound in lovely small houses constructed of the local stone, originally of one room and built no earlier than the seventeenth century, particularly in the Banbury area.

Further east, the Northamptonshire stone becomes a more yellow colour on the uplands around Daventry, Weedon and Braunston, part of the limestone belt running up to the Humber with a series of important quarries along its whole length. Although separated from the Edge Hills by part of the Avon and Nene valleys, these stone-bearing areas form part of a line from the south to east coasts upon which lie most of the stone-built villages and towns of central England.

In the Northamptonshire area, stone buildings can be found in Braunston, Brixworth, Everden, Great Weldon, Flore, Rockingham, Rothwell and Stanford-on-Avon and the larger towns of Higham Ferrers,

Oundle, Stamford and as far south as Towcester. The Northampton-shire and Rutland buildings have steeply pitched roofs, typical of the former use of thatch, the gables have parapets, dormer windows and stone-mullioned bay windows are common, but the most distinctive feature is the use of what can best be described as striped stonework in which the walls have alternate courses of different coloured stone, grey and brown being the most usual. A variation in the pattern is the use of grey stone quoins with the main walls of brown stone. This type of con-struction, common in villages of rural Northamptonshire, is rarely found elsewhere, even within a short distance of this particular district.

Northwards, in Leicestershire, there are ancient granite rocks in the Charnwood Forest area, particularly near Mountsorrel, but being too hard to work easily for building it was not often used, although the older buildings are of stone, the later ones are of brick from a very early date. This county has no really good building stone although some limestone was used around Market Harborough and in the north near Ashby-de-la-Zouch, in which areas stone-mullioned windows were only replaced by the later 'Stuart'-style sashes as recently as the eighteenth century. Here the stone was expensive to quarry, unlike the softer Cotswold stone, so that it was used only for larger houses and until brick became cheaper small cottages were timber-framed or cob, a situation which prevailed well into the eighteenth century.

Everywhere else in the Midlands brick predominates, ranging in period from St John's Hospital at Lichfield, dating from 1495, the Tudor house of Compton Wynyates, built in 1520, the large Victorian villas at Malvern or further afield in Pangbourne and Maidenhead along the Thames Valley (in their period as elaborately designed as the earlier manor-house) to the neo-Georgian houses of the earliest of the 'New Towns' – Welwyn Garden City, built just after the First World War. All the surviving earliest known examples of houses, or other buildings, with brickwork dating from 1450 to 1550, have been listed by Jane Wight and their location illustrates the extent of brick buildings across the Midlands and also the location of the wealthy and noble families who built these early mansions. The four in Worcestershire and five in War-wickshire represent the average for the Midland counties, but there are eight in Buckinghamshire, ten in Berkshire and thirteen in Hereford-shire, indicating the long tradition of building in brick in the southern Midlands. The oldest house in Hertfordshire, the Brick House, Great Hormead, existed before the reign of Elizabeth I and as the name sug-gests was an unusual building when it was first erected.

Throughout central England, without exception, brick can be seen in every town and village, down to the smallest hamlet, and the older the settlement the greater the variety of buildings. In the oldest towns, apart from those in the upland stone areas, timber-framed and brick houses will be found side by side, largely dating from the seventeenth century onwards. It is here that the humbler and older domestic buildings survive while in the prosperous areas the rebuilding of the existing towns, or the building of completely new towns or villages, resulted in the Georgian town centres of Ampthill, Bedford, Huntingdon, Kimbolton, Woburn and of course Bath. Probably the most varied groups of brick buildings of all periods are lining the streets of the towns along the old coaching routes out of London, where the centres of Dunstable and Stoney Stratford on the old Watling Street, for example, are still composed of timber-framed and brick houses of all periods, of which many have been converted from domestic to commercial uses for shops and offices.

The Midland roof-coverings are typical of the rest of the country, thatch being traditionally used wherever timber-framing or stone was used for building, particularly in those areas where stone slabs were not found. There are however lowland areas where brick houses and cottages are also thatched but these are usually of a later date, and doubtless among the most famous thatched dwellings is Anne Hathaway's Cottage at Shottery. Thatched buildings are usually limited to the rural areas as the material was banned from built-up areas because of fire risk long ago and was replaced by clay tiles or Welsh slates if there were no stone slabs in the locality, although even in these areas clay tiles appeared on many seventeenth-century buildings. Plain tiles were the most common but pantiles, which could be transported by water from the east-coast ports, were used along the Trent Valley in Nottinghamshire. The colour of the tiles always matched that of the local brick and the light-coloured tiles of East Anglia are unknown in the Midlands, but nineteenth-century mass production made standard materials available all over the country.

13

Northern England

The counties of Cheshire, Derbyshire, Durham, Lancashire, Northumberland, Yorkshire and Cumbria (formerly the counties of Cumberland and Westmorland) contain the main highland areas of England. The Pennines, the backbone of the region, cover half of the area and reach across the borders to the Scottish Highlands, while on each side are the gently undulating coastal plains. The narrow western plain is occupied by Lancashire and the much wider eastern plain includes the Vale of York and the Wolds of the old East Riding, now part of Humberside, while the Dales leading up to the eastern slopes of the Peak District each have their own character. Although stone is used for building throughout this region its colour is not uniform so that each area has it characteristic buildings, the oldest being the longhouses of the farmers on the lower slopes of the highlands. The region is mostly sandstone with millstone grit on the Pennines and limestone in Durham and North Yorkshire, with slate in the Lake District and brick clays on both coastal plains.

In the southernmost county, Cheshire, the many surviving timber-framed buildings indicate the vast numbers which were once inhabited in a county which has perhaps an exceptionally high proportion of timber buildings. Along the Welsh borders many cottages can be seen with exposed crucks although in other districts these are often concealed inside walls of clay or brick and therefore not seen from outside. The northern cruck buildings are almost always associated with mud or stone external walls while those further south have timber-framed walls rarely seen in northern counties. Probably the most frequently seen type of timbering uses the simple post and panel construction, usually dating from the seventeenth century or later, the humbler cottages having large square panels surrounded by flimsy timbering. These cottages now have the frames filled in with eighteenth-or nineteenth-century brickwork replacing the older infilling of lime plaster on oak laths which was preferred to the usual wattle and daub. In all cases these houses are distinctly "black and white", the timbers being coloured with pitch and the panels whitewashed rather than being left in the natural colours as was the case further south.

But the larger houses in Cheshire include some of the most spectacular timber-framed houses in the country, with elaborate patterns of diagonal and curved braces following the style of many in Shropshire, often with a feature not seen further south. This is where the top of the external timber-framed walls is joined to the overhang of the roof with a smooth unbroken cove uniting the walls and edge of the roof; this cove is also of curved timbers with the spaces filled in with wattle and daub or plaster-work. These date from the sixteenth century, the earlier houses having close-set vertical struts and herring-bone patterns of diagonal braces.

The centre of Chester is full of timber-framed buildings but many similar buildings can be seen all over the county, and among the largest are Little Moreton Hall, built in 1559, now owned by the National Trust and visited by thousands every year, Churche's Mansion built at Nant-wich in 1577, the sixteenth-century Soss Moss Hall, at Nether Alderley, and Hampton Old Hall at Malpas. Such houses form only a small propor-tion of the Cheshire timber-framed domestic buildings to be seen away from the industrial areas such as Crewe or further north, while at Port Sunlight, south of the River Mersey, are some of the best examples of Victorian half-timbered houses in this country; an indication of the popularity of this style of building even in modern times.

The timber buildings found within the old walled city of Chester are unique and many were originally the houses of wealthy merchants although now used for commercial purposes. These buildings, known as The Rows, have continuous galleried walkways at first-floor level forming part of the timber-framed houses built on top of vaulted base-ments at street level. Some of the timber houses in Chester date from the thirteenth century when The Rows first started to develop, although there is no apparent satisfactory explanation for this, but most of those seen today date from the fifteenth or sixteenth centuries. There was, however, much rebuilding during the Victorian period to replace missing sections of the continuous façades and perhaps the best of the older houses are Leche House, dating from the sixteenth century, with a timber front altered by the insertion of later sash-windows, and Bishop Lloyd's House built a century later. But mentioning a few such houses does not do justice to the large numers of timber-framed houses still to be seen in the city.

These houses, requiring large quantities of wood, were of course the homes of the richer people as the expensive timber was hardly used by the poorer yeomen. They had to be content with the smaller cruck sup-ports, the most widespread form of timber building in the region, while the lack of trees to supply building timber in highland areas means that the further north one goes, the rarer are sizeable old timber-framed houses. Cruck buildings certainly remained in use into the eighteenth century in some parts of the Yorkshire Dales, records confirming the existence of a number of such cottages in Wharfedale during the pre-vious century.

The coastal plain stretching from Cheshire northwards through Lancashire to Cumberland is now divided by the vast industrial conurbations forming the Greater Manchester area, all developed in the last two centuries, early nineteenth-century Manchester being a small medieval town with many timber buildings. A few of the larger ones have survived, now standing isolated in the middle of later industrial or residential developments, and looking rather out of place among red-brick factories and rows of terrace houses, often slum properties. Among these are fourteenth-century Baguley Hall at Wythenshawe, Manchester, and Ordsall Hall, in Salford, now used as a museum.

North of the industrial belt in the more rural parts of Lancashire there are no large concentrations of timber houses as in the south, but there are a few large mansions dating from a period long after similar houses were going out of fashion in the Midlands. The best are Rufford Old Hall, built in the fifteenth century as was Samlesbury Hall; the latter was extended in brickwork in 1545 making it the earliest example of dated brickwork in the county.

In Cumbria the remnants of the very few timber houses that were ever built in the area are represented by several cruck cottages of a comparatively late date, often with the timbers hidden behind brick or mud walls. Cruck cottages of this kind are not uncommon in the more isolated parts of northern England, either side of the Pennines, but there are no elaborately patterned small timber-framed domestic buildings as in the south-eastern counties.

Yorkshire forms most of the eastern coastal plain and the pattern is similar but considering the county as a whole, rather than as three separate administrative units, there is very little timber building throughout Yorkshire except in York itself. The number of small timber houses and cottages outside the city was never very large even when timber was available for building, and the survivors are to be found in the villages of the coastal plain south of the Cleveland Hills and Whitby, particularly in the Vale of Pickering and the Wolds of the old East Riding. A few cruck cottages remain in the industrial areas but many recorded in the Sheffield area during the last few years are now disappearing through modern developments. Although examples can be found elsewhere there is no evidence of a long tradition of timber building in any part of Yorkshire or further north into Durham or Northumberland.

The few Yorkshire survivors are in the rural areas to the north and east, particularly in the Helmsley – Hutton-le-Hole district, and some with crucks or close-set studs and diagonal braces can be found around Coxwold and Easingwold, and also the villages between Pickering and the coast. In the older streets and the market-place of the original port of Whitby there are still a number of timber-framed houses with the jettied upper floors leaning out over the narrow street below, but many of these have the timberwork hidden under layers of plaster or whitewash. A reconstruction of a cruck cottage, moved from another site not far away, stands in the grounds of the Folk Museum at Hutton-le-Hole, not far from Pickering. This building is thatched and typical of the smaller cottages which were once to be found on the fringe of the North Yorkshire Moors. Perhaps the thatched buildings at Etal, in Northumberland, are the northernmost of such cottages, elsewhere thatch is rare and in Lancashire rye straw was normally used in preference to other materials.

York, always the richest city of the eastern coastal plain, has the most important timber-framed houses in the area, and although many of the original timber houses were rebuilt or refaced with brick during the Georgian period there are some interesting survivals. The best are in The Shambles, the most famous street in the city and according to Dr Pevsner, "the picture-book example of timber-framed houses because it is so narrow and picturesque particularly where two timber-framed houses almost touch with their overhangs. Hand shaking anyway ought not to be difficult." There are many good timber houses in this street although somewhat over-restored, and the timbering of many is hardly original, but nowhere else in the country can the visitor gain such a vivid impression of a street in a medieval town.

York may represent the last outpost of the timber tradition because, except for isolated cases or Victorian reproductions, there is a dearth of timber-framed houses as one goes further north into the Durham coalfield and Northumberland. An unexpected oddity is the only large timber building in Newcastle upon Tyne, Surtees House, a five-storeyed, seventeenth-century, timber-framed house, five bays wide flanked by Georgian-style brick houses of the same period and suggesting the last flourish of a method of building that was old-fashioned, particularly in the centre of large towns, for that period.

The other building materials of northern England, brick and stone, are found in distinctly separate areas, a least until the late nineteenth century industrial expansion. Brick was widely used on both coastal plains, particularly west of the Pennines where suitable clays were found, while stone was exclusively used on the highlands, but where the hills sloped down towards the plains, brick and stone were often used side by side.

The earliest brick buildings are in the Wolds of the old East Riding near Beverley and Hull as some of the first brickworks in the country were established in these two places as described in Chapter 8. Since the time that the first brick buildings, like the North Bar at Beverley, appeared in the fourteenth and fifteenth centuries there has been a continuous tradition of building in brick which gradually spread north-

Castle Street, Bridgwater, Somerset. Late Georgian houses, built after the London Building Act of 1774, but the curved window heads are not typical of the earlier Georgian period

Early nineteenth-century brick house, characteristic of the Midlands, the recessed central arch feature only being found in the smaller market towns of central England. The windows have lost their original glazing bars

(*Above*) Wootton Wawen, Warwickshire. A late eighteenth- or early nineteenth-century brick farmhouse similar to those found in many parts of the Midlands

7 Lower High Street, Stourbridge, Worcestershire. Gothic Revival house of the late Georgian period

Royal Crescent, Brighton, Sussex. Regency building on a grand scale between
1798 and 1801

Sidmouth, Devonshire, a group of Regency houses typical of the newly developed south-coast resorts

Parade, Leamington Spa, Warwickshire. Regency houses built in 1836, although now largely altered internally; the front walls rendered and the window frames recessed as required under the original London Building Act of 1774 then being adopted as standard construction in most towns outside London

Houses in Clarendon Square, Leamington Spa, built in 1836 with ironwork characteristic of the Regency period

Ravenstone, Northamptonshire. An early nineteenth-century canal lock-keeper's house

Swindon, Wiltshire. The houses built in the town centre for the workers employed by the Great Western Railway Company, dating from the early nineteenth century

Hampstead, London. A group of nineteenth-century workers' houses, now altered and in demand as houses for the more prosperous middle class of the present day

Blaise Hamlet, Avon. A cottage in this 'picturesque style' village designed by John Nash, the famous Regency architect, perhaps better known for his Regent's Park buildings

The Lodge, Charlecote House, Warwickshire. A nineteenth-century Gothic romantic lodge gatehouse built in the last part of the century

The Lodge, Welcombe House, Stratford-upon-Avon, Warwickshire. A Victorian lodge with later additions

Brooke End, New Road, Henley-in-Arden, Warwickshire, built in 1909 and designed by C. F. Voysey

wards along the coastal plain with the wider understanding of making bricks from the local clays.

Naturally, most of the market towns and villages of the coastal plain, and of course York itself, have many pleasant brick houses, mostly Georgian although some are earlier, but nowhere, even in York, is the brickwork of the quality found in London. The orange-red bricks commonly used in the Vale of York tend to emphasize the regional characteristics of the houses which are just plain and straightforward, after the designs found in prosperous farming districts anywhere in the country, usually two storeys high with pantile roofs, the later ones with sash-windows, although many of the smaller houses are often rendered over to resemble stone, or heavily whitewashed.

In north and east Yorkshire the brick colours vary slightly depending on the local clay, but as the region escaped the industrial pressures of Lancashire or the West Riding, large-scale production of bricks was not established in the Vale of York as in other areas. Therefore many more houses were of hand-made bricks in contrast to the harsh red machine-made bricks in use west of the Pennines during the Victorian period, and this absence of industrial growth in what is now rural Yorkshire, prevented the market and coaching towns from expanding during that period. Fine terraces of Georgian houses may still be seen in Richmond, North Allerton, Thirsk, Helmsley, Pickering and Malton, all in their day important and prosperous towns, as well as Scarborough, then developing into a popular spa and coastal resort, and the port of Whitby. Here in St Hilda's Terrace a fine group of Georgian brick houses was built in 1779 for occupation by master mariners whose ships sailed from the port; such domestic buildings equal those inhabited by the wealthy merchants of southern England, like the contemporary houses in Leeds, Halifax, Durham or Stockton-on-Tees. These places are not usually associated with the period but all had Georgian houses, now overshadowed by Victorian developments. Further north in Durham and Northumberland there are few examples of pre-sixteenth-century brick and most brick houses are early eighteenth century onwards. In the highlands areas brick came into general use much later than in the lowlands and usually in conjunction with the local stone, for bonding together rubble walls, or for decorative purposes rather than for complete buildings.

West of the Pennines the abundance of local brick clays enabled large-scale brick production to keep pace with the needs of the vast industrial growth in Lancashire. Brickmaking from the clays of the coal measures started in about 1800 when machine-made bricks first began to appear, the most typical being the bright red ones of the Accrington district which became known as Accrington Bloods because of their colour. All the local bricks were commonly much larger than those produced further south being a full 9 × 3 × 4½ inches, a size retained in the northern counties right up to the last war.

Thousands of early nineteenth century small brick-built houses survive in the towns and villages of rural Lancashire and there are Georgian brick houses almost lost in the vast connurbation of southern Lancashire. Streets of the Georgian period are to be seen in Liverpool, Manchester, Preston and Lancaster and other industrial towns but are being steadily reduced by modern rebuilding schemes. Little remains of large-scale developments but some of the smaller northern towns have the best examples, for until recently these towns were not subject to the same rebuilding pressures as places further south, and Maryport, Whitehaven, and the villages around the Solway Firth, still have many older brick houses and cottages.

The port of Whitehaven, created almost entirely in about 1680, is the earliest post-medieval planned town in England and is changing under the pressures of redevelopment, therefore many of its eighteenth-century houses may well disappear. In 1633 the village contained only nine cottages but by 1693 the population was 2,272 persons mostly working in the local collieries owned by Sir John Lowther, who laid out the town in order to export his coal. By 1811, at the peak of its prosperity, there were 10,106 inhabitants in nearly two thousand houses, then followed a gradual decline as the collieries were worked out. The centre of the old town was built as a complete unit, laid out on a grid plan, composed of houses of the same date, making it the largest eighteenth-century development in the northern counties; a similar but smaller development followed in Maryport in 1748–9.

Further north in rural Cumberland, early small brick dwellings are rarely pre-nineteenth century, and many workers' cottages built then have become modern holiday homes, but numerous clay buildings used in particular by poorer farmers around the Solway Firth have survived from the period extending from the seventeenth century to the end of the nineteenth.

Eighteenth- and nineteenth-century writers described in some detail the clay houses they had seen over much of north-west England, for example Celia Fiennes, visiting remote areas of Cumberland in 1698, saw cottages with mud walls. Up to the early years of the last century clay cottages and farm buildings were common there in spite of plentiful local stone as these buildings were cheaper to construct. The main walls were usually placed on top of rows of stones used as foundations, or low stone walls perhaps rising up to the sills of the ground-floor windows. Some buildings also had internal crucks to support the roof coverings, originally stone slabs but later tiles or slates.

A more recent survey by Dr Brunskill, printed in Volume 10 of the

Transactions of the Ancient Monuments Society, located approximately one hundred such cottages still surviving in the Solway Firth area, particularly in the parishes of Rockcliffe, Orton and Burgh-by-Sands, all north-east of Carlisle; many of these dwellings were built before 1840 and some very much earlier.

The 'Great Rebuilding' following the increased prosperity of the farmers took place in southern England during 1570–1640 but the poor system of communications prevented ideas about new styles of building reaching the north-western counties quickly. Buildings in the south, whose design shows them to be of that period, occur in Cumbria about a century later, particularly the smaller stone houses of which the oldest are in the valleys, with variations in style and colour of stone between one valley and the next. The oldest ones were the farmhouses which were often in groups rather than isolated on the separate farms and there were few cottages until the workers' cottages began to be built near the quarries and mines newly developed during the late eighteenth and early nineteenth centuries. Northern, and especially Cumbrian, landowners were conservative in their outlook, particularly in the seventeenth century, and numerous houses and cottages built from this period onwards bear a date showing that patterns of local building were almost unchanged for quite a long time.

Either side of the Pennines the oldest farmhouses were of the longhouse type, described in Chapter 7, a type of dwelling with the barn, or byre, under the same roof as the house, the two being divided by a cross passage with one common entrance for both farmer and stock. Longhouses were traditionally used by hill farmers who did not possess large numbers of cattle, but during severe winter weather they had to be housed under cover so that this type of house remained in use in the highlands longer than on the coastal plains. In some northern areas where snow was a problem longhouses frequently have projecting stone slabs forming canopies, known as pentices, over the doorways to keep off the snow.

In the upland parishes of the West Riding of Yorkshire there evolved 'laithe houses', very similar in layout to longhouses, and these were often built into the sloping hillside where the site was a difficult one, with a combined barn and byre, known as a laithe, built with the farmhouse under a continuous roof. But, unlike the longhouses, each part had a separate entrance, that into the laithe often being a large archway to allow access for hay carts. Most surviving laithe houses are in the Halifax and Huddersfield area, and a fine group may be seen in the Malham district; although the earliest of those still standing dates from about 1650 most were built in the following century and one even as late as 1880. Very few longhouses or laithe houses remain in their original state, mostly having been converted into larger houses or two separate dwellings, but until quite recently it was possible to find unaltered longhouses in the remoter parts of Wales or Scotland, although the numbers are dwindling as changes in farming methods affect even the smaller and more isolated farms.

On the edges of the North Yorkshire moors there are other farmhouse types dating from the eighteenth-century land enclosures, and these houses have two storeys with a single-storey byre built on to one or both gable ends, so that the roofline is not continuous as in the case of a longhouse. The outline of the building was different and easily distinguishable from the traditional pattern, and other outbuildings such as barns were built away from the house in an adjacent farmyard or, as was typical in the Yorkshire Dales, isolated from the farmhouse. Almost every field in these areas is still surrounded by a dry-stone wall which also encloses a stone-built byre with a hayloft above, some of which originated in the seventeenth century, while the farmers lived away from their land in the nearby villages on lower ground more sheltered from severe winter conditions.

Sheep farming started in the Pennines in the Middle Ages, therefore woollen mills developed in the West Riding where water power was available to work the machinery. In many places large numbers of seventeenth- and eighteenth-century farmhouses and cottages had weavers' shops on the upper floor, and although no longer used, the evidence of the workshops' existence remains in the rows of long windows which lighted them. The windows often have as many as nine sashes in a row, divided by stone mullions, with wooden frames fitted into the stonework, and these indicate the thriving woollen industry carried on in the homes of weavers, some working part-time while also carrying on farming on a small scale.

The medieval farmhouses were usually of clay or timber-framing, but later the local stone was always used and as the highland stone was harder to cut than the stones further south, buildings were plain and simple looking. Only a few larger houses were of worked ashlar, the usual form being rubble giving a rough texture to the exposed stonework, with no precise courses so that many houses were rendered over to conceal the surfaces or heavily colour-washed for the same reason. This was particularly the case in the north-western coastal areas where cobbles rather than stone were often used for building, while chalk clunch was used similarly on the Yorkshire Wolds to the south. If ashlar was used it was almost always as stone quoins at the corner of the rubble walls.

A typical feature on both sides of the Pennines was to build the smaller cottages, and other farm buildings, with dry-stone walls using a technique similar to that used for the walls around the local fields. To strengthen the structure large stones were placed right through the walls, often projecting slightly beyond the main wall surface on the outside of the building; cottages with these "throughs" can be seen in the Lake District and also in the Yorkshire Dales. The use of dry-stone walls for these smaller domestic buildings is wider than commonly supposed and many cottages which look like normal stone buildings prove on close examination to be built in this way, some being rendered over after completion, but the absence of projecting "throughs" does not mean that the structure is not composed of dry-stone walls.

What distinguishes the buildings of one part of northern England from those of another are the varying and localized, different coloured stones. In Cumberland, for example, houses may be of stones coloured red, pink, brown, yellow, buff, fawn, green, grey and black while outside the Lake District most of the stone used in Cumbria was red or pink granite, sandstone of the same colours being prevalent in Lancashire especially around Morecambe Bay. On the Pennines the colours are grey or buff, the darker stones on the highlands, and pale grey limestone found in the Yorkshire Dales or further south in parts of Derbyshire. The dividing line between brick with timber and stone runs a few miles north of Derby where the limestones and millstone grits are found along with the sandstones of the coal-measures which appear in the Ashbourne district.

The Pennine millstone grit varying from dark grey to buff-coloured becomes black when exposed to the atmosphere and is hard to cut, so houses were plain and rectangular without mouldings or carved decoration until the last century, and traditionally were roofed with stone slabs of various types. These older farms are long and squat, even if of two storeys, with the staircase in a projecting wing at the rear, and the shallow pitched roofs have very little overhang. The simple styles prevailed until the nineteenth century brought better methods of cutting stone, and large pieces of irregularly shaped millstone grit or granite could be cut into squared ashlar, and the window or door jambs moulded.

In the Dales in particular, door and window surrounds in the older houses were made of three or four large blocks of millstone grit projecting slightly from the main walls, and these were the only stones in the whole building which were cut to a shape. The walls were often rendered over and painted in one colour while door and window surrounds were painted in a contrasting black or white. On later houses the door lintels often had carved patterns incorporating the initials of the original owner and the date of the building. Similar surrounds are also found in Cumbria where the local slate or granite is used, dark grey or green in colour, and always in a comparatively rough, unworked state. Invariably the early houses had small windows, usually horizontally proportioned, the larger and taller sash-windows being much later.

Formerly the roofs were covered with standstone slabs, particularly in the Rossendale area of Lancashire, while further south, slabs from the quarry at Kerridge were extensively used. Thatch was rare, and the Westmorland slate of the Lake District was much used in the form of thick heavy pieces resembling stone rather than thin Welsh slate. Depending on such materials meant that dormer windows and hips at the ends of roofs, being hard to construct, were not used until the last century when clay tiles or Welsh slates came into general use.

The plain gable ends of the roofs had low parapet walls, sometimes stepped, and stone brackets or kneelers of varying designs, used to terminate the gables at eaves level, were characteristic features of the Pennine houses. During the eighteenth and nineteenth centuries, houses also had cornices of wood or stone, supported on carved projecting brackets which also held up the wooden gutters of that period. The chimney-stacks were usually at the gable end, many in the form of large circular stacks, sometimes with ovens, but there are examples of chimney-stacks corbelled at the top of the gable wall with no brick or stonework below it. In these cases the flues would have been taken up inside the house, made of lath and plaster, but for obvious reasons most have now gone and the original corbelled stack remains on the outside of the building. The top is often finished off with two slates leaning together to form an inverted V to prevent the strong highland winds from blowing the smoke down the flue.

Although longhouses are the most widely distributed buildings designed to shelter men and beasts under one roof they are uncommon just south of the Scottish border. In Cumberland and Northumberland, within 20 miles of the border, there are stone houses of a type unknown elsewhere except for a few along the Welsh borders. These are a kind of defensive tower house known as Bastel or Pele towers, the word pele meaning an enclosure. Such houses are not easily dated but the first was built about 1267 and others followed up to the seventeenth century, for the borders were still troubled by Scottish raiders. There were numbers of these houses resembling either square or rectangular towers, their average size 36 feet by 20 feet, their walls between 3 and 4 feet thick, with two or three storeys. The main living-room occupied the first floor with bedrooms above if a third floor existed, and the floors were connected by a spiral staircase in one corner starting at first-floor level. The first floor was normally undivided and had a fireplace at one end with a few small windows for ventilation. Access to the first floor was by a ladder leading up through a hole in the centre of the stone vault which always covered the ground floor. In Bastel houses the undivided ground floor was always used for cattle which entered by a single narrow doorway in one end, with slots set in a deep reveal to take a door, and the only other openings were narrow slits to provide ventilation for the cattle. In later houses the ground floor was often used for living accommodation, never having been used for anything else.

The Northumberland volume of the *Buildings of England* series contains a list of one hundred and fifty possible Pele towers but few have survived and all have been altered or incorporated in larger houses during the last two centuries, often hiding their origins.

One distinct group which never housed cattle can be identified as Vicars' Peles, houses used as vicars' residences and always situated near churches, which were also subject to attack from the northern raiders while the vicars had to protect themselves in defensive towers. Those surviving in Northumberland include the Pele towers at Corbridge, built about 1300, and during the fifteenth and sixteenth centuries others appeared at Alnham, Elsdon, Embleton, Ford, Ponteland and Whitton. Most of these have, more recently, been extended or now form part of modern vicarages.

But many of the cottages admired nowadays in the Yorkshire Dales and other northern areas which are assumed to be farm workers' cottages are actually dwellings formerly occupied by the thousands of miners or quarrymen who once lived in the area with their families. Many of these cottages were built in terraces and therefore the rural cottages of northern England, especially when built for miners, were of a more uniform pattern than those further south. During the late eighteenth and early nineteenth century increasing numbers of labourers needed houses as many mines were being sunk in that part of Yorkshire in places that have now become depopulated rural areas, showing little trace of past industrial activity.

Such cottages followed an almost standard plan of two rooms side by side on the ground floor and two rooms over, creating a long, narrow house with the staircase either in a projection at the rear or in between the two rooms. The chimneys were always at the gable ends, and the rooms were as low as practicable to keep the height, and therefore the cost of the building, as small as possible. The first cottages and houses had long and low windows with a special type of sliding sash peculiar to Yorkshire, the familar sash-window appearing later and usually only on the ground floor.

Another feature of northern rather than southern England was the laying out of model villages where all the houses were built by wealthy landowners or industrialists anxious to provide better living conditions for their workers. The first of these, Whitehaven, was followed by villages at Blanchland in Northumberland, built by Lord Crewe in 1752 to house lead miners, then Harewood in Yorkshire and Lowther in

Cumbria, both started in the 1760s. The first houses at Etal in Northumberland came late in the eighteenth century and at Bamburgh the first cottages, in the "Tudor" style were begun in 1800. One of the most famous of these villages, Saltaire, was established in 1853 by Sir Titus Salt on the banks of the River Aire near Bradford, and Port Sunlight was built later in the same century.

Another feature of northern England was the "discovery" of the Lake District by Victorian travellers after which large numbers of houses and hotels were built based on the "Swiss cottage" style, with large overhanging eaves, low pitched roofs, turrets and elaborate barge-boards as well as other decorative features, and may still be seen overlooking the Westmorland lakes.

14

The Georgian House

The Georgian house, found throughout the country even in many of the smallest villages, and readily distinguished by the simple brick elevations, incorporated, after about 1700, the newly invented sash-windows. So popular were these houses that it has been estimated that even today about a million are still in use and, allowing for the numbers demolished in recent years, it can be seen that during the years 1700 to 1830 more houses were built than in any previous period, all classes of people living in houses of a similar style, the only difference being the size.

These houses originated from the rigid requirements of the fire laws, first introduced in London after the Great Fire of 1666 and copied elsewhere when people found such houses fire-proof as well as fashionable. To understand why this style was so widely used one must look at what was happening before 1666, as the fire laws in force after the Great Fire included only the best building practice of the time in an Act of Parliament which proved successful, unlike many previous Acts of the same type.

In 1615, when Inigo Jones was appointed Surveyor to James I, the City of London had many timber buildings and an old-fashioned appearance compared to the rest of Europe where the classical ideals of the Renaissance were appearing in the buildings of the period. Inigo Jones's opportunity came when he designed the Queen's House at Greenwich, a house still existing as part of the National Maritime Museum. With its plain brick front this building was unlike any others in London, its windows tall and narrow, unlike the low horizontal windows of the earlier timber-framed buildings. The proportions of the windows were similar to the later sash types, the openings divided up by a vertical mullion with the horizontal transom about two-thirds of the way up, the spaces being filled with leaded lights; these at first had rectangular panes and later diamond-shaped ones. (*See* Figure 14.) About the middle of the seventeenth century these casement windows were replaced by sliding sash-windows and although it is uncertain who invented this window, it is believed that they were first used in this country at Chatsworth House between 1676 and 1680, and soon afterwards in such buildings as the Banqueting Hall in Whitehall and the later extensions to Hampton Court Palace.

Such was the impact of the new style that in 1630 the Duke of Bedford, starting to develop his land outside the City of London, adopted it for the construction of the Covent Garden Piazza. Here the plain brick houses were built in terraces forming an open space on the Italian pattern, the first in England, although such squares were already familiar to many noblemen who had been on the Grand Tour.

Very little of the piazza survives to show what it looked like although the north-west corner does indicate the original design greatly admired by the king, so that other influential people started to build similar housing schemes in the surrounding areas. Great Queen Street close by was laid out with these red brick houses, complete with tall and narrow casements and a classical cornice made of wood at eaves level, forming continuous terraces on both sides of what was the first "street" in London, using the word in the modern sense. In the following years similar streets were built as a speculation, to let or sell. This was the dawn of the "spec." builder; previously houses had always been built for a definite person and although such schemes halted during the Civil Wars, they re-started after the Restoration, particularly in the Bloomsbury area.

All these developments on land outside the overcrowded City could only be carried out by persons who had enough influence to obtain from the Crown licences to build, since Queen Elizabeth, James I, Charles I and Cromwell had all issued decrees to restrict building in or around London, with little or no success. An Act of 1605 issued by James I decreed that all new houses within the City were to be of brick or stone and none could be built outside the walls within a distance of one mile. Two years later this distance was extended to two miles and new buildings were only allowed if being built on existing foundations or within a courtyard of an existing building, the first hint of future overcrowding. So ineffective were these decrees that in 1615 yet another effort was required; this time no licences for any type of building were permitted while those already being built had to be finished by Michaelmas of that year or a fine was incurred. A three-year period of grace was, however, given before all existing licences were revoked in 1618.

Such was the demand for houses near London that building soon started again and in the following year James I issued another decree for builders in an effort to prevent illegal, poorly constructed houses springing up in any available space both inside and outside the City walls.

For the first time precise rules for the control of building began to appear in a legal form proclaiming, among other things, that:

> if the saide buildings do not exceed two stories in height then the walles thereof shall be of the thickness of one brick and halfe a brickes length from the ground unto the uppermost part of the said walles. And where the build-

ings shall be [over] the height of two stories the walles of the first storey shall be the thickness of two bricks length and from hence to the uppermost part of the walles of the thickness of one brick and half a brickes length.

All rooms on the lower floor had to be 10 feet high and those above, including all half storey or attics in roofs, 7½ feet; it is interesting to note that three hundred and fifty years later, and before metrication, the minimum floor to ceiling height allowed under modern building regulations was 7 feet 6 inches. The minimum distance allowed is now 2.3 metres (7 feet 7½ inches), which shows only a minor variation from the decree of 1619.

This decree also required the other walls, jambs and heads of the openings to be formed before the windows were fixed, and bay windows or projecting floors, traditional in the earlier timber-framed buildings, were forbidden. Uniform types of elevations resulting from these regulations were very similar to those which were first built in the Covent Garden Piazza. The window openings were higher than their width at the end of any rooms, with a sufficient "peere of bricke" left between the windows for strengthening the structure. A year later a further proclamation confirmed the earlier standards and required the piers between the windows to be not less than half the breadth of the windows themselves; this indicates how building laws influenced the external design of houses of the period, which was impossible when timber was the normal building material.

Such regulations for new houses were useless regarding the vast number of timber-framed buildings crowded inside the City walls and in other medieval towns throughout the country. Inevitably people began to find ways around the statutory requirements, obviously on a large scale, so that in 1625 Charles I had to issue yet more rules forbidding the digging of cellars for rooms below ground level and the construction of dormer windows to light rooms in roof spaces. The restrictions on new buildings within 2 miles of the City were repeated except for those in brick or stone being built on existing foundations; yet another unsuccessful attempt to replace the existing old timber-framed houses.

The digging of cellars had to be controlled because as brick became obligatory for building, the clay dug out of cellars was moulded into bricks and burnt in temporary kilns on the site. Under such conditions poorly burnt bricks were produced and used in the walls of houses being built above the cellars, and by the early seventeenth century there was a lot of evidence that such practices were becoming widespread. The proclamation, issued on 2nd May 1625, also dealt with the making of bricks, controlling all stages of their manufacture as well as fixing the prices at which the bricks could be sold. The finished bricks had to be $9 \times 4\frac{3}{8} \times 2\frac{1}{4}$

inches in size.

Five years later Charles I tried even tougher measures by trying to imprison all workmen engaged on new buildings without licences if within 3 miles of London; the attempt failed as a survey of 1637 discovered four hundred and fifty culprits and over thirteen hundred houses which had been built without licences. Yet in spite of all Charles I's failures to control building, Cromwell tried in 1657 without success and further Acts passed after the Reformation also failed. Yet such efforts were necessary to try and control the outward spread of London, and all other large towns, and the threat of large-scale fires was always present when large numbers of timber buildings were crowded into confined spaces inside City walls.

In the early seventeenth century there had been large fires in many places including London, Northampton, Marlborough and Bury St Edmunds which preceded the Great Fire, the one chiefly remembered. After the Great Fire the Rebuilding Act was approved by Parliament on 8th February 1667 and, as well as dealing with the re-arrangement of some roads, this Act also controlled the rebuilding of the houses, imposing stricter regulations than ever before to ensure that the new buildings were as fire-proof as possible.

Under this Act four classes of houses were to be allowed; houses of the first and least sort, facing streets and lanes, were to be two storeys in height, the height of the rooms on both floors being 9 feet. Houses of the second sort fronting streets and lanes of note as well as the River Thames were three storeys high, the rooms on the two lower floors being 10 feet high with 9 feet being allowed on the upper floor. Houses of the third sort in the principal streets, of which there were only four, were to be four storeys whilst the fourth sort of houses, the largest standing in their own grounds, were to have the same number of floors. In both cases the two lower floors were to be 10 feet high, the next floor 9 feet and the upper floor 8½ feet. In all cases cellars and garrets were permitted, the minimum height for these to be always 6½ feet. These larger houses also had to have an external balcony at first-floor level, a feature which continued throughout the Georgian period. (*See* Figure 21.)

The Act was based on the idea of new houses being built as continuous terraces forming a frontage along both sides of a street and the construction was also standardized with the precise thickness of the walls at various heights in the building being fixed, depending on the type of house being erected, as were the sizes of timbers to be used for floors and roofs. These sizes were set down in tables at the end of the Act and followed what was considered good practice at that time. In three-storey houses, the walls up to first-floor level usually had to be two and a half bricks thick, otherwise they were to be of two bricks' thickness, with one

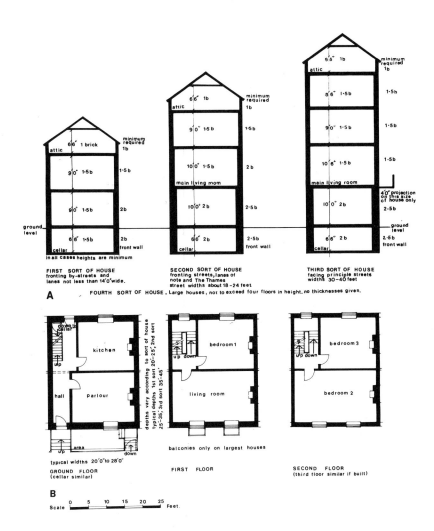

Fig. 21 London Building Act of 1667. Standard houses types which were later used throughout the whole country: A. wall thicknesses and room heights; B. typical plans which later became standard for all Georgian and Regency houses

and a half bricks to garret level and above this no less than one brick. The party-walls in superior houses were usually as thick as the external walls, but in the first and poorest quality houses slightly thinner dividing walls were permitted. No wood was to be placed within 12 inches of the front of any chimneys and all joists at the rear were to be at least 6 inches from the flue, and no timbers were to be used inside any chimney or in the walls around the actual flues. All these, and many other, structural requirements were observed in all the better-class houses right through the Georgian period, although building standards were certainly lower for the poorer houses, particularly in the Victorian period.

Although the internal layout was not originally standardized this tended to become so in time due to the limitations of the sites and building acts, the plan being in effect the same for all classes of houses although poorer houses had smaller rooms and cheaper internal finishes. The better-class terrace houses had almost always a 24-foot frontage, the building itself being the same depth, a square shape on plan and this became almost standard throughout the country as the London houses were eagerly copied in other cities and large towns, and there are very few places in the British Isles not possessing some Georgian houses. In all terrace houses there was a room at the front and back, on each floor, the stairs being at one side of the rear allowing the front room to be the full width of the house on the upper floors. On the ground floor a passage led from the front entrance to the staircase, resulting in slightly smaller rooms on this floor. As the houses were built in terraces the flues serving the fireplaces had to be placed within the party-walls, often back to back with those of the adjacent houses, forming recesses on both sides of the fireplace filled with cupboards or shelves. (*See* Figure 21.) During later periods additional accommodation was achieved by building annexes projecting from the backs of the houses into the garden space.

The plots, typical of those of the medieval period, were long and narrow, the width varying from 12 feet to the usual 24, and most new houses had basements formed by a shallow excavation, the depth being fixed under the Rebuilding Act. The garden level at the rear was usually at approximately natural ground level, but the road in front was made up to a new level, therefore an open area in front of the house was essential to allow light into the basement windows; the wall in front of the area helped to retain the road in place. (*See* Figure 21.)

The 1667 Act almost designed the individual house, standardizing the height of the storeys throughout all new houses built in the City and fixing the relationship of the ground floor and street levels. So successful was the pattern that similar designs appeared in many parts of the country soon after the Act came into force, many towns adopting similar building acts for their expansion. The requirements of the Act were so precise that once details of the site and levels of the adjacent road were known builders could easily estimate the cost of building a house in one of the particular classes. All agreements between owners and builders could just use the phrase "according to the Act for rebuilding of the second sort of building", or the third sort, etc., and all this made the rebuilding of the City easier as well as maintaining high standards.

Wood was banned from the outside of all houses except for beams over openings in the walls, and for this oak had to be used, as even then it was realized that oak withstood fire better than softwood. But this wood was so scarce that the Privy Council allowed the importing of timber in order to reserve oak for shipbuilding and the substitution of fir for oak was later allowed. In 1608, for example, the New Forest had 123,000 oaks suitable for the Navy, but a century later the number was down to 12,000 and building a ship needed 4,000 oaks.

Before the Fire most houses were of timber, filled in with wattle and daub, many of the exteriors plastered over completely which helped to protect the timber framework from fire damage in minor outbreaks but was useless in the case of major fires. Even less fire-proof were the poorer houses of thin weather-boarding on a light timber frame, as by this period wood in suitable sizes for building was very expensive even if available. Some timber buildings in the area unaffected by the Fire survived for a long time, but most have now vanished; the only timber-framed building in London dating from before the Fire is Staples Inn in High Holborn which is well outside the City, a building which has naturally been heavily restored, particularly in the last century. In the City and surrounding districts, old timber houses were supplanted by paved streets and lanes lined by terraces of brick houses built to a standard height and design, with few variations in the external appearance, similar terraces appearing throughout the country in the following decades.

The question is, why should this particular Act have achieved so much success when all previous attempts to improve building standards had failed? Firstly, because the Act was more detailed than anything previously attempted and fixed everything possible; besides the construction of the houses it fixed the position of cellar flaps and the laying out of the first sewers. Even though untreated waste was discharged direct into the River Thames, this was better than tipping it into the streets.

The City commissioners abolished the projecting jetties at the upper levels of buildings and dealt with the laying out, paving and levelling of the streets. It was necessary to raise the street levels to allow them to drain properly, as well as to prevent the muddy conditions and the rubble from the fire-damaged buildings from stopping the passage of traffic through the City. Rules for the pitching and levelling were issued in 1667, followed by more detailed procedures in 1671. The narrowest streets had to be a minimum width of 14 feet to allow two carts to pass, but exceptions were allowed where this was impracticable, and as all houses were of a standard size and layout new parts of the City had almost no slums; later, overcrowding caused many of these houses to degenerate into the slums familiar to Victorian writers and philanthropists.

The key to the Act was undoubtedly the appointment of the first building surveyors, the start of a system which has continued without interruption up to the present. This Act specified the fines to be imposed for contravention of the various sections, while "knowing and intelligent persons in building" were appointed to detect infringements, resulting in the banning of "jerry-building", for if no controls had existed cheap, badly constructed, badly sited houses would have been put up, recreating the overcrowding which preceded the Great Fire. Charles II recognized that without inspectors the Act would have been as powerless to stop building in the suburbs as the previous attempts, and with a proper system of inspection, backed by a series of administrative procedures, a partial success was attainable and rebuilding could start promptly.

Probably the most difficult problem when building terrace houses, if each site is owned by a different person, is how to deal with "party-walls", those essential walls dividing one house from another and normally built partly on each site with the boundary line running through the centre of the wall. Two party-walls, one at each side of the house, are necessary if a terrace house is to be built and if all the houses are not built simultaneously there are problems over which owner should carry out the work and who should pay the costs; without the settlement of this problem no building can proceed.

The Rebuilding Act overcame this problem by allowing for the party-walls to be set out only by one of the City surveyors at a fee fixed at 6s. 8d., which was a considerable sum in 1667. When each builder was ready he went to the City Chamberlain, entered his name and the place of the site in a register and paid his fee, and was given a receipt to take to the surveyor for his district, who set out the foundations of the wall. If one building was put up before those on the next sites the owner was entitled to build the party-wall on both sites and recover half the cost of the work from the other owner when he started to build. Since it was illegal for a party-wall to be set out by anyone else, and as there was a register of licences, it was possible to check all the new houses being erected within the City walls and so prevent almost all illegal building.

In the Stuart period the height of a town house was related to the width of the street it faced, while the proportions of the windows were fixed, all the casements being fixed flush with the front face of the external walls;

the frames were wide and the glazing bars quite thick when compared with later windows. All roofs were steeply pitched and of plain clay tiles while just below the overhanging eaves was a wooden cornice of classical design; the only other exterior ornamental feature was the surround to the entrance door, again of classical design.

While terrace houses could have four floors, most detached houses had two, the chief rooms being on the ground floor whereas in terrace houses these were on the first floor, a constant characteristic of the Georgian period. Many detached houses also had attics lit by dormer windows forming a feature of the roofline, each covered with a small pitched roof, giving a triangular gable over the window itself, typical of the small late seventeenth-century manor-house. Few of these detached houses had basement rooms, but where they did they were not completely below ground level, so that the floor above was raised several feet and the front entrance reached by a flight of steps.

It is therefore possible, at least in London, to date precisely houses of this pattern, whether terraced or detached, to the years between 1667 and 1707 when the next Act of Parliament changed the regulations which affected their external design. It is impossible to date similar houses elsewhere in the country as accurately as in London, since it took some time for them to become fashionable in the distant northern counties. It is certain that houses of this type are always the oldest houses of the Stuart and Georgian period in any particular district even if they were built a century after the style first appeared in London.

The Act of 1707 was preceded by a tax, first imposed in 1695, which affected house design, even if negatively. In that year the Window Tax first appeared and all houses having more than six windows, as well as being worth over £5 per annum, were taxed for each additional window. This tax was increased several times in the following century and not finally repealed until as late as 1857, and the detailed tax returns afford a picture of the standard of housing and the wealth of the residents of most English towns during the eighteenth century, many of the new spa towns, like Bath, paying more tax than the medieval towns. The tax was quite severe and in 1747 any surveyor making false returns could be fined £100; quarterly payments were demanded from each house having between ten and fourteen lights at 6d. each window, between fifteen and nineteen at 9d. each, while twenty and above paid 1s. each. All houses with less than ten windows were exempt although every inhabited house in England was taxed 2s. annually.

Some of the larger houses still have blocked windows which obviously existed before the introduction of the tax, as once this was in force builders would only use the minimum number of windows. Where windows have been blocked the spaces remain either as recesses in the brickwork, sometimes rendered with imitation windows painted on, or with the window frames in place and blocked by building walls inside. As most smaller houses were exempt the number of windows blocked because of tax is less than might be expected in the average Georgian and Regency house. Frequently the blank windows expressed the need to maintain symmetry, an essential feature of Georgian design, and dummy windows sometimes appeared on front elevations, especially when a square or terrace was being developed as a complete unit. There are also examples of internal walls or even party-walls running behind the middle of dummy windows proving that the buildings were designed in this way, and most of the blocked windows seen in spa towns are of this type rather than being due to tax.

The 1707 Act introduced other changes which included arrangements for fire-fighting for the first time, and detailed the thickness of the party-walls. Eighteen inches thick at basement and ground-floor level, 13½ inches above this, the party-walls were to project 18 inches above the roof-covering to prevent the spread of fire, for the first time interrupting the continuous roofline so that individual dwellings became obvious from the outside. More significant was the abolition of wooden eaves cornices, up to that time a prominent feature; in the words of the Act: "no cornice of timber or wood under the eaves shall hereafter be made or suffered", so the roof was thereafter hidden behind a parapet wall with a cornice of stone, brick, or later stucco, a little way down from the top of the wall at the approximate level of the original eaves. In later Georgian terraces the parapet walls were raised into a pediment over the central houses, particularly when stucco covered the frontages.

From this year can be dated the typical Georgian, rather than Stuart house, with its brick elevation rising to a parapet wall, the only ornament being the cornice, the first-floor balcony and the elaborate door surround at the entrance. At this time the windows, whether casements or early examples of the sliding sash-windows were still fixed without reveals, which dates such houses in London to between 1707 and 1709 when a new Act was passed by Queen Anne. It was decreed that from 1st June of that year no door-frame or window-frame of wood to be fixed in any new house or building should be set nearer than 4 inches to the outside face of the wall. (*See* Figure 22.) Thereafter reveals to windows appeared, first in London and later throughout the country, but C.F. Innocent, writing in 1916, stated that in some country districts frames were commonly set flush with the outside of the wall until the Model Building By-laws were introduced early in this century. This change to setting back the frames originated not from fashion but from yet another effort to prevent fire spreading from one house to another through the window openings. About this time also the tall narrow casements of the

Stuart period gave way to the sliding sash which then became a character-istic of all Georgian houses. These windows were in general use in London as early as 1688 when in the *London Gazette* an advertisement offered "glasses for sash windows" for sale. The provinces were more re-luctant to use such windows but they were known in Yorkshire in 1702 and Oxfordshire in 1728.

Sash-windows became so fashionable that nineteenth-century la-bourers were known to object to casements in their cottages, consider-ing them to indicate an inferior social status, which makes accurate dating of ordinary small houses difficult without other evidence.

Normally these windows had two equally sized sashes, although some of the larger windows had two unequal sections, the lower often being two-thirds of the height. The proportions varied depending upon which floor the windows were used; on the first floor where the reception rooms were situated the windows often reached almost from floor to ceiling and the height was twice that of the width, these windows allowing access to a balcony outside. On the upper floors windows were smaller, and although the widths were the same the heights varied, diminishing in size from the first floor upwards. Richard Neve in his *Compleat Builders Guide*, written in 1726, tells us that for middle-sized houses windows would be 4½ to 5 feet wide and double this in height for the first storey. The windows for the second may be one third part lower than the first and the third storey one fourth part lower than the second, the widths being the same. In smaller houses the window heights are always between one and a quarter to one and three-quarters the width, the tallest windows dating from the Regency period.

The first sashes were kept open by a series of hooks or by using wedges to hold up the lower sash, the top being fixed, a practice common in smaller houses until well into the last century. Later windows were kept open by a series of counterbalancing weights held by cords over pulleys fixed into the frames. This method was thought to have been introduced from France but the first patent in this country for such a mechanism was granted in 1774, while the first fastener, the barrel type with screw and spring, was patented in 1776, followed by many different types right up to the present.

The earliest glazing bars were substantial, cut by hand out of solid wood and it is often possible to estimate the date of the sash by looking at the thickness of the individual bars which became thinner after the middle of the eighteenth century. The thinnest ones occurred in Regency buildings when the bars were often no wider than an eighth of an inch on the outside face; in such cases the bars were often kept in place by the glass fixed between them. The earliest frames do not have mitred joints to the surrounds or joining the glazing bars which were fixed with

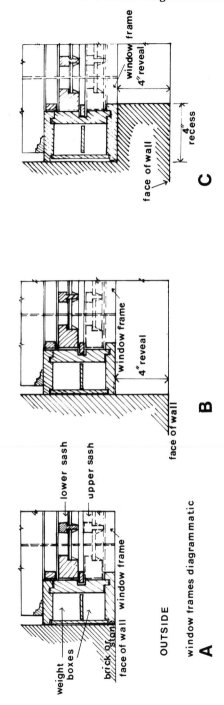

Fig. 22 Sash-windows as fixed in Georgian houses: A. window frame flush with face of wall as allowed under the Rebuilding Act of 1667; B. window frame set back 4 inches as required under the Rebuilding Act of 1707; C. window frame set back 4 inches as well as in a 4-inch recess as required under the Rebuilding Act of 1774

square joints, the wood being thickened out to form blocks in the corners. The first frames were massive in construction as the whole frame, including the groove for the weights, was worked out of solid wood and it was only later that the weight boxes formed part of the jamb itself, constructed of separate jointed members giving a much lighter window and economizing on timber.

Sash-windows were subject to the strains of being raised and lowered and their general use only became possible as glass-making techniques improved during the early eighteenth century, although the invention of better machinery for moulding and planing wood was important as the glazing bars had to be made to fine limits.

Window glass, first made in this country by the Romans, was reintroduced in the early medieval period by French glass-workers who, according to Bede, came in 675 to glaze the church windows at Monkwearmouth and taught glass-making to local craftsmen. Even in the sixteenth century greased linen cloth was still being used to cover the windows of the poorer people's homes instead of costly glass, and where glass was fixed in the form of leaded lights, the fixed panes were regarded as part of the property but opening casements were valuable and belonged to the tenant, who could remove them when he left.

Roman glass was cast in slabs, pieces as large as 28×21 inches having been found, but during the medieval period it was made only with difficulty being blown so that the sheets were small and irregular in size and thickness as well as being slightly tinted due to impurities in the silica sand used to make it. In the Tudor period diamond-shaped or rectangular lattice panes were the only type of glazing used as these pieces were the largest size it was possible to cut out of the blown glass. The small panes were held together by strips of lead packed with tallow to keep out the rain, and these larger sections were fixed to iron saddle bars keeping the glass in place and strengthening the window.

Up to the early nineteenth century most glazing was in crown glass which was blown into circular discs up to 5 feet in diameter and the lump in the centre created by this process was discarded as useless when the usable glass was cut. These lumps, cheaper than clear glass, may have been used for glazing windows by poorer people, but such glass was certainly not used for the windows of larger houses. It is a fallacy that such bottle, or bullion, glass was used in all Tudor buildings but, to give an air of quaint authenticity to many others built at a much later date, such glass has been widely reproduced for glazing the now popular Tudor-style windows.

Crown glass, still found in some old buildings, is recognizable by its pale, light-blue colour, caused by impurities in the silica sand, and the faint concentric rings which can be seen on the surface. The earliest crown glass was French but during the seventeenth and eighteenth centuries Newcastle upon Tyne, Bristol and Staffordshire were the most important sources in Britain apart from the Lambeth works in London. This glass was expensive and according to Neve the cost in 1726 was about 8d. a square foot; normally it was not used outside its own immediate locality unless it could be transported by water to avoid breakages, for taking glass by road was risky because of the unsatisfactory surfaces and the carts available. The cheapest glass in London and the most widely used in southern England was from Newcastle upon Tyne as, owing to unusual circumstances, it was the only glass easily transportable by sea. The glass was packed with straw into frames or crates and brought to London in coal ships which regularly traded between these two ports. The crates, set on end, were packed in the coal to more than half their depth which kept them steady and prevented them from falling and being broken due to the motion of the ship. Even after being transported in this way the cost of Newcastle glass was as low as 6d. per square foot, in comparison with London glass costing 2d. more.

Glass was also produced by the cylinder method, practised by the Romans and reintroduced during the medieval period. By the seventeenth century improved manufacture enabled sheets large enough for sash-windows to be made. Cylinders of flint glass were blown and, while still hot, were cut longitudinally with iron shears and then opened up onto a smooth iron plate, coated with sand, forming flat sheets as the glass cooled. Lucan Chance improved the method in the 1830s and eventually became one of the country's largest glass manufacturers, supplying glass for the Crystal Palace in 1851. The cylinders of glass were allowed to cool before being cut with a diamond cutter and then reheated, allowing the curved glass to be flattened onto a sheet of smooth glass instead of an iron plate. Perhaps the best way of recognizing pieces of old cylinder glass is by the impurities and bubbles, which appear parallel and elongated rather than curved as in crown glass.

Both types were eventually replaced by cast glass, first introduced into England in the late seventeenth century and made by pouring molten glass onto a heavy iron table coated with sand. This glass, made on a large scale as production techniques improved and continued well into the present century, was in turn replaced by glass made by more modern methods such as the continuous drawn or rolling processes.

At this period grey or brown bricks were generally used in London with red rubbed bricks forming arches over the openings, the bricks needing to be fine in texture and soft to allow cutting, and most of these bricks came from near Windsor where suitable clay was available. Little changed until 1739 when a statute decreed that bricks made within fifteen miles of London had to be $8\frac{3}{4} \times 4\frac{1}{4} \times 2\frac{1}{8}$ inches and so the standard four courses of brickwork to 11 or 12 inches became established.

In the last half of the eighteenth century other Acts were passed to improve building standards, among them the 1764 Act aiming to abolish all bonding timbers in brick walls. This succeeded only in the larger cities, as this method of building persisted until the end of the last century in isolated places where builders thought that such timbers helped to strengthen brickwork, increasingly badly built during the Victorian period.

Although Welsh slates became preferred to roof tiles about 1700 the outside appearance of town houses remained almost unchanged until the next important building Act of 1774, the first to introduce "status" into housing as well as to enforce most rigid fire-prevention measures. These had a considerable influence on the appearance of the new houses of the period. Under this Act houses were put into separate categories or "rates", each having specific limits placed on their value and size; thus a "first rate" house was one valued at over £850 with a floor space over "nine squares" of building, which is nine hundred square feet, while at the other extreme was the "fourth rate" house valued at less than £150 and occupying less than three hundred and fifty square feet, in both cases excluding all outbuildings.

In all there were seven "rates", six covering houses and the other workshop buildings. The second rate houses were of a value between £300 and £850 with a floor space of between five and nine hundred square feet. The third rate was for houses valued between £150 and £300 with a floor space of between three hundred and fifty and five hundred square feet. Rates for the fifth and sixth classes were for detached houses and need not be considered here.

Each "class" or "rate" had to conform to its own structural code regarding foundations, thicknesses of external and party-walls, and the positions of windows in the outside walls. These eventually became the minimum requirements of the speculative builders when erecting new houses, particularly those to be occupied by less wealthy people. This Act tended to produce standard types of houses as the requirements of each category allowed few variations in the internal layout, so that second, third and fourth rate houses became standardized throughout the country during the next fifty or so years. This Act did provide a minimum standard of housing for poorer families, at least when only dimensions were considered, but since there was no legislation about overcrowding, conditions did not greatly improve. The smaller houses were more and more shoddily built as the rents they produced were very low but even so overcrowding reached such proportions that later in the nineteenth century the Public Health Acts were brought in to ameliorate housing conditions in the major cities.

The 1774 Act, as well as restricting the use of ornamentation such as projecting cornices and exposed timberwork, also required window frames to be concealed in brick reveals, or recesses, at least 4 inches deep as well as being the same distance back from the front face of the walls. The whole of the frame, apart from the sill, had to be concealed in this way to prevent the spread of fire from adjacent houses and so only a small strip of frame was visible when the front elevation was studied. This again enables such houses to be dated later than 1774, as obviously the full width of the frame was exposed, either flush with the face of the wall or set back with a 4-inch reveal depending on the date of the house.

Bay windows and shop fronts were allowed to project only 10 inches or less from the face of the building depending on the width of the street. This resulted in the shallow bays surviving in some older villages and towns where the urge to modernize has not been great enough to cause their replacement with the present semi-circular "Georgian-style" bay window projecting much further than the original true Georgian bay window. But as this Act did not relate the height of the houses to the width of the street, like the Rebuilding Act of 1667, many streets built after 1774 tended to be dark and gloomy, always being in the shade of the large houses lining both sides.

This was the last important building Act of the eighteenth century but throughout that century and the nineteenth it was difficult to achieve any improvements at all in the construction of new houses, particularly those intended for the poor classes. The problem was so intractable that many contemporary writers drew attention to the serious defects and overcrowding of the smaller houses in both urban and rural areas.

Many of the defects resulted from skimping the work in order to build houses as cheaply as possible, a practice often forced on the builder by the inflated price of land and materials due to the Napoleonic Wars which dragged on for over twenty years from 1793 to 1814, during which period building costs almost doubled. To cut the costs, the party- and rear walls of houses, in many cases three or four storeys high, were often erected to the height of a whole storey, and in extreme cases to the full height of the building, by the less skilled workers before the front wall was added by skilled bricklayers, perhaps the only ones capable of producing the fine brickwork worthy of being exposed to view. This was not a new practice as in 1678, nearly a century before the 1774 Act, Joseph Moxon writing in his *Mechanick Exercises*, an early book on building, mentioned the "Ill custom of some bricklayers to carry up a whole storey of party walls before they work up the fronts that should be bonded with them". While there is no doubt that in the case of the larger houses brickwork on the front elevations was of a very high standard, as may still be observed, this was often a sham, hiding inferior work at the rear. Building the front and rear walls at different times produced problems in bonding the work together, often leaving many structural cracks where this was not properly done, and investigations have revealed examples where the front wall was not even keyed into the rear walls at all, leaving a straight joint right up the building at the junction of the front and party-walls. This was concealed internally by plaster and outside hidden by the next house in the row, or in later houses concealed by stucco, in which case the brickwork was even shoddier as all defects could be covered up. It must be remembered however that such houses have survived for over two hundred years, standing today and still in use as houses or offices, and they have lasted very much longer than anticipated by Isaac Ware, an architect of the eighteenth century, who wrote in 1735:

> The nature of the tenures in London has introduced the art of building slightly [flimsily]. The ground landlord is to come into possession at the end of a short term and the builder, unless his grace ties him down to articles, does not choose to employ his money to his advantage. . . . It is for this reason we see houses built for 60, 70 or, the stoutest of the kind, for 99 years. They care they shall not stand longer than their time occasions, many to fall before it is expired; nay some have carried the art of building slightly so far that their houses have fallen before they were tenanted.

Other problems were caused by using "bonding timbers", many of soft-wood, in foundations where beams placed at the base of the wall just above the footings took the full weight of the brickwork, and when the beams decayed the whole building started to settle. This practice of attempting to strengthen poor brickwork by inserting timbers in apparently casual positions in the walls was pointless; usually the result was a weakened building. In 1678 Moxon recommended it to builders at a time when brickwork was increasingly used for new homes, in what we now call the Stuart and Georgian styles, therefore many of these houses were badly built. In spite of all contradictory evidence, builders were convinced that bonding timbers helped to strengthen brick walls and in 1796 the Foundling Hospital governors feared that buildings construc-ted for them in London had "insufficient bond timbers to hold them together and therefore the walls would be apt in settling to give way and separate". This practice persisted well into the nineteenth century until stopped by the enforcement of stringent building standards.

During the middle of the seventeenth century home-grown hard-woods became very scarce and from then onwards fir and pine became the most widely used timbers, causing great problems during the Napol-eonic Wars when supplies depended on imports from Scandinavia or America. The trade was well organized to cope with the emergency as

Scandinavian deal was used as early as the thirteenth century, but the modern trade in imported squared logs really dates from about 1738 when the first book on the subject was published. Seventeenth-century imports from the colonies were mostly Spanish mahogany, and mahogany planks from the West Indies first appeared in this country in 1774, but the cheaper deal was most frequently used for building work, encouraged by the invention in 1791 of a mechanical planing machine. White deal was used for almost all internal fittings, floors, doors and windows, a practice starting in the 1770s, so that in 1790, 200,000 loads of fir were imported, rising to two million by 1846.

Shortage of timber, and joists smaller in section, meant that from the seventeenth century timber had to be used more scientifically and economically. This sometimes resulted in poorly constructed floors so that some leases of early nineteenth-century houses contained a condition "that there shall be no dances given in them".

Formerly, oak floor joists had been larger than really necessary and the rectangular timbers had always been laid on their side which, it is now known, was the weakest way to use them. From the time of Wren it was realized that using rectangular softwood joists with the longer dimension upwards made the most of the structural strength of the timber, and it was found that the size of the timbers could be reduced, so from then onwards floor joists have always been used in this way.

This in turn produced changes in the interior of houses as the small sections of softwood used for supporting the floors were unsuitable for exposure to heat; the wood warped and twisted and it became increasingly common for the undersides of such floors to be covered with plaster ceilings. Plaster had been known for many centuries, though not often found in smaller houses up to this period, and medieval building records show that purchases of lime and sand were among the commonest entries in the accounts, these materials being essential for mortar and also for plasterwork. This was a skilled craft and when Henry III visited Paris in 1254 he noted the elegant houses covered with plaster made from the material found under Montmartre, giving the name "plaster of Paris" which is still used. Much English plaster was made from local materials chiefly found in the Isle of Purbeck, near Knaresborough in Yorkshire, and along the Trent Valley, and was used for finishing walls, for flues, fireplaces and floors. Very little medieval plasterwork survives and only in the more important buildings as it was too expensive for general use. During and after the Tudor period royal palaces had elaborately moulded ceilings of plaster but it was not used as a wall and ceiling covering in the smaller houses until the late eighteenth and early nineteenth centuries. Elaborate plaster ceilings as seen in many "stately homes" were abandoned for a simple moulded cornice around the top of the walls in the main living-rooms of Georgian houses, but this was missing from the poorer houses. It became so fashionable that even oak beams, and moulded timber ceilings, were covered over, surviving intact under the later plasterwork until rediscovered in modern times. One guide to the age of a ceiling is the type of laths used; older ones were riven – rent or split – from trees by hand and therefore are thick and uneven in shape. The regularly shaped, sawn laths still used today were first introduced during the Victorian period, and indicate that the ceiling is later than the mid-nineteenth century.

The interior of a house changed with the use of softwood joists and plastered ceilings, the outside, when slates started to supersede tiles in the Georgian period and were used country-wide until at the end of the nineteenth century machine-made tiles appeared. Slates had a long history, certainly having been used by the Romans, and in south-west England were quarried even in the twelfth century, being taken by water to Winchester where their use was recorded in 1160. The medieval use of slates was largely restricted to the localities where they were quarried or places easily reached by water.

The Romans certainly obtained slate in North Wales but the industry expanded during the eighteenth and nineteenth centuries, the main quarries of Penrhyn and Dinorwic exporting most of their slate through the port of Bangor. The largest quarry in South Wales at Prescelly was worked for over four hundred years up to the 1950s but Delabole in Cornwall is perhaps the oldest quarry, producing since 1555, and the Westmorland quarries have a life of three hundred years. But even during the Georgian period slates from anywhere except North Wales were too expensive for general use and Welsh blue-grey slates became the predominant roof-covering. The Penrhyn quarry started in 1765 and by 1792 that one source produced 12,000 tons of slate annually, perhaps equalled by Dinorwic.

Slates were originally fixed with oak pegs in the same way as stone slabs, but from the seventeenth century onwards fixing by nails became the general method. Welsh slates were produced in a number of regularly shaped stock sizes and about 1750 were given the titles of ladies of the aristocracy, allegedly by General Warburton, the proprietor of one of the largest Welsh quarries. These names, commonly used until well into the present century, are singles, the smallest at 12×8 inches, ladies, viscountesses, countesses, marchionesses, duchesses, princesses, empresses, imperials, rags and queens, the largest at 36×24 inches.

Slates permitted shallower roof pitches than were possible with plain tiles; with the largest slates it could be as low as thirty degrees, and as the sizes graduated from the largest at the eaves to the smallest at the ridge, rain was kept out more efficiently than with tiles. Softwood joists planed to regular sizes were developed successfully during the Victorian period, giving many special roof trusses, thus achieving larger spans with the minimum amount of timber. The fact that slates were lighter than stone slabs or tiles enabled timber to be saved, according to an advertisement in the *Sheffield Courant* of 1827 which stated "the advantages of blue slates are many and important, being more durable and so light that 24 cwt. will cover 60 yards and great saving in timber is also effected making a difference of 5d. per square yard after allowing for a good substantial roof".

So the pattern of the typical Georgian house was set and adopted by all classes of people, with the result that for over a century all inhabited similar houses, a thing unknown in the rest of Europe. Standards of accommodation were strictly regulated but little was done to ensure hygiene; very few houses had water laid on, even less had any form of drainage, and not until the mid-nineteenth century could various Public Health Acts enforce better standards of hygiene. In the Georgian period what drains existed were of brick and laid just under the floors of the cellar giving little protection in the case of leaks which were frequent. The concealed drains were often badly constructed, leading to brick-lined cesspits in the rear yard or garden. In some larger towns drains were connected to public sewers in the roads and the untreated sewage was always taken to the nearest river, in London, for example, the Thames.

The privy was at the end of the garden, or at the rear of the house, and methods of disposal were primitive until the first w.c. was patented by Alexander Cummings in 1775, the first reliable one being produced by Joseph Bramah three years later. These might have been fitted into first and second rate houses but others had to depend on the cesspits emptied at night, and though the houses had fashionable exteriors conditions inside were not improved until the widespread development of public drainage systems during the late nineteenth century.

Although the building Acts controlled the style and construction of Georgian houses the regulations allowed the use of stone for houses as well as brick and in many cases where stone was the natural building material local stone was used. All that has been said in this chapter applies equally to stone houses, the finest examples of which are the terraces, crescents and squares of Bath, mostly built during the early Georgian period.

At this time many owners, feeling that timber-framed houses were beginning to look rather old-fashioned, began to modernize them by inserting sash-windows in place of the small medieval casements, even though this meant cutting through the timber framework to create openings large enough, weakening the framework and causing future structural problems. False brick façades added to the front of timber-framed buildings are quite common and the superficial front is hard to detect from the street if the house forms part of a continuous row. In many medieval towns, for example Warwick, brick-fronted Georgian houses still have timber-framed buildings behind the brick façade, while some detached timber houses have been cased in brick on all four sides.

After sash-windows had been inserted there were other ruses to conceal the timber frame, and boards, tiles and lath with stucco were all used, sometimes all three on the same building; but brick was generally used on the lower floor, particularly in Kent and Sussex.

The last change affecting houses of this period was probably in 1784 when a brick tax was imposed to provide funds to fight the American War of Independence. Amounts ranged from 2s. 6d. per 1,000 bricks up to 4s. in 1799, and even higher in 1803 when 5s. per thousand was charged for small bricks and 10s. for bricks not larger than 150 cubic inches; large bricks $10 \times 5 \times 3$ inches originated in that year being exactly the maximum size allowed. The tax was finally repealed in 1850 but as it related to numbers rather than size it had resulted in the development of bricks larger than the normally acceptable $9 \times 4\frac{1}{2} \times 3$ inches, 121 cubic inches. Bricks twice the normal size were certainly used in Leicestershire and Hertfordshire; during the 1780s buildings in Lincolnshire had bricks measuring $11 \times 5 \times 3\frac{1}{4}$ inches, and some as large as $12 \times 6 \times 3\frac{1}{4}$ inches have been discovered.

The brick tax also made tile-hanging popular on walls or timber framework, as roof tiles were untaxed, and having first started in the southeast of England during the late seventeenth century this soon spread, particularly in Sussex, Surrey, Berkshire and Hampshire. At first plain titles were used but Victorian manufacturers produced many types of ornamental tiles especially for this purpose. Slate-hangings, longer established and popular in the Stuart period, continued well into the nineteenth century in Devon and Cornwall. The tax also made other cladding materials desirable, including weather-boarding, examples of which still exist in the Weald of Kent and Essex, but was then rarely seen elsewhere. These boards with feather edges were laid horizontally, overlapping at the edges; oak and elm were unpainted but during the Georgian period the more commonly used softwood was painted or tarred.

Perhaps the most interesting and effective covering developed as a result of the brick tax is the late eighteenth-century mathematical tiles. The origin of the name is obscure, but the tiles were so well made that their use invites the closest inspection and many think the buildings on which they are used are of brick. The tiles fit one above the other so that only the lower section moulded in the shape of a brick shows, and the upper part holds the tile in place by being nailed to the battens or to the timber framework of the house being modernized. The joints were then pointed up to resemble brickwork convincingly as it is possible to stagger the tiles to form an imitation bond; Flemish bond, created by a combination of whole and half tiles, was commonly used, English bond but rarely.

These tiles were widely used between 1784 and 1850 and although the brick tax was repealed their use continued until the middle of the last century. Mathematical tiles were not cheap and as a result were largely used for the better-class houses although small houses covered in this way can be found, but the majority of examples date from the early nineteenth century. As might be expected these tiles were normally found in areas where bricks were made, the tiles being made in the same type of kilns. Being a thin veneer the tiles are harder to detect on a terrace of houses as the awkward problem of dealing with the corners disappears, but normally the ends are stopped by boards or by quoins of wood painted to imitate stone, while 9×4 inch angle tiles are also used.

Tiles of this type are restricted to the southern counties as far west as Salisbury and as far north as Cambridge, being rarely seen north of the Thames Valley except for a few isolated examples in Durham and Nottinghamshire. The principal centres are Brighton, Canterbury, Lewes, Marlborough, Rye and Salisbury.

Perhaps the popularity of the Georgian house was best summed up by Louis Simond writing his journal of a tour and residence in Britain, dated 1810: "These narrow houses, three or four storeys high – one for eating, one for sleeping, a third for company, a fourth underground for the kitchen, a fifth perhaps at the top for the servants – and the agility, the ease, the quickness with which individuals run up and down and perch on the different storeys give the idea of a cage with its sticks and birds."

15

Regency and Victorian Houses

Jacobean and Georgian buildings were laid out with rigid symmetry but during the Regency there was a reaction against such formality and houses generally acquired a more light-hearted and frivolous air. The Regency period as applied to buildings does not correspond exactly with the constitutional Regency, as this architectural style lasted throughout the following reigns and well into the years of Victoria's, buildings becoming less formal and generally less well built. In the Georgian period columns, pilasters, cornices and other similar features laid out according to classical principles were reproductions of the originals. On Regency buildings these elements were used as decorative features in ways unknown in classical times, while features from other cultures and civilizations – Egyptian, Assyrian, Indian and, later, Chinese – began to appear, often jumbled together on a single building. The size and layout of houses hardly varied from those of the earlier period, but Georgian straight lines gave way to the use of curved walls, bay windows, iron balconies and other decorative features.

Nothing odd was seen in brick buildings being disguised as stone by using stucco, or "Roman" cement, which was left in its natural colour similar to that of stone; it is the whims of later generations which changed the original appearance of these stuccoed houses by painting them in the so-called "Regency" colours. Early in the nineteenth century brick was out of fashion, being associated with industrial buildings and workers' cheaply built houses so that anyone of consequence – and many who were not – wanted a house of stone. If they could not afford one or already had a brick house, this was often covered with a thin veneer of stone either when the house was built or long afterwards, and those who could not have stone had to be content with a stucco imitation of the real thing. This finish was being commonly used in the expanding Regency towns such as Cheltenham and Leamington, two spa towns developed long after Bath, the first of them all, with its stone-built houses. Stucco also appeared on many houses in the coastal resorts of Brighton, Hove, Scarborough, Sidmouth and Weymouth, among others; most of these houses date from the 1780s to the 1830s when brick again became fashionable.

The first really successful rendering was patented by a Swiss named Lardet in 1773 and the famous British architects, the Adam brothers, acquired the patent rights and used it copiously, after which it became known as Adam's Patent Cement. Similar products subsequently included one invented by Mr Dahl in 1815, followed two years later by Hamelin's cement.

These renderings, which were not cement as understood today, frequently failed in practice, for if the rain penetrated the bond weakened, especially if the oil dried out, with disastrous results. Therefore as a preventive most of these buildings were finished with limewash since oil paints were not in general use until the 1840s. These protective materials also included Johns' "patent permanent stucco wash and paint", developed by Ambrose Johns, who was granted a series of patents in the years 1806, 1838 and 1839 for compositions for covering and facing houses.

Many of the later "Regency" houses were covered with stucco of a composition similar to lime mortar as used for the brickwork, this being porous enough to allow any rain to dry out from the outside surface. Later on, problems were often created when the original stuccoed surface was covered with impervious oil paints so that any dampness behind the coating could not dry out, but most early stucco houses still have their original covering, although occasionally it may have been replaced by a rendering based on the use of Portland cement.

The first manufacturer of natural cement was James Parker of North-fleet under patents granted to him in 1791 and 1796. He burned the calcareous clay nodules found in the shale, or embedded in the shoreline around the coast of Essex and the Isle of Sheppey. This material, when mixed with water, set rapidly and as it kept out water it was widely used mixed with sand as a coating for damp walls. It acquired the name Parker's Roman Cement, although it was unlike the original Roman materal, being a substance somewhere between lime mortar and later Portland cement. As the demand for "Roman" cement increased, nodules were dredged up from the sea bed, but the raw materials became scarcer and by the 1840s this cement had almost gone out of use.

Portland cement is the modern equivalent, so called because its colour resembles Portland stone, and it was invented by Joseph Aspdin of Leeds in 1824. It was made by burning slaked lime, or chalk, and clay and after pounding up the resulting clinker, the mixture used with water and sand formed a hard-setting mortar suitable for bricklaying. It was made around the lower reaches of the Thames and Medway where suitable raw materials were plentiful and it is still made in these districts on a very large scale, the manufacture being based on various successive patents, including one of 1852 granted to Patrick Anaspie.

The stucco-covered houses of the Regency and early Victorian periods are easily recognizable and distinctly different from the earlier houses. The floor heights and window sizes are still those of the Georgian period, but the front walls of many houses were formed into shallow curved bays often running the full height of the building. The shallowness of these bays contrasts with the large semi-circular bays of the Victorian house, the windows still having sash bars and small panes and there are many decorative mouldings, cornices and plaster pilasters or columns.

Speculative builders, then beginning to operate on a large scale, could therefore produce impressive-looking houses by using cheap bricks covered with stucco, leaving more money available for features such as curved front walls, semi-circular bay windows, window shutters and broad overhanging eaves to the shallow pitched roofs typical of the period, which were achieved by the mass production of larger and thinner Welsh slates. Wrought- or cast-iron balconies, canopies, porches and railings, as well as smaller items like scrapers, door-knockers and lamps are undoubtedly characteristic and attractive features of the "Regency" house, many of which still grace the spas and seaside towns which developed during the early years of the nineteenth century. Hundreds of the Regency bow fronts, often extending up the whole height of the house, remain in Regency spa towns or coastal resorts like Brighton. The bow front could be either segmental, or semi-hexagonal, and used not only in connected terraces but also for individual free-standing villas.

During the Georgian period it became fashionable to put the main living accommodation on the first floor of a house and later the large windows used in these rooms opened onto balconies, often considered essential by the London Building Acts which required the structure to be fire-proof. This obviously required the use of iron for balconies and, apart from railings, these were the first ironwork features to appear, soon becoming used on a wide scale throughout the country. Usually these balconies run the full width of the house, but there are also examples of separate smaller balconies, one outside each window, instead of a continuous structure. The ironwork of the Georgian period used classical motifs, mainly Greek, with very formal designs being based on the palmette, volute, acroterion, acanthus leaf and the Greek fret, all standard decoration on classical buildings. All of these appeared in, and were copied from, numerous eighteenth-century pattern books which included drawings of Greek buildings, many produced by designers like Robert Adam, who visited Greece and measured the actual buildings. In contrast "Regency" ironwork used motifs based on scrolls, circles and many naturalistic features such as flowers, leaves, vines and all kinds of foliage, followed later by designs based on Gothic arches, Egyptian motifs and the popular Chinese fret pattern. All were very free adaptations of the originals rather than faithful copies, and the Chinese patterns stemmed from the great eighteenth-century interest in the products of the Far East. These designs, adapted to English taste and applied imaginatively not only for ironwork but also furniture and buildings, are part of the style now called "Chinoiserie". Many examples can be seen on houses which have the balconies covered by concave-shaped roofs of copper or lead, the shape suggested by the curved roof line of a Chinese pagoda, or the English version of this type of building the most famous one being the pagoda still surviving in Kew Gardens, dating from *c*.1757.

There were very many designs, some variations on well-tried patterns and others entirely original, but comparatively little is known about the designers and manufacturers of this very fine metalwork requiring great skill to make. Mostly made for purely decorative purposes, much of it had functional use, the balconies for sitting on or for use when cleaning the windows, while the smaller essential items such as door-knockers were at the same time transformed into objects of considerable beauty. Some of the original pattern books survive but considering the quantity of ironwork made there are very few, and most of them are in the collections of the Victoria and Albert Museum and the Coalbrookdale Museum which is housed in old buildings once part of the iron-foundry which flourished on the site of Abraham Darby's ironworks, one of the earliest sites of the Industrial Revolution.

Among the surviving pattern books are those of Robert and James Adam dated 1769, Isaac Ware's, issued from 1725–56, I. and J. Taylor's dated 1795, Isaac Bottomley's of 1793 and one from the Birmingham firm of M. and G. Skidmore in 1811, one of the few issued by an actual manufacturer apart from those of the Carron Company, iron-founders, of Falkirk. One of the most comprehensive was C. N. Cottingham's *The Smith and Founder's Directory* of 1823, but this merely reproduces the work of other designers, including those of the Carron Company, and very little information is given in any of the books regarding the names of the designers or makers responsible.

A larger number of firms obviously made decorative ironwork to order as well as general cast-iron products; this was certainly the case with the Coalbrookdale Company, but more research is required if the names of many of the manufacturers of this ironwork are to be established, and it was certainly made on a wide scale, often in small foundries in places not usually associated with the iron-making industry. At one time or another the spa towns of Bath, Cheltenham and Leamington all had their own local iron-founders and the ironwork of these spas has been the subject of recent studies by local historians. In Bath it appears that the largest quantity of ironwork made during the early years of the town's development came from two firms a considerable distance from the spa, the Carron Company of Falkirk and the Dale Company of Coalbrookdale.

The Dale Company made bridges and other large castings and also made most of the balconies and iron fireplaces up to the 1830s but undoubtedly the Carron Company had the strongest countrywide influence on the design of the ironwork used on the houses of the Regency period. The firm, founded in 1759, had as one of its directors John Adam, the brother of the famous architect Robert, who was responsible for the firm's original neo-classical designs, many published in his own pattern book in 1769. The Carron Company's ironwork was widely used not only in Bath, Cheltenham, Dublin and the new town of Edinburgh but also in most of the newly developing coastal resorts which were following the later London fashions in building.

Robert and James Adam built the Adelphi in London in 1774 and one of the houses forming part of this development, No. 7 Adam Street, was probably the earliest to have balconies cast by Carron's using the "heart and honeysuckle" pattern copied later by many of their competitors. In his 1823 Directory Cottingham included it as one of the patterns then being widely used in London. Two heart-shapes face the centre of the panel with formalized honeysuckle flowers on either side and it was so popular that the Carron Company kept it in their catalogue until 1868 at least.

Like all ironwork the "heart" pattern was made in standard panels of varying widths so that balconies could be made up for almost any type of house. The design, perhaps the most typical of the period, was in such demand that in Cheltenham, for example, one hundred and thirty-eight of the surviving houses show it in their balconies dating over a period of at least twenty years, although not all of this ironwork was made by the Carron Company. That this type of decorative ironwork was made on a large scale cannot be in doubt, as some patterns which appear in spa towns like Cheltenham and Leamington are found all over the country, other patterns are only found in a small group of towns, not necessarily all close together, and finally there are the rarer designs found in only one town.

Before the railway this ironwork was certainly transported by water, the Carron Company's own ships serving London and other ports whence their products travelled farther inland by river or canal. Ironwork cast in Falkirk came to Cheltenham via Bristol in this way, while much of the Leamington ironwork came from the newly developed foundries of the Black Country, whose ironmasters obviously supplied other Midland towns in the same way.

By the early nineteenth century most of the larger towns had their own local iron-foundry making all types of products, but rarely with enough skill to make the elaborate ironwork required for the houses of the Regency period. The greatest demand came from the newly developing spa towns so that was where the most skilled founders were established with the experience to copy the patterns made popular by larger companies as well as develop their own individual designs.

At the same time that Regency towns were acquiring their elaborate houses, surveys published by the Board of Agriculture at the end of the eighteenth century revealed bad rural housing conditions, mud cottages still being common throughout the country except in Kent where brick was generally used. These labourers' cottages, hardly more than hovels, were often worse than the cattle sheds or stables built to house the stock, and most were replaced during the following century so that very few small "Regency" cottages still exist and certainly none in its original state.

Many other writers had described the appalling conditions so that landowners began to realize that the agricultural labourer and his family needed better housing and many new dwellings were built near the more important estates whose owners made better provision for their workers. The first rows, as opposed to individual cottages, appeared during the middle of the eighteenth century in the more prosperous districts, and in giving evidence to the enquiry into the sanitary conditions of the labouring population of Great Britain, a century later in 1842, J. C. Loudon said, "The cottage should be placed alongside a public road as being more cheerful than a solitary situation and in order that the cottager may enjoy the applause of the public when he has his garden in good order and keeping."

New villages were also specially built by landowners improving their parks, the new landscaping often requiring the removal of complete villages to allow such schemes to be carried out. Outstanding among these were Blanchard in Northumberland built in 1752 to house lead miners employed on Lord Crewe's estate, followed in 1760 by Harewood village erected by Lord Harewood, and Sir James Lowther's new village at Lowther in Westmorland, and during 1761 the Oxfordshire village of Nuneham Courtenay on Lord Harcourt's estate.

These villages had a formal layout based on the squares and crescents then appearing in Georgian towns throughout the country. They were the exception rather than the rule and many contemporary observers thought them rather old-fashioned even when newly built, hoping for more informality perhaps along the lines suggested by J.C. Loudon in his *Encyclopaedia of Cottages, Farms and Villa Architecture*, written in 1836, in which he states that "houses should never be put down in rows, even though detached, unless the ground and other circumstances are favourable for a strictly regular or symmetrical congregation of dwellings. There is not a greater error in forming artificial villages than always having one side of the buildings parallel with the road".

It became fashionable therefore to design estates and houses in the "picturesque" manner to look as natural as possible, like the landscapes being painted by the artists of the late eighteenth century. The houses had elaborate porches, carved barge-boards at the eaves of the shallow pitched slate-covered roofs, bay windows and casements of the "Gothick" style based on medieval Gothic windows but really nothing like the originals, rising in popularity as the Gothic Revival affected all classes of property owners. The achievement of Regency builders was in employing new materials in new ways and this freedom allowed them for the first time consciously to design buildings for their appearance rather than for the structural limitations of their materials. They began to adopt the styles of other civilizations for decorative purposes which frequently resulted in the addition of quite inappropriate features such as arches, pinnacles and domes to existing houses, or building copies of structures such as Greek temples, particularly as lodge-keepers' houses at entrances to estates.

Pattern books published by late eighteenth-century architects illustrated picturesque houses and cottages which were neither classical in design nor conformed to the formal patterns of the previous Georgian houses. The picturesque movement is not easy to define but James Malton in his book *An Essay on British Cottage Architecture* published in 1798, suggested that "such buildings should try to preserve the vernacular by adopting the peculiar mode of building which was originally the effect of chance". This required new houses or cottages to be irregular-looking with walls of unequal height, projecting windows and eaves, all to achieve the effect of accident, and the idea that irregularity was essential to make a building interesting prevailed throughout the Victorian period.

The first village demonstrating picturesque principles was Blaise Hamlet near Bristol, designed by John Nash, the Regency architect, for J.S. Harford, a Quaker banker. This hamlet, now in the care of the National Trust, built between 1810 and 1812, consists of nine cottages, eight single and one double, arranged in an undulating line around a green. All the dwellings are different, some being thatched and some tiled, in a determined effort to create dissimilarity. This village made an immediate impact and though small became a model for other villages, such as Edensor, in Derbyshire, built in 1839 for the Duke of Devonshire. Laid out by Paxton, it was an attempt to copy the Blaise Hamlet type of artificial village with solid brick and masonry houses of various architectural styles. The buildings include Swiss chalets and Italian-looking houses such as Loudon commended in his encyclopaedia published three years earlier, and there are also Jacobean gables, barge-boarding, Norman window surrounds and Tudor chimneys.

The first book to discuss this fashion, Sir Uvedale Price's *Essay on the Picturesque*, set out in 1794 the principles of the picturesque doctrine, if so vague an idea can be defined. Numerous other works followed, some more practical than others, all containing plans to help a landowner to design and build his cottages to suit his fancy. Other works included Plaw's *Rural Architecture*, 1794, Pocock's *Architectural Designs for Rustic Cottages and Picturesque Dwellings*, 1807, and J.B. Papworth's *Rural residences, a series of designs for cottages, decorated cottages and small villas*, published in various editions from 1818 to 1832. The architect P.F. Robinson was a prolific writer whose books included *Rural Architecture, or a series of designs for ornamental cottages*, 1823, and *Ornamental Villas* and *Villa Architecture*, both published in 1837. Though many contained plans of cottages already built, there were also many unpractical designs for "ornamental cottages" which were hardly homes for labourers, and were both difficult to build and almost impossible to live in.

Many of these unusual buildings were in the "cottage *orné*" style, the early nineteenth-century name for something difficult to describe. When the term was first used is uncertain but Joseph Gwilt's *Encyclopaedia of Architecture*, also early nineteenth century, defined it as "a building only subject to the rules which the architect chooses to impose on himself", giving a wide scope to the imagination. These romantic "picture-book" houses were usually one-and-a-half storeys high, the roofs, particularly the thatched ones, having undulating eaves instead of the straight lines of earlier buildings, and french windows opening onto cast-iron verandas, or cast-iron Gothic-style casements partly filled with coloured glass. But unlike genuine labourers' homes these had outbuildings for the owner's horse and carriage.

The growing middle class, consisting of the wealthier professional or tradespeople cherished the ideal of life in a romantic thatched country cottage, a sentiment still prevalent today, ignoring the real squalor of the labourers' dwellings which these wealthy families, and their servants, did not have to endure. As life in a small country cottage was no longer a social disgrace, provided the cottage was sufficiently ornate, the demand increased for residences smaller than the grander manor-houses so that most small country houses date from this period onwards. This is reflected in Jane Austen's novels, and other writers of the period extolled the "cottage" as a country dwelling in contrast to the owner's town house; many of these rural dwellings had as many rooms as a farmhouse of several generations before.

Enthusiasm for the picturesque produced villas in the most unsuitable places, provided the view was romantic, and houses were often perched on hilltops or other exposed sites. Malvern, the Peak District, areas near the coastal resorts of Devon and Cornwall or up the sides of Welsh valleys have many villas with names like Prospect House, Bellevue, Mount Pleasant, Montpelier, Belmont, and "Groves" of various kinds, such as Ivy or Willow Grove, unknown before the last century.

Gothic Revival, or "Gothick" houses, first appeared in the mid-eighteenth century following the passion for romanticism and mystery suggested by the medieval abbey ruins still surviving throughout the country. The first writer to discuss this revival was Batty Langley in his book *Gothic Architecture Restored and Improved*, printed in 1742, but the earliest houses were of course those created from the original ruins and many manor-houses became called "abbey", though their connection with an ancient religious house was tenuous. Abbey ruins, even when altered, made inconvenient dwellings so new houses were built, or earlier Georgian houses remodelled in the "Gothick" manner; the word "Gothick" is now applied to this imitation Gothic style which in reality was only a fanciful version of the original.

Although there were a few Gothic Revival houses in the early eighteenth century the person who undoubtedly made the style popular was Horace Walpole, fourth Earl Orford, and the youngest son of Sir Robert Walpole, who having acquired a house at Strawberry Hill by the Thames at Twickenham, began remodelling it in the early 1750s, taking twenty years in the process; his success commemorated whenever the style is described as "Strawberry Hill Gothic". At this time, however, "Gothick" was used only for small garden buildings, summer houses, mock ruins or entrance gates; Strawberry Hill was the first known example of its application to a complete house.

Strawberry Hill was the home of an eighteenth-century gentleman, it was essentially a Georgian house ornamented with details from the fourteenth and fifteenth centuries. The outside was almost untouched apart from some additional Tudor chimneys, Gothic windows and battlements, but the inside was covered with medieval ornament used purely for its decorative value, all cribbed from ancient sources but copied as accurately as was possible at that time. Scale was disregarded, the original design being increased or decreased in size to suit its new application, and certain medieval tombs, from places like Canterbury Cathedral, or altars and screens, may be recognized in doorways, bookcases and ceilings, all reproduced in plaster to create a visionary world.

Soon after the Strawberry Hill remodelling began similar schemes were carried out at Bishopthorpe, in York, in 1765, now the home of the Archbishop, and in 1776 at Milton House, near Didcot in Berkshire, but the most notable was the remodelling of Arbury Hall, in Warwickshire, famous for its associations with George Eliot. This house is one of the finest examples of early Gothic Revival houses in England; work on the earlier sixteenth-century house continued from 1750 to 1796, and was on a larger scale than that at Strawberry Hill.

Originally the Gothic Revival was fostered by the wealthy or the well-to-do and the fashion spread, following Walpole's example, and was fed by the romantic writings of the period, particularly those of Sir Walter Scott whose first novel appeared in 1814, all set in ruined abbeys or mountain scenery. Those who could not have a new house built in the style adorned their parks with sham ruins, or little villas, mansions or fake castles. The richer landowners demolished the houses and cottages of their Georgian ancestors and rebuilt extravagantly in the Gothic style, or in Scotland using the "Scottish baronial" style, so that on estates like that of the Duke of Westminster, in Cheshire, almost all existing buildings both large and small, date from the nineteenth century.

Such Gothic dwellings, regardless of size, had battlements, and occasional cross-shaped windows imitating the medieval archer's loophole, while traceried windows and small circular towers were essential for larger villas. Most popular was the faithfully reproduced Norman keep, but the sash-windows in the towers disclosed the true origins and date. Many such fake castles appeared in Scotland and Ireland during the last half of the nineteenth century but with few exceptions the earliest examples of the style are Georgian houses with Gothic ornamental additions to the original structure, only skin deep.

Up to 1820 only houses were built in this way, but it became the Victorians' most favoured style after it was used for the new House of Commons, started in 1836, and was chosen for many ecclesiastical and public buildings. But there were failures and Fonthill illustrates the worst excesses of the style. The owner wished to build a "ruined convent" as a country retreat, but the building evolved into an abbey, a vast gimcrack place impossible to live in. Started in 1795 and finished in 1822, then opened for public inspection when Beckford sold it to pay his debts, it was certainly badly and flimsily built; much of the house was in the form of "theatrical scenery" being of timber and plaster, so the huge central tower collapsed in a storm in 1825 and the rest of the house was demolished a few years later.

A few lesser houses were built in the Indian style but the only sizeable one remaining is at Sezincote, in Gloucestershire; much of the detail is authentic for the owner, Samuel Cockerell, had lived in India. It was finished in 1805, ten years before John Nash began his famous remodelling of the Royal Pavilion at Brighton, with unique results. This residence, taking ten years to build, was completed in 1825; afterwards Nash worked on Regent's Park, Buckingham Palace, and many less noted country houses in various styles throughout the land. Nash achieved a great variety of contrasting buildings before he died in 1835, and a reference to his use of stucco is recorded in the lines:

But is not our Nash too, a very great master,
He finds us all brick and leaves us all plaister.

By 1862 tastes had changed and James Fergusson writing in his *History of the Modern Styles of Architecture* said, "Nash was prepared to build pagodas, pavilions, Grecian temples, Gothic Castles, Gothic churches or abbeys suited either for suburban residences or manorial dwellings – anything at any price; for if stone or brick were too dear brick noggings and lath and plaster or stucco would produce the most splendid effects at the least possible price", and this undoubtedly emphasizes the flimsiness of many of the buildings of the Regency period.

Nash's buildings around Regent's Park were superb examples of architectural scenery; the front elevations of the terraces finished with stucco created impressive-looking buildings, the backs of which were plain unadorned brickwork. These groups of identical houses had a classical appearance, plaster columns or pilasters at intervals breaking up the long uniform frontages, the individual blocks linked together by triumphal arches leading to the stables at the rear. The blocks, built between 1822 and 1827, were finished after Nash's death, but the detailing was crude and clumsy, slightly sham and badly built, a discovery which caused alarm when the terraces had to be reconstructed a few years ago. But the distant effect was to provide a romantic background to the park in which fifty villas were to have been built, but this part of the plan was never completed although Nash laid out the neighbouring Park Villages, east and west; only part of the eastern group has survived but the western village is intact.

This was one of the most influential residential developments of the early nineteenth century, these villages heralding all subsequent picturesque suburban developments right up to the present day. These houses were in Italian, French, Swiss, Gothic and other less recognizable styles but the important feature of the design allowed two houses to be joined together to look like a single villa. The dwellings, similar in size and plan, were all pairs of semi-detached houses, a type previously suitable only for labourers' dwellings, but Nash made this type of house acceptable to well-to-do middle-class families by designing the two houses to look like a single unified and rather impressive villa, even if small in size. This was achieved by giving the pairs of houses a central feature, such as a pediment, gable, carved panel or fake windows, almost anything which would conceal the fact that the single block contained two houses not one.

Thus began the age of the villa, a name which, during the nineteenth century, finally meant any house slightly out of the ordinary, with a suggestion of architectural pretensions. The name was certainly applied to any house, excluding the purely classical ones, during the 1780s, half a century or so after the English versions of the original symmetrical classical houses of the Italian Renaissance began to appear. Precise copies of these, the true villas, first appeared early in the eighteenth century, the most famous of which, Chiswick House, was by Lord Burlington in 1720, and still exists, in the ownership of the Department of the Environment. These were followed in the nineteenth century by smaller and less faithful copies of the original buildings, usually with two main storeys, unlike the earlier Georgian houses. The basement was eliminated, or where it existed was partly built above ground so that the main floor was approached up a flight of steps from the garden level. The main living-rooms also had communicating doors instead of being individual box-like rooms as formerly.

The first villas in this country were small luxurious houses situated in open country on the outskirts of towns and surrounded by large gardens planted with shrubs and trees, but many became surrounded by crowded streets as the towns expanded rapidly during the Victorian period. Afterwards the "villa", or rather its name, descended in the social scale so that by the 1870s almost every small semi-detached house acquired the title.

After the suburbs of London the best places to see villas are the spa towns where many Italianate villas line the tree-shaded roads, usually dating from the early nineteenth century. By then they were usually asymmetrical, stucco-covered, in Tuscan style with low pitched roofs, wide eaves supported on ornamental brackets and often with a flat-roofed tower at one corner or over the main entrance doors. They survive in the outlying districts of Bath, Cheltenham, Leamington Spa, and coastal resorts such as Sidmouth and Weymouth.

These houses represent the beginning of the end for stucco-covered buildings although the tradition lingered on during the later Victorian period, when some artisans' terraced houses had stucco up to first-floor level to hide the poor brickwork underneath.

During the early eighteen hundreds, brickwork fell from favour as a building material for better-class houses, for the public now associated brick with the poorer workers' houses, all types of industrial buildings, and canal and railway warehouses. These functional buildings, now objects of admiration, were considered by affluent people at the time of building, to be plain and ugly, and it was not until the 1880s that opinions began to change encouraged by the very influential writings of Ruskin. In *The Stones of Venice*, 1852, he suggested that wherever possible buildings of all types should be ornamented with patterns of coloured bricks, the glazed ones being the most popular. As a result decorations of polychrome brickwork brightened the more prosperous industrial towns and cities and even the smaller houses or cottages had simple, coloured-brick string courses at eaves level and often around window and door openings.

This revived fashion for brick coincided almost by accident with a rapid increase in population which may indeed have stimulated the interest, so rows of brick houses, often badly built, appeared wherever building land was available. The impact on towns and cities meant that between 1860 and 1870, 53,000 new houses were built in England and Scotland, while in the following decade, 1870–80, the number rose to 80,000.

Mass-production methods coped with the demand for vast quantities of bricks thanks to machines developed throughout the nineteenth century by the inventive Victorian brickmakers, so output doubled during the period 1850–1900. Men, women and sometimes very young children were engaged in this, working in filthy conditions for as long as fifteen hours a day moulding bricks for burning in the new types of kilns such as the tunnel kiln, invented in 1845, and later the Hoffmann continuous kiln, which ceased operation only when repairs became necessary.

Clay was still hand-moulded into unburnt bricks until the machines first appeared in the 1820s, including in 1825 Lyle and Stainford's pugmill which could mould fifteen bricks simultaneously, and by 1846 Mr Hall's horse-powered machine had a daily production of ten thousand. These machines moulded clay into forms as previously done by hand, but in the 1840s the process was revolutionized by a new method in which the clay was forced by pressure through a die, or nozzle, issuing as a continuous ribbon which was cut up by wires into bricks known as "wire cuts" even to the present day. The first of these machines was William Irving's in 1841, and the number of wire cuts made by a single machine increased from eight thousand a day until by 1861 the Bulmer and Sharpland steam-operated machine was making as many as twenty-five thousand.

Mass-produced bricks transported easily and cheaply by rail meant the closure of many small works and the loss of their characteristic local bricks. Henceforth identical, precisely shaped, smooth, red bricks appeared in the farthest corners of the country ousting the traditional hand-made bricks, whose extinction is now complete. The most popular colour was bright red, and increased demand matched increased brightness, the most typical of these harsh-looking late Victorian bricks being the reds made in the Accrington district of Lancashire.

The Accrington "bloods", as they were informally known, bright red with smooth almost glazed surfaces, were produced in the 1860s by compressing local shale into unburnt bricks needing very little water, being a semi-dry method similar to the process used for making Fletton bricks. These were made in the late Victorian period from the lower Oxford shale clays found at greater depths than the previously used brick clays. The use of this material, although excellent for brickmaking, was made possible only by better moulding equipment, hydraulic presses, kilns, and by the development of engineering machinery such as steam shovels, first used for laying out the railways, as these made possible deep excavations where clay could be dug easily and cheaply.

Flettons, named after the village of Fletton near Peterborough where they were first made, became the most commonly used brick for building during this period, particularly for the small houses for the working classes. They were cheaply made and were mass produced by a number of firms in the Peterborough area; these firms eventually amalgamated to form the London Brick Company, the largest brickmakers in the British Isles and perhaps in the world. Flettons were first made in the early 1880s by compressing semi-dry shale into unburnt bricks, the advantage being that these contained little moisture, while the shale itself contained natural oils so that less fuel was required for the burning. This took place in the Hoffmann continuous burning furnaces in which the combustion gases passed from one chamber to another before cooling down and being released into the atmosphere. So successful was this process that fifty million flettons were made and sold in 1890 and ten times that number annually during the early 1900s. Nowadays flettons represent almost all those used in this country, and though previously used for concealed work they are now faced in various ways and used for the outsides of most modern houses; the chief form of finishing by dipping them in sand before burning gives the bricks a coloured face and they are known as "sand faced".

However, large supplies of cheap bricks did not guarantee good building and in keeping pace with the demand for housing, standards of construction deteriorated especially in the poorer houses and "jerry-building" became almost standard practice during the late Victorian period. Brick walls of the minimum practicable thickness were used and frequently they were not even weatherproof; half-brick walls were normally used for labourers' houses whether urban or rural.

Even when brick walls were thick enough they were not necessarily structurally sound as builders often used poor mortar, incorrectly mixed and of bad quality using very little lime and poor sand. But this was better than using ash from fires instead of lime, and earth instead of sand. Mortar was also mixed from the dust made by grinding up old bricks which were themselves often inferior, containing ashes or clinker instead of being entirely clay. To encourage poor mortar to set, fires were often lit against the walls of a house and all these practices inevitably weakened the walls so that houses in terraces often helped to support each other by virtue of being built one against another. The strength of the walls was even further diminished by the insertion of bonding timbers or hoop-iron binders to tie walls together, rather than by bonding the brickwork correctly.

"Jerry-building" was probably at its height in the decade 1870 to 1880, coinciding with the great surge in house building throughout the country, and many local authority surveyors were bringing increasing numbers of offenders before the courts for infringing the building regulations then being introduced under the new Public Health Acts. Problems arose because these Acts laid down minimum standards which then became regarded as maximum standards by all but the best builders.

While bricklaying standards declined, methods hardly differed from those known for centuries, the only Victorian innovation being the use of cavity walls for the external brickwork of better-class houses. Such walls were used only in a few buildings, and were adopted hesitantly; cavity walls became the general rule in the early 1930s and are now used in a modified form for all houses. They were first used in the early nineteenth century and William Atkinson's *Views of Picturesque Cottages with Plans*, dated 1805, suggested the use of hollow walls of two leaves of brickwork tied together across a 6-inch cavity by headers, to save materials as well as to make the cottages cosier. Air being one of the best non-conductors of heat and cold, cavity walls are warmer than solid ones, although later builders thought the cavity should be ventilated to allow air to circulate, keeping damp out of the walls. In 1821 Thomas Deane in his *Hints on an Improved Method of Building* advocated a cavity wall of two 4½ inch single brick leaves with a 2-inch cavity again tied across by headers, a form of construction used in some Regency houses where the bonding was concealed from view by stucco. (*See* Figure 17.)

A slightly different type of construction using "rat-trap bond" was detailed in Gwilt's *Encyclopaedia of Architecture* first published in 1842 and was still included in the 1903 edition. He stated that "many people consider this arrangement produces a disagreeable appearance on the outside face", but this was easier to build than the second method suggested in which "all the bricks are laid flat but the stretchers are sawn in half so as to leave a space of 4½ inches between them to take the headers". It was stressed that the mortar should only be laid where the stretchers crossed the headers and not in the centre of the ties.

In 1846 Henry Roberts is known to have used patent hollow bricks in building model dwelling-houses for the poor in the St Giles district of London and later promoted the same construction in his book on *The Dwellings of the Labouring Classes* printed in 1850. Mr Roberts also used cavity walls in his design for Prince Albert's "model houses for labourers" which were erected in Hyde Park at the time of the Great Exhibition of 1851, dwellings which were later removed and rebuilt at Kennington Park. Many hollow bricks were patented and used, perhaps the most popular being the Jennings brick, but gradually there was a preference for cavity walls using metal ties, similar to the modern method.

Later editions of Gwilt's book describing cavity walls held together with wrought-iron ties, state that this technique was being used in southern England especially in the Southampton area, so by the 1870s it was acknowledged that the use of slate damp-proof courses kept rising damp out of walls and that a cavity wall gave dry conditions in a house provided that the two skins of the wall were not tied together by bricks which could attract moisture across the cavity. Unlike modern cavity walls where the two leaves are normally of the same half-brick thickness, Victorian builders thought the best cavity wall had an inner leaf of a half-brick thick and an outer wall as thick as possible, and by the 1880s J.J. Stevenson had put these ideas into practice at 8 Palace Gate, SW7. Dr Brunskill in his book *English Brickwork*, written with Alec Clifton-Taylor, quotes this as one of the earliest examples of such construction in London.

Although cavity walls were adopted reluctantly, other inventions more rapidly affected the character of the English house, especially in the more expensive dwellings, by making improvements unforeseen in the late eighteenth century. Perhaps the most obvious external difference was large panes of window glass manufactured by a process introduced into England in 1832, enabling sash-windows to be made without the intermediate glazing bars necessary in Georgian and Regency houses. The removal of excise duty from glass in 1845 made it much cheaper, and the abolition of the Window Tax in 1851 made windows much larger so that sashes usually had single sheet of glass in both portions from then onwards. Many of the glazing bars were then removed from the windows of earlier houses, a change in fashion obviously altering the character of large numbers of the Georgian houses still surviving. About the same time semi-circular bays lost popularity to three-sided bays with canted sides, eventually one of the outstanding features of the Victorian house. As time went on, increasingly elaborate ornament surrounded the bay windows, and indeed most of the windows, in ostentatious middle-class houses.

Inventions which were the novelties of the Great Exhibition of 1851 became the basis of many modern domestic appliances and services, perhaps the most important ones concerning the heating, sanitary fittings, water supply and drainage, or the lack of these services. In 1838

J.C. Loudon in *The Suburban Gardener and Villa Companion* had empha-
sized the need for a separate room for the bath, instead of using it in a
bedroom or sitting-room, and a properly constructed small boiler
behind the kitchen fire to supply hot water, at a time when baths were not
always found even in affluent households, but by the late 1850s special
rooms with fixed baths, complete with taps and water supplies, were
more widely used.

One of the first boilers behind a kitchen range was patented by
William Armitage in 1792 and many others followed, some exhibited at
the Great Exhibition of 1851. Mr Loudon also proposed heating houses
using a greenhouse stove invented by Mr Strutt of Belper to produce
warm air which could circulate in ducts to the main rooms, stale air
escaping up the chimney. In 1839 Samuel Brooks, in *Designs for Cottages
and Villas*, offered a plan to heat houses by circulating hot water in pipes.

Such ideas obviously had little effect on the heating of most houses, for
nearly fifty years later in 1880, J.J. Stevenson stated in *House Architecture* that, "for heating English houses the best system on the whole is the
old one of open fires. No doubt it is unscientific . . . as well as wasteful.
But it has the advantage that everyone understands it and it is so pleasant
that we are not likely to abandon it as long as the coal lasts." After the
Great Exhibition, among the many inventions including improved
kitchen stoves, baths and gas lighting which changed the living conditions for the wealthier families, the foremost was the supply of water to
individual houses and the gradual improvement in sanitary conditions
resulting from proper drainage systems.

The poor gained little benefit from these developments; their housing
problems seemed almost insoluble by this time because of the rapid
increase in population, and its influence on the buildings then being
erected in London, the Midlands and Lancashire is shown by the fact
that in 1700 the population of London was about 400 per square mile, in
Worcestershire between 100 and 150, while Stafford, Cheshire and Lancashire had less than 100 in the same area. By 1900 the population of
London was over 1,600 per square mile, equalled by Lancashire, and
other counties had between 500 and 1,600, the density in Lancashire
explained by the nineteenth-century migration north to the cotton-
manufacturing areas.

This increase in population led for the first time to the concept of different types of houses for different sections of the community. Formerly, particularly in the Georgian period, everybody occupied similar
houses using standard designs and all that distinguished one class of
house from another was the size and number of floors, therefore whole
streets, and even towns, acquired the unity so admired today. The Victorian period changed all this and in the process many fine Georgian

streets and squares disappeared, replaced by endless streets of mediocre "by-law" houses.

Eighteenth-century laws had concentrated upon improving the construction of houses, particularly to make them more fire-proof, but the nineteenth-century laws were almost entirely concerned with the worst aspects of layout and sanitary conditions. These Acts were almost powerless to prevent extensive slum properties being built in all the industrial cities, for in the scramble to house the poorer people, houses to rent were erected on any land available. Row upon row of poorly built houses formed mean streets and crowded courts, dwellings surrounded mines and factories without any consideration except to squeeze in as many as possible; the worst type were the "back-to-back" houses built by many factory owners, but even these were better than nothing although very soon condemned by the more enlightened Victorian philanthropists. (*See* Figure 23.)

Among the most important of the nineteenth-century building Acts was that of 1844 which controlled the sizes of underground rooms, the areas lighting them, and limited the size of buildings in relation to the open space around them. Each new street had to be at least 40 feet wide and the height of buildings alongside controlled by the width of the street. Under this Act buildings were divided into classes, and houses were in four standard classifications, the largest type being restricted to a maximum permitted height of eighty feet.

This Act controlled structures alongside new highways only; there were no limitations on heights of buildings adjacent to existing streets, so the later Victorian period saw much rebuilding on old sites, and demolition of many Georgian houses. So many dwellings were crammed into the older parts of existing cities, particularly London, that the London Building Act of 1855 was introduced to prevent building on the gardens of these earlier houses. These smaller houses filled up any available space and were intended for labourers, meanwhile many more of the poor packed themselves into the existing Georgian houses creating slums out of fine houses formerly occupied by the wealthier families, now settled in villas in the suburbs.

The Public Health Act of 1848 also dealt with sewers and there followed a series of reports compiled by Government inspectors on "the state of sewage, drainage, water supply and sanitary conditions of the inhabitants" of any town wishing to construct new drainage schemes as this Act was meant to be adopted voluntarily by the local people rather than to be enforced like later Acts. Reports made under the 1848 Act covered small towns the size of Stratford-upon-Avon and Warwick, providing evidence of the horrifying sanitary conditions prevalent in the important towns and revealing the squalid situation of the poor between

1848 and the early 1850s even in towns like Leamington Spa newly developed during the Regency period some thirty years earlier.

The Public Health Act of 1858 empowered towns to make by-laws to control building, while that of 1875 provided for proper sanitation, drainage, water supplies and refuse disposal, all to be the responsibility of the local town councils.

In 1868 the Artisans' Dwellings Act was introduced followed by the Labourers' Dwellings Improvement Act of 1875 which enabled the local authorities for the first time to clear away slum properties and build new houses for the "working class". Previously, housing for poorer people was at the mercy of the speculative builder who could build whatever type of house proved the most profitable, achieved by crowding as many back-to-back houses as possible on any plot of land available. These were rows of houses two rooms deep with a wall down the middle separating one side from the other. There was a cellar below and another room above, all rooms being about 11 feet square with the staircase tucked into one corner. The rows were barely 3 or 4 yards apart with communal water taps and privies opening onto these narrow courts. (*See* Figure 23.)

The 1875 Act offered a chance to improve on these conditions by inaugurating schemes for slum clearance and the rebuilding of whole areas; in the same year Birmingham embarked on one of the earliest and largest projects of this kind. The 1890 Act for the Housing of the Working Classes extended the powers of the town councils to buy land and raise money to provide houses for poorer people, but councils were often sluggish and private charities had to provide many of these first housing schemes, most of which were in city centres where the problem was greatest. Some schemes were little better than the slums they replaced, with new buildings introducing flats for the first time, multi-storey dwellings of a type previously used only on the Continent. These large blocks were erected on land even then hard to find and valuable, and those of better quality were designed for more affluent families whereas those for the poor have a very dreary appearance with their bare brick walls, open staircases and access galleries grouped round gloomy courtyards. Some of the earliest London flats for labourers were erected by the Peabody Trust and several blocks still remain tucked away behind more modern buildings; the first Peabody flats built in Spitalfields in 1864 were ahead of anything else being done at that time.

Although most schemes for housing the less well off were realized as long narrow streets of rows of small red brick houses, many with a bay window directly onto the pavement, they were far better than anything previously built for this type of family. These were "by-law" houses, the by-laws controlling not only the minimum size and construction of the dwelling but also the width of the streets along which they were built,

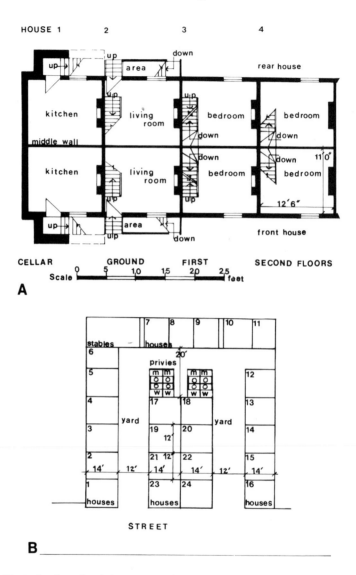

Fig. 23 A. back-to-back houses, typical of those found in any large industrial
town during the nineteenth century. All such houses are now forbidden under
modern public health acts. (These examples are based on back-to-back houses
found in Nottingham in the last century.); B. St John's Court, Satchwell Street,
Leamington Spa. Back-to-back houses built in 1836 in a new Regency spa town,
and during the 1850s, 130 persons were recorded as living in this court which has
now been demolished. (Plan not to scale.) It stood immediately to the rear of
     large houses facing the main street of the town known as The Parade

and such houses represent most of those lining the streets on the fringes of all industrial town centres. Even tighter by-law controls later resulted in row after row of "tunnel backs" opening direct onto the road with the tiny spaces at the back reached by tunnels at ground level, passing through the terraces at intervals, the bedrooms of the adjoining houses being over these access passages. These houses, mainly found in the densely populated parts of the country, were by no means badly built but certainly did not provide a good environment to live in. Invariably the minimum size became that normally used by the speculative builder, and the contrast between these houses and those for the wealthier people is still obvious. (*See* Figure 24.)

According to Joseph Gwilt's encyclopaedia, the smallest site on which such houses should be built was 20 feet by 30 feet but frequently less land was used, some houses having frontages only 12 feet wide. These two-storey houses had two rooms on each floor, those on the ground floor being smaller as the entrance passage and staircase were at one side. The earlier dwellings had the kitchen below ground level, later in a small projecting wing at the rear of the house containing the bathroom also, if one was provided; the only open space was a small yard at the back.

In contrast, superior houses, although following roughly the same layout, had a first-floor living-room and study, and bedrooms on the upper floors. Gwilt stated that the minimum site required for these houses was 100 feet by 30 feet, giving room for stables at the end of the garden. Sites of this size were obtainable only on the outskirts of the cities, therefore the better-class houses formed suburbs extending into the countryside where the smallest site for a country villa was given as 80 feet by 60 feet for the house, plus any garden. It established the pattern of the rich living in the country, the middle class in the suburbs and the poor in the city centres.

This represented the rigid standardized approach to housing layout but there had been earlier innovations and these experiments, although modest, have influenced present-day housing developments. The first schemes were undertaken by industrialists to provide better housing for their workers; most comprised conventional terraces with open spaces simply as adjuncts to the houses, with other features such as church, schools and libraries. Other industrialists built small groups of workers' cottages, examples surviving at Cromford, Belper and Darley Abbey, all in Derbyshire, Papplewick near Nottingham and Mayfield in Staffordshire, but the first of the new industrial settlements, complete villages rather than a few houses, was at New Lanark in Scotland.

Started by Richard Arkwright in 1782 and completed in the early 1800s by Robert Owen, by 1816 the village with its houses grouped round the cotton mill housed 2,297 people. So revolutionary was this

Fig. 24 Typical house-plans of the nineteenth century: A. second half of the century, two rooms up and down; B. house with a single-storey annexe, typical of all industrial towns. Late nineteenth century. (Based on a house in Leamington Spa); C. house with a two-storey rear annexe. (Based on a house in Coventry built about 1900); D. typical large Victorian house, ground-floor plan only. (Based on houses built in Leamington Spa from about 1836 to the end of the reign of Queen Victoria)

settlement that it had approximately 20,000 visitors between 1815 and 1825.

The first English scheme, similar but smaller in scale, was at Belper, near Derby, where William Strutt built some workers' cottages in 1792, but nothing more extensive appeared until the mid-nineteenth century when several larger industrial villages were built near the woollen towns of Yorkshire. Colonel Ackroyd, a mill-owner in the Halifax district, laid out several estates, the first at Copley in 1847 was of terraces of back to back houses followed by a school, library and workers' canteen, all completed by 1853. So successful was this group of workers' houses that a second development followed in 1859 known as Ackroydon, where several rows of cottages were built, the first being York Terrace, designed in a simplified Gothic style by Sir Gilbert Scott although later completed by a local architect, W.H. Crossland. This estate near Shipley was grouped round Bankfield House, the Victorian Gothic mansion of the mill-owner, which is now a museum.

Better known is Saltaire, laid out between 1850 and 1870 by Sir Titus Salt, another prosperous mill-owner. Here eight hundred and fifty two-bedroomed houses were followed by forty-five almshouses, a church, institute, baths, shops, hospital and park; the houses all had proper sanitation, something rare for that period. The twenty-two streets were laid out on a grid-iron pattern surrounding the mill which, opening in 1853, employed four thousand at the height of its prosperity.

Among other early pioneers, George and James Wilson, owning the Price's Patent Candle Company, moved from London to Cheshire where some workers' houses were built at Bromborough Pool Village, about a mile from the place which became the site of Port Sunlight. At Bromborough the first few parallel streets, with terraces or pairs of houses, were built in 1853, followed by a chapel and school, and by 1901 there were nearly one hundred and fifty houses.

In these schemes the layout was unremarkable and the houses were usually conventional plain brick or stone buildings erected as cheaply as possible, and the village of Bromborough was no exception. But at Port Sunlight less than a mile away, William Lever, later Lord Leverhulme, achieved a housing development that was exceptionally advanced in its layout and design and although it had many imitators it was the creation of this village which influenced the housing layouts and New Towns of the present day.

In this estate, started in 1888, houses and landscape together made the whole design, rather than arranging small formally laid out open spaces as adjuncts to the buildings. Port Sunlight echoed the romantic landscape ideas of the eighteenth century and the concept was similar to some of the middle-class suburbs of the period, particularly Bedford Park in

London. The original 32 acres of Port Sunlight were laid out to take advantage of natural features in placing the houses and other public buildings. The site was divided by a series of channels, formerly tidal inlets from Bromborough Pool, part of the Mersey Estuary, skirted by the curving roads of the village planned around them, though these channels were later filled in, providing sunken gardens and more conventional open spaces. The four hundred houses built by 1900 have now increased to about a thousand, all occupied by company employees.

Though simple in design, the first houses were grouped in blocks varying between two and ten in number, no two blocks being alike. This variation gives the village an oddly Victorian "half-timbered" look, the predominant style, Elizabethan, naturally bears little resemblance to the genuine thing. Although other styles were imitated many of the public buildings also were "half-timbered" and among them, now demolished, was a replica of Shakespeare's birthplace. The houses were smaller versions of the reproduction timber-framed mansions so desirable to the prosperous Lancashire cotton merchants and many of the details which originally featured in Port Sunlight were copied by speculative builders when "half-timbered" houses became popular in the 1930s. Such houses are not true half-timbered buildings as the thin pieces of wood fixed to the face of the brick walls were merely applied decoration.

Building at Port Sunlight continued until the late 1920s; shortly after work began, a similar scheme was started by Richard and George Cadbury at Bournville, then on the outskirts of Birmingham. The Cadbury family business started at Bournville about 1879 and a few pairs of semi-detached houses for the workers were built near the factory. In 1893, 120 acres of land were purchased for housing with the aim of providing improved dwellings together with gardens and open spaces to be enjoyed by "the working class and labouring population in and around Birmingham". The houses were not limited to Cadbury's employees but were available to all working people; the estate, intended to be self-supporting, had 300 houses by 1900 and 3,500 by 1955.

Pevsner describes Bournville as "an area of controlled suburban development and of all the contemporary experiments it most closely resembles the Hampstead Garden suburb started in 1906". There is a difference, for the Hampstead estate was built for middle-class occupation rather than "the labouring population", nevertheless the houses were very similar in design and layout. All the houses had two storeys and gardens, the roads were laid out in an informal way unlike the rigid formality of earlier estates. The Hampstead houses were simplified Georgian, really unlike the original houses, but the elements of Georgian design such as sash-windows, classical doors and porches appeared in a new guise, becoming popular thereafter in a rather more debased form.

Other houses were "Queen Anne" in design, a style revived – or rather adapted – by Norman Shaw about thirty years earlier in 1876 when he designed the first of the garden suburbs at Bedford Park, then on the outskirts of London. Although this style became fashionable some contemporary critics considered it a debased form of English architecture, in contrast to the Swiss, Tudor, Gothic or other historical styles of building then popular with wealthier families.

These small estates had little effect on the real difficulty of housing the population of the overcrowded cities and although architects tried to improve the design of individual houses, in competition with the speculative builders responsible for the bulk of the housing it was Ebenezer Howard, a court reporter, who inspired what was perhaps the most important movement of the early twentieth century. In 1898 he published a book called *Tomorrow*, re-issued in 1902 as the more familiar *Garden Cities of Tomorrow*, in which he proposed that instead of living in crowded cities people should live in a new type of community which he named a Garden City.

Howard was following the tradition of two lesser-known authors whose works were too advanced for their time; the first of these, James Buckingham, suggested in 1849 the setting up of "The Model Town Association" to build a new town named "Victoria". Although based on a type of communal living unlikely to succeed, Buckingham was sufficiently advanced to insist upon public baths, water closets and a supply of pure water in each house, and surprisingly suggested electric light to illuminate the main public spaces. In 1876 there followed Benjamin Richardson's plan for *Hygeia – A City of Health*, another ideal form of community, but Howard succeeded through the well-planned practical nature of his project, particularly in its financial aspects which should enable such towns eventually to become to some degree self-supporting.

Howard's new city was to be small enough for the people to enjoy a community life and yet large enough to provide enough industry to enable them to work in the district where they lived, avoiding long journeys to work. The maximum diameter of the city was to be one and a half miles and the maximum population 30,000, occupying an area of a thousand acres surrounded by six thousand acres of agricultural land, a "green belt" supplying some of the town's food. There were to be public buildings, churches, schools, community buildings and parks, and houses in tree-lined avenues, the scheme being based on twelve to fourteen houses per acre, providing accommodation for thirty people.

In 1903 Howard established the First Garden City Ltd., and started to build Letchworth Garden City, followed in 1920 by a second scheme, Welwyn Garden City. The towns did not follow Howard's principles completely as, for example, his space standards proved inadequate for twentieth-century planning. The idea of New Towns surrounded by a green belt was quickly accepted but was only put into practice on a large scale after the passing of the New Towns Act of 1946, the starting point for the present day new towns. The first group, Stevenage, Crawley, Hemel Hempstead and Harlow, now over thirty years old, have been followed by over twenty similar projects.

While Howard was advocating better town-planning standards there were glimmers of a reaction against the ugliness of the buildings themselves, a movement led by William Morris. He died in 1896 before Howard's city at Letchworth started, believing that ugliness in daily life was wrong, unnecessary, and could be avoided by returning to the high standards of craftsmanship of the Middle Ages. His teachings inspired the Arts and Crafts Movement which attracted many of the most progressive contemporary designers, including Philip Webb, Joseph Ashbee and Charles Voysey.

It was the houses designed by Voysey, with steeply pitched roofs, usually tiled, small simple casement windows set in plain brickwork either whitewashed or rendered, which came to represent the typical English country cottage. They were almost always long and low in outline, having large chimneys and often dressings of Bath stone round doors and windows, and soon became freely copied. Before he died in 1941 Voysey had seen his style so debased in imitation that it was unrecognizable in the confusion of house styles which thrived in the first half of this century – ornament and individuality receding before simple uniform-looking buildings with mass-produced windows and doors, which can be placed with certainty in their particular decade.

The ebb and flow of fashion is swifter than before; perhaps future historians will be able to recognize amongst the multitude of styles the one which truly represents the twentieth century.

References and further reading

Please note that some of these books have long been out of print, but the public library may be helpful.

Addy, Sidney Oldall, *The Evolution of the English House*

Alcock, N.W., (editor), *C.B.A. Research Report No. 42. Cruck Construction: An Introduction and Catalogue*

Ancient Monuments Society Transactions. Various volumes

Andrews, Francis B., *The Medieval Builder*

Atkinson, T.D., *Local Style in English Architecture*

Bailey, M.W., *The English Farmhouse and Cottage*

Beresford, Maurice, *History on the Ground*

Billett, Michael, *Thatching and Thatched Buildings*

Briggs, Martin, *The English Farmhouse*

Brown, R.J., *The English Country Cottage*

Brunskill, R.W., *The Illustrated Handbook of Vernacular Architecture*

Brunskill, R.W., *Vernacular Architecture of the Lake Counties*

Brunskill, R.W., *Clay Houses in Cumberland* (Ancient Monuments Society Transactions)

Brunskill, R.W., and Clifton-Taylor, Alec, *English Brickwork*

Bunker, R., *Cruck Buildings*

Charles, F.W., *Medieval Cruck Buildings*

Clifton-Taylor, Alec, *The Pattern of English Building*

Clifton-Taylor, Alec, and Brunskill, R.W., *English Brickwork*

Cordingley, R.A., *British Historical Roof Types* (Ancient Monuments Society, 1961)

Crossley, R., *Timber Building in England*

Davey, Norman, *Building Stones of England and Wales*

Davey, N., *A History of Building Materials*

Field, John, *English Field Names – A Dictionary*

Fletcher, Valentine, *Chimney Pots and Stacks*

Hale, Robert, Limited. The Village Series

Hall, Robert de Zouche, *A Bibliography on Vernacular Architecture*

Harris, R., *Discovering Timber Framed Houses*

Harvey, John, *The Medieval Craftsman*

Hewett, Cecil, *The Development of Carpentry 1200–1700*

Hoskins, W.G., *The Making of the English Landscape*

Hoskins, W.G., *The Rebuilding of Rural England*

Hudson, Kenneth, *The Fashionable Stone*

Innocent, C.F., *The Development of English Building Construction*

Iredale, David, *This Old House*

Jope, E.M., *Studies in Building History*

Lloyd, Nathaniel, *The History of English Brickwork*

Mason, R.T., *Framed Buildings of England*
Mason, R.T., *Framed Buildings of the Weald*
Mercer, Eric, *English Vernacular Houses*
Penoyre, John and Jane, *Houses in the Landscape*
Pevsner, Nikolaus, (with various co-authors), The Buildings of England Series
Platt, Colin, *The English Medieval Town*
Rackham, Oliver, *Trees and Woodlands in the British Landscape*
Raistrick, Arthur, *Buildings in the Yorkshire Dales*
Reddaway, T.F., *The Rebuilding of London after the Great Fire*
Reid, Richard, *The Shell Book of Cottages*
Rubinstein, David, *Victorian Homes*
Salzman, L.F., *Building in England down to 1540*
Smith, J.T., and Yates, E.M., *On the Dating of English Houses from External Evidence*
Smith, J.T., *Timber framed building in England – its development and regional differences* (Archaeological Journal 1965)
Smith, J.T., *The Evolution of the English Peasant House in the late seventeenth century* (Journal of the British Archaeological Association, 1970)
Summerson, John, *Georgian London*
West, Trudy, *The Timber Framed House in England*
Williams-Ellis, Clough, *Cottage Building in Cob, Pisé, Chalk and Clay*
Wight, Jan, *Brick Building in England – From the Middle Ages to 1550*
Woods, Margaret, *The Medieval House*
Woodforde, John, *The Truth About Cottages*
Woodforde, John, *Georgian Houses for All*
Woodforde, John, *Bricks to Build a House*
Wood-Jones, R.B., *Traditional Domestic Architecture of the Banbury Region*
Yates, E.M., and Smith, J.T. *On the Dating of English Houses from External Evidence*

Index